SHEPHERD GIRL:
A Dog Story

By Cat L Needham

This book is dedicated to Sharon Dodd, my amazing, brilliant, funny mom. I wouldn't have been able to do any of this without you, and not just for the obvious reasons. Thanks for being everything to me.

Contents

Foreword

Going into a stranger's home to gently boss her around for an hour in the name of dog training is a daunting task, particularly at 8:00 a.m. on a rainy Saturday morning. Add to that the tension radiating from a new dog owner not quite sure about her furry best friend, and you have my introduction to Cat and Athena.

Nervous new puppy owners fall into a few different categories. There's the list maker, who greets me with a sheet of paper filled with questions. There's the "OH MY GOD, WHAT DID I DO?" type, who is wild-eyed and near tears during the Q & A portion of our meeting. There's the "fun parent," who is more concerned with playing with the new puppy than figuring out how to live with it. And then there's the type I discovered when I met Cat and Athena: the slow burn.

At our intro session I initially saw a typical clever pup/overachiever parent relationship. Athena was gorgeous and charming, and her proud mama knew it. Both parties seemed ready to soak up some training.

We got to work, and then I started to notice little . . . hiccups. Cat's tentative treat delivery. Her extreme personal space protection around her jumpy puppy.

Oh no, I thought. *Cat is afraid of her new dog!*

I'd worked with flat-out fearful puppy parents before, but never in a situation where the dog side of the equation was a *German. Shepherd.* Being afraid of a squirmy, bitey Bichon is something entirely different from being afraid of a brilliant GSD who can read your mind and program your cell phone if necessary. GSDs need charismatic, confident guides. Not bosses or Alphas, but mentors. Without a leader, chaos reigns. It seemed that Cat wasn't ready to provide that for Athena, and I walked out of our first lesson very worried about the state of their union.

Six years later, at the launch party for my first book, who strolled in but a very assured-looking Cat and her shadow, Athena. They showed off their bond for me, and their skills put the other hooligan dogs to shame. I wasn't above telling other party guests that Athena was a student from way back when, hoping that I could claim some of their glory. Cat regaled me with tales of Athena's jaw-dropping recalls and civility around lesser-mannered mongrels, while Athena gazed up at her, seeming to share Cat's pride. I was amazed by how far the two of them had come, though I don't kid myself that six short weeks of training all those years ago had much to do with it.

Their journey, from a tentative beginning to a triumphant partnership is enough to, well, fill a book. May their slow burn bond give hope to those puppy owners struggling with their new best friends and serve as a fond reminder to those who have walked the same path.

Victoria Schade
Dog trainer and author of *Bonding with Your Dog: A Trainer's Secrets for Building a Better Relationship*
Consultant, Animal Planet *Puppy Bowl*
Trainer, Animal Planet *Faithful Friends*
Trainer/Creator, DVD *New Puppy, Now What?*

Acknowledgements

I first have to thank Megan Judge, breeder and owner of Haus Juris Kennels in Nokesville, Virginia. None of this book would have been possible if I hadn't found Megan. If you are looking for a fantastic representative of the German Shepherd Dog, do yourself a favor and go to Megan's for one of her puppies.

Thanks also to Victoria Schade, phenomenal puppy-and-person trainer and my mentor. Victoria, you gave me the crucial tools for establishing a bond with my dog, but you also gave this struggling writer encouragement and confidence. I strive to be one-tenth as cool as you are.

Heidi Bell, editor extraordinaire—thanks for your help in trimming the fat.

Thank you, Dr. Martin Tohill and the awesome staff at Chantilly Animal Hospital in Chantilly, Virginia. You have kept my pets and me healthy.

To the staff at the Hope Center Emergency Vet Clinic in Vienna, Virginia: thank you for your compassion during some very painful moments.

To the staff at Milwaukee Frozen Custard in Chantilly, Virginia, and Kazan Turkish Restaurant in McLean, Virginia: thank you for always making Athena feel welcome and for your delicious food.

Thanks to the grooming staff at Featherle Pet Care in Chantilly, Virginia, for keeping Athena pretty.

Janelle Cooley and Doggie Walkers, Inc., in Great Falls, Virginia, I appreciate your dedication and care when I couldn't be there. I always knew my babies were in good hands with you.

To my friends Diana, Lauren, Liz, Jim, Greg, Sam, Liz C, Margaret Pirk, and Craig, who offered me shoulders to cry on, ears to listen, helping hands, belly laughs, and rooms in New York: thank you. Robin Orr, you get your own special shout-out; you are the one friend I know who would help me bury a body. You know my every secret, and I'm glad.

To Sandi Wilson, who inspired me to believe that I could write a whole book, and to my fellow Algonkian Conference writers who helped me hone my vision—thanks. I'm looking forward to reading all your books next.

To the rest of my family: Mary Dodd, Ethan Pirk, Mike Dodd, the Needhams, thank you for all your support. I would be calling my dog something really dumb without you, Mary, and my cover art wouldn't have popped without your expertise, (Unkie) Ethan.

To Nonny and Pop Pop—I did it! I wish you two were still here to read it, but something tells me you know the whole story, anyway. I miss you, but it must be so beautiful there.

To all Athena's friends—Mindi, Kiera, Carman, Cody, Fireball, Raleigh, Kaiser, Rocky, Maya, Josie, Timber, and the Huskies: woof and meow.

Kashka, thank you for proving that it's possible to be as suave as Cary Grant but also unfailingly kind. I wish more human beings could be like you.

And finally, thank you to Athena Justagirl Haus Juris. Not only have you made me a better, happier person, but you have made it patently impossible for me to imagine my life without a dog. Clicka, clicka.

1. Pet Expo Trance

Sure, she was sullen, and in hindsight I would recognize her as a thin donkey of a shepherd with the strained, suspicious look and nervous pulled-up groin of a potential fear-biter. But I wanted to cuddle a puppy. In the Virginia German Shepherd Rescue booth, I scratched Sasha 1's chest, and she burrowed her head into my lap.

"Are you really thinking of getting a dog?" my friend Robin asked, in the same tone one would ask, "Are you really thinking of licking that spider?" We were at the Chantilly, Virginia, *Super Pet Expo!*, an annual event held in an echoing warehouse and featuring vendor booths, exhibits, and various animals for adoption or sale.

Robin, a tall, laconic redhead, is my favorite friend to take along to crowded places like the *Expo!*, which tend to overwhelm me with noise. While I get cranky quickly after having to say, "Excuse me, excuse me; sorry, go ahead," over and over, she's always relaxed and amused by her surroundings and points out things to me in her melodic, slow voice that sounds like she's comfortably talking around a mouthful of pudding.

I wasn't surprised by the hint of betrayal that spilled over into Robin's voice when she asked that question. She and I loved cats, and she disliked dogs, even though she coexisted with her husband's dog Logan. I hesitated to answer her, and the rescue lady saw it as an opportunity to advocate for the puppy burrowing into my lap. "She really likes you!" she said. "She's afraid of most everyone else!" People who visit homeless animals love to hear things like that, and I was no exception. I felt like I alone had unlocked Sasha 1's dormant love.

"Yes, I think I am going to get a dog," I said to Robin and, as if in a trance, picked up the clipboard and filled out an application. Then I dragged Robin over to the small *Super Pet Expo!* stage, on which the rescue volunteers paraded the potential adoptees around in a circle. When it was Sasha 1's turn, she eyed the crowd with dismay and stiffly trotted behind her person.

"Look at her walk!" I said to Robin. "Look at her gait!" I didn't know the difference then between a German shepherd with a skittish, shy temperament and the more outgoing self-confident type desirable to the breed. I only saw a cute puppy.

"What about poor Kashi?" Robin asked with doubtful, accusatory notes in her voice. She stared at me like I had just suggested we steal from the homeless pet donation jar to buy crystal meth.

I felt a guilty twinge. Kashi. Kashka. My beloved, beautiful cat I had had since he was a baby. Now twelve years old, he had been with me through five moves and three serious breakups, and he had never done a petty or malicious thing to anyone in his life. I even had evidence that he liked dogs. Surely he would do fine with a dog.

"Oh, I think Kashka could handle a dog," I said to Robin as I watched Sasha 1 scoot away from an imaginary hand reaching for her backside.

Robin pursed her mouth and said, "If you think so," and started to walk away from me, as if I were embarrassing her.

"Kashka's been around dogs before, and he was cool with them!" I called after her.

Kashka came into my life in 1991. I was a recent college graduate working at a local newspaper, taking classified advertisements over the telephone. I had an abrupt, absurd thought when I woke up one morning, an ordinary Tuesday. "I'm getting my cat today," I said to myself, as if I were deciding to buy a slice of pizza for lunch. The thought crossing my mind wasn't completely outlandish only because one of my roommates had moved out a few weeks before, taking her cat with her. The remaining roommates and I had decided as a household that I would be the next roommate to get a cat. I yearned for a cat more than I had ever yearned for anything in my life, except maybe a bicycle when I was eight that had lowrider handlebars and a banana saddle. Some nights I actually felt the sudden pounce onto my bed, followed by a settled weight, but it was only me wishing for my own cat so hard I hallucinated.

My family had had cats while I was growing up, and I'd loved those family members dearly, but I wanted one for my own. I had a vision of what I wanted—a gray, long-haired male. I even had his name picked out. My fiancé in college (we did not get married, but that's a different tale) had taken Russian, and when he said "Kashka" meant "kitty," I knew it was the perfect name for my future cat.

Sitting at my computer terminal at work that day, waiting for the front desk to dispatch a call to me, I forgot my earlier declaration about my cat. Around 9:30 a.m., I was doodling pictures of animals when a call was put through. It was a representative from the local chapter of the American Society for the Prevention of Cruelty to Animals, ASPCA for short. I adjusted my headphones and prepared to take dictation for the ad.

"We want to place an ad in the *Gazette* for Saturday's kitten fair," the lady said.

"Okay, I can do that," I said. She dictated the time and the place, and I offered the stunningly creative headline "Kitten Fair."

When she had finished with the details but before she could hang up, I blurted, "What kind of kittens will be at the fair?"

"Uh, we won't know that until they arrive. They're coming from all over the county. From other rescue groups." Her tone had grown a little brusque, maybe because I had so blatantly breached the professional boundary between service provider and customer.

"Oh," I said. "Well, do you have any kittens at your headquarters, now, by any chance?"

"Of course," she snapped, as if I were a complete idiot. I suppose it was a stupid question, but I was undaunted.

"What do you have there now? What sorts?" I asked.

"Well, we have two brothers right now."

"Uh huh, and what do they look like?" I asked.

"Well one is gray and white, long haired."

Silence.

I felt like we were playing "Is it bigger than a breadbox?"

"And the other one?"

"He's solid gray. Long hair."

"Hold that one. I'll be by at lunch to pick him up," I said.

Sounding skeptical and, if possible, even more irritated, she said, "Okaaay."

I took a few more calls and doodled and looked at the clock too many times, waiting for my lunch break. I talked one of my co-workers into coming with me, and she eyed me suspiciously, noting that I had no carrier. *Are you really getting a cat? Today?* The ASPCA chapter was near the *Gazette* offices, but I had only a vague notion as to where it was. Having come to terms with my stellar sense of direction, I knew I would get lost if I tried to go alone.

The center turned out to be a trailer, conspicuous enough to find easily. Inside, the left wall was covered floor to ceiling with cages containing platforms, litter boxes, and, of course, cats. I spotted the two brothers immediately, lying next to each other on a platform. The all-gray kitten was batting the tail of his gray-and-white brother. When I came in, the gray kitten stopped and stared into my soul with his leaf-green round eyes. A slight shiver of pleasure went through me. The look was lazy, a little insolent, and said, "Well, what took you so long?"

"That's him!" I said to the room. "That's Kashka." The lady at the desk sold me a cardboard traveling box that snapped shut with tabs at the top and had holes in the sides. I paid the adoption fee, filled out the paperwork agreeing to get him neutered, and we left. This was in the old days, before pet adoption included waiting periods and home checks. The whole procedure took only fifteen minutes.

I carried Kashka into work and set his box next to me on the floor. I periodically opened the top and peered in at him. With the unflinching confidence he showed later in life, he blinked up at me, meeting my eyes, as he lay on his side apparently not flustered in the least that some strange lady had taken him out of his big cage and put him in a cardboard box. I couldn't believe that this silver long-limbed vulpine beauty was actually mine.

I later found out that Kashka's mellow demeanor was likely due to a bad case of roundworms; he was more rambunctious after his deworming. The first night at my house, however, I had expected a mewling, needy kitten who would want to snuggle with me in my bed. Kashka instead silently walked to my bedroom door, looking at it and then at me. I opened the door, and without a backward glance, he walked down the stairs to explore the rest of the house. My roommate said later that she followed my kitten to the basement, where he discovered a basket of cat toys. My roommate watched as Kashka removed every toy from the basket, looked around at the toys with supreme boredom, and then left. He came back to my room later to visit. It took him a few weeks to jump up in bed with me. But when he finally did, I had the settled little weight I had coveted. I believed after getting Kashka that truly wanted pets and their owners find one another when the time is right.

What I'd said to Robin was technically true: Kashka had been around dogs. As a one-year old kitten, he play-boxed with a friend's Rottweiler puppy while perched on the back of our couch. But that was eleven years ago. Kashka as a yearling had a robust, Jack Lalanne vigor about him and feared nothing. He would lope around the neighborhood, visiting people in their homes, his tail either held straight up, the tip bouncing like a wind sock, or curved low and relaxed, like a lion's.

During Kashka's early years, a neighbor stopped me on my way to the front door. "Is that cat yours?" she asked as Kashka came trilling up the walkway, his heavy paw falls jarring each quiet twinkling burr from him.

"Yes he is!" I answered, smiling. Kashka, with his silver Angora-rabbit-like fur, pointy fox face, bright green eyes, and fluffy tail, was a truly stunning cat. I was as proud of his prettiness as if I had borne him myself.

"Oh, we just love him," the neighbor said. "He always comes into our house for a visit every day, at least for a few minutes," she said, "and I have seen him coming out of that house, and that one . . . "

I laughed and blushed and apologized, making a mental note to thank everyone on the street for showing him such hospitality. I hoped they didn't mind that he liked to visit. But it turned out my apologies would soon be unnecessary, because Kashka's love of visiting the neighbors seemed to vanish overnight.

Even though he stopped his rounds, Kashka was still a charmingly placid and friendly animal, greeting people who visited us and becoming pals with the cats acquired by my roommates over the years. He stared at everyone with round glassy stuffed-animal eyes, rarely vocalizing except for an occasional soft chortle. Although he was a heavy, muscular cat, he never used his bulk to intimidate other animals. Everywhere we moved, he made friends easily with any neighborhood cats and, indeed, almost always picked up some random younger male sycophant who followed him around, worshipping the large, benevolent king of the sidewalk.

He was exceptionally gentle to weaker animals, particularly ones who were scared, as he demonstrated once at my veterinarian's office when he was eight years old. He walked well on a leash, and that's how we went to our vet's, where he stalked around the room sniffing everything. While other cats yowled and shrank in their carriers, Kashka tried to get back behind the front desk to show all the staff how pretty he was. (Another of his qualities was a tremendous vanity. He knew he was handsome and would make a grand entrance just to hear, "He's SOO pretty!") "Fifteen pounds," the vet tech announced as Kashka stood on the scale blinking up at her.

While we waited our turn, we noticed a man a few chairs down with a female terrier puppy about Kashka's size who whimpered anxiously, jittering in front of her owner's feet, clearly frightened. Kashka pulled on his leash toward the puppy, and I walked him over to her. He stood directly in front of the puppy and allowed her to snuffle all over his face; the only emotion registering was one of mild surprise (his default expression). "She loves cats for some reason," the puppy's owner said, and we both watched Kashka stand motionless, letting the puppy frantically lick his chin and cheeks. Kashka calmly backed away when he decided he had had enough. "Your cat's good with dogs," the man said, as the puppy seemed to temporarily forget about her fear and plopped down at his feet.

"I'm kind of surprised at him, actually," I said, "but he seemed to know your little one was scared." That was Kashka, my kind, gentle giant.

When I decided to adopt a puppy, I mentally played this reel in my head, ignoring the fact that it had happened four years ago. Older age made Kashka a bit grumpy, a little more fearful of strangers, and not particularly interested in doing much. He didn't seem keen on anything except eating and sleeping, although from time to time he ventured out into the tiny fenced-in yard of the house I finally bought. He would sit under a bush while I stood in the yard with him for about five minutes, and then we'd go inside again.

I didn't let him outside unsupervised after one of his forays beyond my fence resulted in him being lost for a week. I was beside myself with worry and cried every day, barely eating or sleeping. I put reward posters all over the neighborhood and made heart-pounding calls to the shelters, alerting them that any dead cats they found on the road might be mine. I received numerous phone call sightings from neighbors—my favorite from an excited Indian lady from the next neighborhood over, who said, "A long-haired gray cat is in my yard! All gray! With veddy green eyes, like on the poster!" When I asked what he was doing, her voice became puzzled and said, "Oh . . . he's just sitting on de grass, staring around. He doesn't even seem scared!" I knew that could only be Kashka, so at least he was alive and finding a way to survive. When

I could leave work, I drove over to the lady's neighborhood, but he had vanished again. He finally made his way home, having lost three pounds in the process, meowing a slew of angry-sounding curses at me the whole way back inside, like the whole thing had been *my* fault. I followed him from room to room petting him, laughing, and weeping.

His being lost was the first thing that made me realize he was getting older. Kashka when he was young was like a homing pigeon; he always found his way home within minutes of me calling for him, no matter what he had been doing. I'd yell his name out the door, and some faraway foliage would move and from it Kashka would emerge bounding, galloping a powerful gallop, chirping his muted greeting. After he came home and I fettered his freedom, he seemed to shrink into a cantankerous, quiet old man who didn't like toys or fun or strangers anymore. Kashka also got neurotic about little things. If I so much as put his food plate a foot from its usual spot, a two-day boycott on eating was likely. I sensed that the old gentleman was maybe a little bored, and I thought he might regain some of his macho swagger if he had a new puppy to boss around. I would turn out to be mistaken.

2. Diana Sets Me Straight

I went home the night after the *Super Pet Expo!* and waited for Virginia German Shepherd Rescue to call me. I sent everyone I knew Sasha 1's picture.

"She looks so scared," was the most common reply.

The day finally came for my phone interview.

"Well, Sasha's been adopted," the volunteer told me.

"Oh. Okay," I said, rationalizing that it wasn't meant to be. I snapped out of my dog trance long enough to wonder why I'd ever thought I wanted to adopt a dog in the first place.

"But we have lots of others to look at," the volunteer said, and instantly the trance kicked in again. I wanted a German shepherd so badly.

I called my friend Diana and promptly burst into tears.

"Why are you crying?" Diana asked. It was with the steely tone I had been secretly hoping to hear. Diana is my extremely logical friend who believes, evidence to the contrary, that I can handle anything.

I considered her question. I wasn't sure precisely what I was crying about, whether it was an irrational feeling of rejection over Sasha 1 or the prospect of drastically changing my daily habits if I got a dog. I suspect it was the latter. I love routine so much I'm surprised I haven't been formally diagnosed with an autism spectrum disorder. I loathe change. I drive the same exact route to and from work each day, and I would get lost if there were ever a detour, even if it only took me two miles from my house. I have always been mystified by the appeal of rearranging one's furniture just to "switch things up." I put my furniture where I want it, and then I leave it there.

I blame these neuroses on moving several times when I was in elementary school, the twice yearly moving in and out of college dormitory rooms, and the post-college temporary housing so many of us experience in our twenties. For decades I've had a tiny, uneasy, humming suspicion that I'll never quite belong anywhere. Even recently when I decided to buy myself a new hairbrush, I stood examining all the models for a stupidly long time, half-wondering if the one I had used since 1985 was really all that bad, in spite of the decaying rubber and the missing spindles. Ironically, while I don't mind eating the same thing for dinner every day for a week, I'm the calmest, most rational voice when there is sudden, chaotic change that calls for immediate action. Unless someone's arm is hydranting blood, a person needs to be talked down from a ledge, or a family's roof has caved in, however, I'm pretty useless.

Diana was the only one in my circle who hadn't asked me if I really thought I was "ready" for a dog. She finds my neurotic love of routine no stranger a habit than deciding which direction to roll the toilet paper, and with icy bluntness she tells me when I'm being a complete ninny. If we were in a war movie together, she'd be the one who would slap me across the face in our foxhole just as I was revving up toward a full, hysterical rant.

"I don't know if I can handle a dog," I blubbered. "You have to alter your whole life, and I can't just go away for the weekend if I want to," I cried, gearing up for a full-blown meltdown. "I'm not sure I even really *like* dogs except for German shepherds, and I thought the German shepherd I would get would be different from the dogs I looked at. I'd be married and have a big yard and Schuyler would run around his big yard, and I'd be settled down. Now I'll have to always be like, 'What about the dog? What will I do with the dog?'"

Diana let me take a breath, saying nothing. I sniffled and prepared myself.

"Um, first of all, you're carrying on like you're adopting a Cambodian orphan," she laughed. "You're thinking of adopting a *puppy*, not a child. I've heard people freak out less over having a baby. Furthermore, you have always wanted a German shepherd ever since I've known you, and, no offense, but what better time than now? You don't run off on weekends as it is, and, well, you may never get married or have a big yard. What are you waiting for?"

There it was, the foxhole slap. As she spoke, I started laughing, too. She was right. All this time I had had in my head a gauzy vision of my dog, a big male named Schuyler, named after my great-grandfather, and he'd be perfect. I'd have a farm and lots of land and a husband. I had this fantasy of what kind of person owns a dog and what kind of person I'd have to be to deserve one. In my mini-breakdown, I had been thinking of all the reasons why I *shouldn't* get a dog, rather than reasons why I would be happy with one. I thought about it more realistically.

I was living alone with Kashka. I finally owned my own house with a small fenced-in yard. I loved German shepherds and read about them on the Internet whenever I looked at dog breeds; I always rooted for them when I watched the Westminster Kennel Club dog show on television. It was also true that more often than not, my weekends consisted of staying home and reading or watching movies. I thought of how much fun it would be to have a dog friend.

I stopped crying entirely and said, "Yeah. Okay! You're right, Di. There's no reason I can't get a dog." I hung up happy. With renewed enthusiasm, I kept tabs on several German shepherds on the rescue website. Nagging me though was the knowledge that I still wasn't totally committed to the idea. Why?

3. Do I Really Even Like Dogs?

I have always preferred cats to dogs. I adore their quiet self-containment, their subtle love. Dogs that slurped and waggled and needed their owner's constant attention struck me as vaguely repellent. Dogs never seemed relaxed. They smelled. They required exercise. Whereas cats had soft coats that fit them all in one piece, like footie pajamas, dog fur seemed patchy and ill-formed, like leftover carpet remnants pieced together.

But I also had a childhood fascination with wolves and their plush ruffs, smart muzzles, alert ears, and bushy tails. I had a recurring daydream of having a protective wolf companion, fed by my voracious appetite for Jack London. Around this impressionable time, I met my Aunt Martha's wolfish German shepherd, Gina, who my aunt had adopted from a nunnery in Pennsylvania. Gina was docile around women and children, but she detested men and would gallop full speed, belly low, snarling down the lane at my aunt's farm to ward off any strange man coming towards the house. The only man of record who didn't panic at the sight was my aunt's vet, an old horse man who treated Gina like it was a completely normal greeting. "Oh, now, hello there," the vet cheerfully said and calmly kept walking to the barn. I guess years of being kicked and bitten by eleven-hundred-pound animals made him pretty blasé around a sixty-five-pound dog. It certainly baffled Gina, and after that, she regarded him as a trusted friend.

I was, upon meeting her, both terrified of and besotted with Gina, who barked furiously at the door when someone knocked but who gently followed me around the house, allowing me to pet her. Gina never slavered over anyone or acted any way except cool and friendly. I never felt embarrassed for her the way I did for other dogs. She moved around my aunt's Arabian horse farm with an aloof dignity that appealed to me. She always wore an expression of gravity, like she had important things to do but didn't mind an interruption now and then. She patiently completed any obstacle course I set up for her in the back field and never looked anything but graceful doing it. From that point on, I was a cat-and-German-Shepherd-Dog person. I liked other dogs well enough but never loved them with the fierce devotion I reserved for the German shepherd.

So why the hesitation over the website adoptees? A memory finally surfaced to help me solve that mystery. The year before, while Robin and I were attending the same Chantilly *Super Pet Expo!*, a pet photographer set up a backdrop and took lovely digital photos of people's pets, and we stood and watched. Years of watching dog shows and reading about various breeds had softened my attitude a bit on dogs in general, though I still wasn't sure I actually wanted one.

Then I saw him.

A teenaged girl had two enormous dogs on leashes, one of which was a male long-haired German shepherd I couldn't take my eyes off. I felt starstruck, hopelessly smitten, my chest aching mildly with covetous longing. I wanted to own that dog. I couldn't imagine another creature so handsome. He looked as if someone had formed a wolf out of black and copper velvet. Long feathers formed a fluffy mane around his solid black nose, and he had almond-shaped, light orange eyes. He was young, as evidenced by his exuberant disregard for doing anything that meant sitting still. His owner placed him in front of the camera, but he kept trotting back to her, his mouth open in a dog smile, and his mammoth caterpillar of a bushy tail wagging slightly.

"No!" the girl said firmly, staring at him, and with a particularly cheeky look, he gracefully stood up on his hind feet and placed two perfect round front paws onto her shoulders and tilted his head. The motion of his tail picked up speed to the point where it resembled those fans used by servants in the old days to keep flies off well-born ladies.

None of the spectators could stifle a laugh, and the dog knew he was being funny. I wanted to grab his collar right then, clip a leash on, and sail around the huge concrete warehouse floor, cantering side by side with this magnificent animal, like I had seen handlers do at Westminster on TV. "Is that your dog?" I imagined people gasping, awed, as we ran by in perfect harmony.

There were no long-haired dogs featured on the Virginia German Shepherd Rescue website, I was sad to realize. I thought each was pretty in his or her own way, and I was touched by their stories, but none of them felt right to me. I knew enough about my personality to know that a shrinking, possibly abused shepherd wouldn't be a good choice for me as my first dog. Since first seeing Sasha 1 at the *Super Pet Expo!*, I had done more reading, and I now had a better idea of what I wanted: a blank-slate impressionable puppy, one that had escaped the kind of poor breeding I'd learned fosters temperament and health problems.

I decided on a whim to look online at area professional breeders. I figured a high-quality small breeder would be the safest. I looked specifically for breeders close to the Washington, DC, area so I could visit the facility and meet the parents. One of my hits was the Haus Juris Kennel in Nokesville, Virginia. On their home page, one of the sires, Manto, lay happily next to a toddler in one photo and in another stood in a regal, strong stack. I decided to read everything on the site and learned that this particular breeder espoused the philosophy of Captain Max von Stephanitz—the "Golden Middle." As the originator of the breed in 1899, von Stephanitz desired to create a herding dog who would be a jack-of-all-trades, with sound build and excellent temperament. In their photos, the kennel's dogs stood or sat in perfect poses with alert, happy, self-confident expressions. They all had the thicker German build with blockier heads and straighter backs, to which I realized I was partial. No mention was made specifically of confirmation for showing; it instead emphasized that the dogs were bred for "balanced structure"—stability, temperament, and health—which appealed to me as well. Puppies were available, but by appointment only, and no prices were listed. This was a serious breeder; I was in the big leagues now. Trying to sound more sure of myself than I felt, I left a message for Megan Judge, the breeder and owner of the kennel.

Megan called me back the same evening. "Are you looking to breed?" she asked. "Because I don't sell my dogs to amateur breeders." She had a no-nonsense, abrupt nature that reminded me of a German shepherd itself. No time for frivolity.

"Um, no, I'm only interested in a pet."

"What's your living situation? I'm very careful with the dogs I place."

"I'm single. I live alone. I own my own place. It's small, but I have a fenced-in yard. And I have a cat."

Megan said she also had a cat.

"I've just always loved German shepherds," I gushed. Megan had that effect on me, of wanting to sell myself somehow.

"What are you interested in, a male or a female? I have some regular-coated puppies that go for—" The amount she quoted was what I would pay for a new air handler or the cost of refinishing the floors in my house. "I also have some long-coated puppies, if you're just looking for a pet," she said. "Those go for—" She named a price a little more than a thousand dollars less than the shorter-haired puppies. "There's absolutely *nothing* wrong with them, other than the coat, but some people don't want a long coat. They can't be shown with that coat. Well, not in a Sieger Show, anyway." She assumed, correctly, that I'd have no idea what a Seiger Show is, so she clarified, "The Sieger is a German breed show that also assesses the character of the dog. The long coat is a disqualifying fault." She sounded as if she were trying to discourage me from the outset, as though she were testing me to see how serious I was.

"*I love long coats!*" I gasped.

There was a pause, and I had a feeling Megan was mildly irritated.

"Well, I have a male and a female. I've sold the male already, but I have the girl."

"Oh. You sold the male?" I asked, disappointed, my vision of Schuyler vanishing.

Another pause.

"Why do you want a male?" Megan asked. "This is your first dog, right?"

I admitted it was.

"You might do better with a female. They're, I think, a bit easier to train and a little less . . . I don't know, I just think they're a little smarter. Just like human girls," she laughed.

"Well, the thing is, I do live alone, and I thought a boy might be more protective."

Megan snorted and then laughed for a good fifteen seconds. "Females are very protective!" she practically shouted. Megan shouted whenever she was educating less-informed dog people, which was most everyone most of the time. "In fact, I think they're more protective. They're less concerned with marking territory, and females by and large want to stay by the family's side more. Anyway, my top Schutzhund dog is a bitch." She laughed some more, and I laughed along, only half aware of what she was talking about. I vaguely knew Schutzhund involved biting a padded sleeve, so when I learned the best at it was a female, I began to reconsider my assumptions.

"Anyway, I'm not going to tell you what to do," Megan said. "If your heart is set on a male, and you like the long coat, I can always keep your information and call you if I get another litter with any long-coated males. It's not that common, but obviously, I do get them sometimes. They're not what most breeders want. But underneath, they're the same dog!" Then Megan practically screamed, "Whatever you do, don't go to a long-coated breeder!" as if I'd suggested the idea (I hadn't even considered it). "That's all I ask. Those Shiloh shepherds you hear about? Big overbred mutants! Horrible for the bones. All kinds of problems. You don't want one. They're not real German shepherds."

Dog breeders have always struck me as partisan and a little quirky, and Megan was proving to be no exception.

"Anyway, if you want to come out, I have an evening appointment open Friday. You're welcome to come see my female. I think she'd be perfect for you, but again, no pressure."

I agreed to come out Friday evening "just to see" the long-coated female I knew I probably wouldn't want. What harm could looking at her do? It would be good practice looking at puppies, I reasoned.

I was doomed.

4. Enter Athena

"I'm going to look at a puppy tomorrow," I said to my sister Mary on the phone.

"Really? Which one?"

"This is a new one; she's not on the rescue site."

"What's she like?" Mary asked. It amazed me that anyone acted interested in the latest dog, as I had cried wolf so many times.

"I don't know; I haven't seen her yet. I called you for some ideas for girl names. I always thought I'd get a male and name it Schuyler, after great-grandfather."

My sister thought for a second. "Let's look on the Internet," she suggested. "I know! I'll look on a website for goddess names." She suggested a few—Hera, Demeter, Artemis, Persephone—and none seemed right. "Oh! What about Athena? The goddess of wisdom and war?"

"That's the one!" I practically yelled. "Goddess of wisdom and war . . . that's *awesome* for a German shepherd. They're smart dogs, and wow, war." I envisioned Megan's top Schutzhund bitch, launched at an imaginary sleeve, which transformed into a vision of a strong, wise dog—my dog—leaping at some faceless assailant who intended to harm me. *Athena*. It was perfect.

"What about Kashka?" my sister asked.

I gave her my *Manchurian Candidate* answer, which had evolved from, "He's been around dogs before," to "He likes dogs."

The next day I kept my plans a secret at work. Since Sasha 1, I had been disappointed with a string of "maybe" and "almost-mine" rescue dogs; either the ones I considered were already taken, or the ones I half-heartedly asked about weren't the ones I really wanted. I didn't want to jinx anything.

I left work early and drove the forty-five minutes to Nokesville, making typical detours to incorrect addresses along the way. I finally found Megan's place, a house with a large building attached—the kennel. Megan came to the front door and told me to move my car, because of course I had driven up a gravel service road and parked it in the wrong area. I hadn't been there three minutes, and I was already annoying her. What if she deemed me unworthy of one of her puppies? The thought made me more certain that I wanted one.

When I walked into the large, tidy living room and kitchen area, Manto, the star of the website, greeting me by barking and then trotting briskly over to me, carrying a partially deflated basketball.

"Oh aren't you cute with your ball?" I cooed. "Is that your toy?"

Megan stared at me, and I felt like an even bigger idiot. But honestly, his majestic stacks and tall proud posture were belied by the comical way he bounced around Megan's kitchen with his ball. It was like hearing a celebrity pee next to you in a bathroom stall.

Also in the room was Iris von der Grafshaft Mark, the dam of the puppies. She approached me with flattened ears and waggley hips and tail, a sweet dog who seemed only to want to be liked.

"Oh, you're the mommy," I said as I petted her.

"Don't look at her coat! She's blown it all away!" Megan shouted. Iris looked like a normal German shepherd to me, and I stroked her sides so her feelings wouldn't be hurt.

"I think she looks beautiful," I said.

Megan stared at me again with a pitying smile. It was obvious I knew nothing about dogs, all my research aside. After shutting Manto and Iris in another part of the house, Megan had me sit at the kitchen table while she went through the door that led to the kennel. Her arrival produced a happy chorus of barks that quieted after a short time.

"Come on! Good girl!" I heard Megan say behind the door. Then the door opened, and Megan stood in the doorway, holding the puppy. She put her down gently on the tile floor, and into the kitchen Athena pranced.

"There she is!" Megan shouted with a mixture of pride, delight, and tenderness.

Athena trotted into the kitchen completely without fear, picking up the pace to a clunky sideways run toward me. I was struck with an almost painful wave of infatuation.

"*Awwww!*" I said, clapping my hands. I launched myself from the chair to my knees. Athena climbed on me. "That. Is. The. Cutest. Thing. I. Have. Ever. Seen!" I screamed, almost hysterically. And she was. Some animals seem to know they're cute, and Athena was one of them. She waltzed around the kitchen with measured exaggeration in her steps, head held high, seeming to dare anyone not to look at her. Her face was almost completely black with small furrows of golden red blossoming across her forehead. I saw that one of her ears stood up in a thick triangle resembling a luxuriant slipper, while the other flopped over like the daintily folded flap of a furry envelope. Her ears took up most of the space on top of her head. She was like a stuffed animal come to life. Her stubby little snout ended with a nose so black and shiny, I was sure it was hard plastic. Her dark brown eyes were clear and merry, and if she could have spoken, I'm sure she would have sung, "Here I aa-am!"

I was especially enchanted by her legs. She had what I term "paw-leg," something I'd seen in large-breed puppies. Each buff-colored leg had no discernible joint between femur and paw and seemed just one column, thick as a little tree. Her thick, downy puppy coat seemed full of static, and it gave her a puffy look. The fur along her back was inky as a panther, and the ruff at her chest the color of rich caramel. Her tail was still a narrow whip. Tiny tufts at the base of her one erect ear and some sparse fur peeking out from between her toes were the only clues that she was a long-coated shepherd. With her cobby body, she resembled a grizzly cub more than a puppy.

"She loves bones!" Megan said. "I mean really loves them! You should see her!" She leaped up from the table, yanked open the refrigerator door, and pulled out a beef bone approximately the size of Athena's head. "These are the best for dogs, by the way," Megan said, and then she yelled, "Do *not* give this puppy rawhide!"

I flinched and said, "Okay," meekly, as if I had been caught offering all the dogs in her kennel rawhides. The truth was, I wasn't crazy about most commercial rawhides, because my ex-boyfriend's Weimaraner had gotten explosive diarrhea after eating one, and all the other dogs I knew who ate them produced witheringly smelly farts for hours afterward.

"I only give them natural beef bones. Stew bones. You can get them at the supermarket!" Megan yelled.

Athena, meanwhile, had gamboled to the refrigerator and stood looking up at Megan. Megan put a vertical forefinger up between her own eyes to train Athena's gaze on her, and when Athena looked up at her and dropped her pudgy rear, Megan said, "Good girl!" and offered the puppy the head-sized bone. Athena took it into her mouth, and all her playfulness abruptly vanished. She furrowed her brow as if concentrating on solving a particularly difficult chemistry formula and began walking slowly around the kitchen before disappearing around a corner. I thought she had taken the bone somewhere to chew it in peace, but seconds later she reemerged, still wearing that fretful expression, this time emitting low whines that sounded vaguely hen like.

"Look at her! Look at her!" Megan screamed. "She's looking for somewhere to hide it! Isn't that *fantastic*?" She actually clapped her hands. "So primitive!"

Athena paid no notice to either of us. It was a trait she would exhibit later whenever she had anything she deemed important in her mouth. She walked by us as if hypnotized, lugging the enormous bone. She carried it into the living room and then back down the hall, out of sight. Every so often, she would drop it, probably out of fatigue, and I'd hear the loud clatter of the bone on tile. I surmised she'd finally found an acceptable spot when she came back into the kitchen without it. She still looked upset that she had had to solve such a weighty matter. I kissed at her, and she stared at me for a second with no emotion, until the mood passed and she bounced like a moving rocking horse over to me.

Megan then reviewed the price with me, in case I chose to buy Athena. I could have easily taken a nice vacation to the Caribbean and spent around the same amount. If I wanted Athena, I would have to leave a good faith deposit and then procure the rest in a money order from my bank.

Then Megan began her litany of rules.

"You may not breed this dog without talking to me first. I can take her back if I find out—"

"That's fine," I interrupted. "She's just for me, for a pet."

"Second—what are you going to do with this dog?"

I stared. The question was a little broad.

"Um . . . put her in a crate? Um . . . for bedtime?"

"Good. Yes. Crate her. What about training?"

"I was going to take her to puppy classes."

"What kind of puppy classes?" she demanded.

"I guess, um, group classes, like at—?" I mentioned a popular pet store chain.

"No. No good. They don't know German shepherds. I teach a puppy class here. She should go to that."

The idea of having to do anything more than sit down across from this woman at a table terrified me. I could imagine myself frozen in indecision as every tiny gesture on my part made her yell, "No! Curl your fingers around the lead *this way*! No! Not all the way like that! No! Don't move! No! Keep your head up; don't look at me!" while Athena spun in crazy disobedient circles at my feet.

"What are you planning on feeding her?" Megan broke into my sweat-inducing imaginary training session.

"I was thinking—" I mentioned a popular high-end commercial dog food brand. I silently congratulated myself for not even considering plain cheap dog food. But Megan recoiled as if I had told her I was planning on feeding Athena nothing but chocolate bars.

"No. No. No. Absolutely not. Those foods have preservatives and grains. They're horrible for dogs. Horrible! Why did you choose those foods?"

"I heard they're recommended by vets."

"That's a scam!" she yelled. "Vets are *paid* to say that! I'll show you the food all my dogs eat," she said, and she pulled from her refrigerator a long tube of meat. It looked like a log of the premade cookie dough you slice up, except those packages don't have blood seeping out of them. "This is K-9 Kraving!" she said. Athena, who had retrieved her bone and was trying to hide it again, brightened, dropped the bone with a clack, and ran over to the refrigerator. Megan did the thing with her finger again, and when Athena sat, Megan fed her a piece of the food off a spoon.

"It has all natural ingredients. Beef, vegetables, potatoes. It keeps their digestive tracts in order. No preservatives." She put the meat tube back and sat down again across from me. She told me she was also a distributor of K-9 Kraving, so I could get it from her. She stared at me. I shifted my gaze to just left of her intense brown stare, like I was deep in thought. But I knew I couldn't afford K-9 Kraving.

"Well, think about the food," Megan said, continuing to fix me with her stare.

Athena broke the tension as she picked up her bone again, and like Caesar's ghost, lugged it through the kitchen and out to the hallway again, muttering to herself discontentedly.

Megan talked more about German shepherds, their special training needs, how they must have "a job," and how attached they are to their owners. I vaguely noticed as Athena waddled back into the kitchen (sans bone) and squatted in the corner. Then she stepped aside, and I suppressed a gasp. "Uh oh," I said, trying to sound cavalier. "She went. She went potty." I was not expecting the huge load of crap that had emerged from such a small dog. I had somehow expected it would be like Kashka's—small, compact, easy to scoop, rather than the large, semi-solid pudding cylinders Athena had dropped.

Megan was completely unfazed and joked, "Ooo stinky girl! Okay, let me get it." I realized that a few of the same large accidents were probably in my future; I just didn't realize how often or how humiliating they would turn out to be.

"Well I'm putting her back now. What do you think?"

"*I love her!*" I practically screamed, forgetting suddenly her large poo and the sleepwalking routine with the bone. I left the sizable good faith deposit and promised to get the rest from my bank the next morning.

"Can I see her one last time before I go?" I asked. I also wanted to see the kennel.

"Sure," Megan said and took me into the spotless kennel. The adult dogs barked a few times but then fell silent. Some lay down; one or two disappeared out of dog doors into their outdoor runs.

The door to the puppy room was open, the entrance blocked with a baby gate. Warm infrared lights turned the thrashing mass of brown and black into Amsterdam, and all five puppies stopped suddenly when they saw us and then as one rushed and clamored on their hind legs at the gate.

"Aw, I really love the face on that one," I said.

Megan fixed me a look of amusement and exasperation. "That's *yours!*" she cackled, shaking her head. And it was. It was Athena. She had no problem knocking her siblings aside to say hello.

"I don't have a baby gate," I said. "I'll probably need one, huh?" Megan rolled her eyes and sold me a used one cheap.

"I want my cat to smell it so he's used to it," I explained.

Megan looked at me like I was crazy and nodded indulgently. "Do you have a craaaate?" she asked slowly, the way you ask a preschooler if she can tie her own shoes yet.

"No," I admitted. "I was going to get one tonight." I almost added, "I swear!" I must have looked alarmed and guilty, because Megan offered to sell me one of those, too.

5. Crate of Laughs

When I got home, I went through the living room to the back of my house and propped the baby gate across my kitchen doorway and stared at it. The bar had fallen in transit, and since I have the mechanical ability of a spiral ham, I moved the bar around, wondering how to fasten it, staring at it as if the solution might appear in front of me in a shiny bubble. It didn't, and I was glad Megan hadn't asked me to demonstrate that I could set up a baby gate. Presumably she had not because the average person with motor skills more advanced than those of a toddler can work one.

"I'll figure it out later," I reasoned and left it propped in the doorway. I retrieved a sleepy, grumpy napping Kashka from atop my bed and carried him to the gate. "Here, Kashi! Look! It smells like doggies, but it's okay." Kashka blinked at me and looked annoyed, barely glancing at the baby gate. He squirmed, demanding to be put down, and when I did, he walked away to resume his nap. I called Robin, my family, everyone I could think of to report I had picked out my puppy.

"She is *so cute*!" I cried, describing her. I left out the parts about the pile the size of a baby elephant's and the hypnotized meandering with the bone. Robin agreed to accompany me to Petco and to go with me the next morning to pick Athena up.

At the store, I settled on Nutro Puppy for the scientific reason that there was a German shepherd puppy on the bag. I picked out a tiny purple collar and an equally tiny leash that were for a cat, because all the regular dog collars and leashes seemed too big. I made a dog tag on one of the do-it-yourself etching machines, and I was so proud to read "Athena Needham." I blurted out to pretty much everyone who crossed my path in the store that I was getting a new puppy. Most smiled indulgently, but a few edged away.

After a fitful sleep, I went to the bank in the morning to withdraw the rest of Athena's price. The bank teller probably didn't wonder or particularly care why I was getting such a large money order, but she was still subjected to my blabbermouth tumble about Athena, my new puppy.

"That's wonderful!" she said, eyeing me with slight alarm.

On the way out of town I warned Robin how scary Megan was, and she laughed unconcernedly, because she was there just to see the puppy and didn't have to talk to Megan. When we pulled up, Megan was outside talking to two other clients.

"She's inside," Megan said. "Let me go get her."

Robin and I followed her inside and sat in the kitchen waiting.

I heard a loud skittering of claws, and when the door opened, Athena ran straight for me—for approximately .0022 seconds—before running to Robin. "She is *so cute!*" Robin began, reaching a hand out to pet her. Athena had already run away by then, though, so we both only had the opportunity to pet the idea of fur. The happy, calm trot she had demonstrated the previous evening was gone. Instead she raced around the kitchen like an excited bee in a flower bush, not standing still for any longer than it took her to place all four feet on the ground. I made a clicking sound with my tongue to get her attention, and with a maniacal, delighted eye roll, she ran back to me, launched, and fixed her sewing-machine-needle teeth on my hand.

"No Ath—" I got out, instinctively reaching to scruff her, like I would a naughty kitten. But she was already scrambling back to Robin, to another pair of unsuspecting hands.

"Aw! C'mere!" Robin cooed, extending the targets. A second later I heard, "Ouch! What a brat!" and saw Robin shaking and examining her fingers.

"I'm sorry, are you okay?" I asked her, as Athena zoomed by again, a black and beige blur. Just then, Megan reemerged from the kennel with a considerable stack of paperwork.

"Wow," I chuckled, "she has a lot of energy this morning!"

I could swear Megan dipped her eyes away from mine briefly, and then she laughed gaily. "She sure does! And she's so smart! Oh . . . I fed her this morning. Sorry." She smiled mischievously and didn't act particularly sorry. I must have looked dismayed, because she quickly said, "I'm sure she'll be fine in her crate. I doubt she'll get carsick."

We turned our attention to the mountain of paperwork. Megan had more rules to go over. Athena, meanwhile, ran over to me again, and looking at a spot directly beyond my line of sight, slapped my leg with her two front paws and then bounced off, running like she was being chased. She fixed her gleaming, feverish eyes on Robin, ran toward her, and then veered off suddenly, thundering around the corner. Megan and I started going over the contract. Robin followed Athena into the other room, and soon I could hear her hissing and saying, "Ow!" Finally, Megan stood and went to the refrigerator, and Athena spun into the kitchen when she heard the sound of the door opening. When Megan lifted the beef bone out, Athena stopped moving suddenly, and a disquieting calmness came over her, except for the frantic look in her eyes. She sat, waiting. Bone in her mouth, her expression shifted then into the hopeless expressionless affect of a patient on Thorazine, and she began the familiar muttering as she plodded around the house.

"Aw, she's so cute with her bone!" Robin said, coming into the now-quiet kitchen.

"I know" Megan said, excitedly. "It's so primitive!" She turned her attention back to me. "First off, you will get this dog some training. Second. This is a dog bred for work. That means her focus should be on you the whole time. My dogs do *not* go to dog parks for that reason!"

I kept my expression carefully neutral.

"Third. You will not breed this dog, unless you receive my consent. Fourth. If you don't feed her K-9 Kraving, then expect high vet bills. I can't give you a lifetime guarantee if you aren't feeding her my food. Fifth. At two years old, you must have her hips X-rayed. Her father has some of the best hips in Germany, supposedly, but you still need to do that."

"Manto has the best hips?" I asked, looking around for the proud papa and his basketball.

"Manto isn't her father!" Megan bellowed, laughing.

"Oh, he isn't? Who's the father?"

Megan rolled her eyes and, still laughing, said, "Romeo!"

"Oh. Is Romeo here?" I asked, looking in the direction of her kennels.

"I don't own Romeo! Romeo is a three-hundred-thousand-dollar dog!" she screamed. "He's in Germany!"

Feeling like I had been part of an elaborate hoax, I looked at Robin. She was wisely averting her eyes, staring at the floor, anywhere out of the vicinity of Megan's intense brown stare.

"So you shipped Romeo's um . . ."

"Nope. Nope. The Germans believe in breeding the old-fashioned way. Iris flew to Germany and then flew back."

"You and Iris flew all the way to Germany for her to mate with the father?" I was flabbergasted.

"I didn't fly. I hate to fly. No, we just put Iris on a plane, and she mated and flew back, and now, here's her litter."

"Oh. Oh. Okay." I was in shock, silently calculating the expense of it all

Megan handed me a chart and showed me both parents' genealogical lines. "You'll have to get the official pedigree once you register with the AKC, of course." She pointed, and indeed, there it was. Sire: Romeo van Pallas Athene. Pallas Athene—another name for Athena. It was reminiscent of the way Kashka and I had found each other, and I saw it as a sign that I had absolutely done the right thing. Besides, my baby girl came from very illustrious lines. I forgot her hand chomping and slack bone-face and the way she seemed to have completely forgotten that fine trot.

I asked Megan about the AKC, if I might have seen Romeo in any of those shows. Megan looked horrified and screamed, "Oh, *no*! Only American shepherds compete in those! Disgusting! All inbred and over-angulated. Skinny! Too long! Weak heads! Can't even do what they were bred for!" She looked at me and may have even gripped my arm. *"Don't ever get an American shepherd!"*

Thinking that I preferred the heavier-boned, stockier German version, anyway (only because I found them cuter), I conspiratorially nodded like I knew what she meant. "Oh no, I won't!" I promised.

After signing the paperwork that I swear took more signatures than when I bought my house, Athena was officially mine. It was time to take my little aristocrat home, a concept Megan sullied slightly by offering to take Athena out "to potty" before we left.

"Did you hear all that, Robin?" I asked, proud of my puppy's German blue blood.

"Yeah," she said mockingly. "I can't believe that little brat comes from such distinctive genes."

"She's a princess!" I gushed and then laughed when Robin raised her eyebrows and went "Uh . . . Yeah. Sure."

Later, when I looked at Megan's website again, I confirmed that Romeo van Pallas Athene was listed as the father of Athena's litter. He was a large, handsome red fellow, who was listed as the "FCI World Winner" in 2002, whatever that meant. I would find out later that the Fédération Cynologique Internationale, or FCI, is an organization of kennel clubs dedicated to preserving healthy breeding stock of breeds from all around the world. In the year 2002, for German Shepherd Dogs, Romeo was the best of breed for all submitted German shepherds as well as the "best dog" (male). I looked at his and Iris's information more closely. Both were Schutzhund IIIs, which meant that both had passed the most rigorous Schutzhund training possible. I called everyone I knew to brag about my fuzzy Brahman. They had no more clue than I about what any of it really meant, but all were obligingly impressed.

Robin and I went outside to find Megan beaming as she held Athena, who was now possessed by a Dr. Jekyll–like calm. "She didn't go," Megan informed me cheerily, "so she may have gone already when she was in her kennel earlier." She put Athena down on the grass and gave me a bumper sticker that read "I love my German shepherd from Haus Juris Kennel" and a bright yellow-and-black windbreaker that read "Haus Juris" and had an embroidered German shepherd head on it.

"Congratulations," she said, and I thanked her for everything. I bent over to pick up Athena, something Megan made look so easy, but apparently I did it wrong, because Athena let out a shriek that I felt in my teeth. I didn't know it at the time, but German shepherds are highly vocal "drama queens" when displeased. I also didn't realize that Athena's initial scream was merely a warm-up for later.

I loaded her into her crate, and we set off for the forty-five minute drive home. Ten minutes into the ride, Robin wrinkled her nose and said, "What's that smell?" It was a rhetorical question, really, since we both knew what "that smell" was. It was as if four children at once had removed their dirty diapers and were waving them around inside my car. "Ew!" we both groaned, and rolled down the windows. "I guess she didn't go at Megan's after all," I said, pointing out the obvious.

"Someone's getting a bath," I added. Poor Athena. Ten minutes later, a dismally familiar bubbling and gagging rose from the crate, followed by seemingly endless splashing and spattering as Athena got prodigiously carsick.

"Poor Athena!" Robin and I agreed, neither of us wanting to contemplate what the crate, the dog, and the back seat of my car might look like. Then a noise began to emanate from the crate, an eerie sound the likes of which I had never heard before and haven't heard since. It began as a low moan and rose to a despondent wail that reverberated up and down my spinal column. Had some keening restless spirit left a bog and invaded my car? Breathing through my mouth, I reached back and put my fingers through the grate on the hard plastic crate, and Athena splashed her way to them, gave them a brief sniff, and then resumed her unearthly cacophony.

"Sweetie, I would cry, too, if I was stuck in all that," I told her.

When we finally pulled up to my house, I carried the whole sloshing affair to the back yard, where I turned on the hose. Then I poured Athena and some of the disgusting contents of her crate out onto the grass. She rolled out in a daze, blinking in the sunshine. Not taking time for niceties, I turned the hose on her and saturated her from neck to tail while she sat limply, shell shocked, as hunks of various bodily wastes skimmed off her. I toweled her vigorously and glanced over at the crate, wincing, girding my loins to tackle the mess inside it.

I am a notorious vomitphobe. I won't even watch a movie in which an actor pretends to vomit. It's not that I have an overdeveloped gag reflex; it's just that vomiting causes an extreme fight or flight reaction in me. No matter how close and dear a friend may be, if she's getting sick, I'd climb drapes to get away from her. I asked Robin to hold Athena, who was still wrapped in the towel, and then I dragged the hard plastic crate through my gate and into the large grassy area beyond my tiny yard. I stuck the hose into the crate and sprayed it full blast. The wave I had created surged out the door of the crate, carrying barf, diarrhea, and, as a special surprise, pee. Robin helped distract me by laughing hysterically and yelling, "Ew! Ewww!"

"I guess this is my trial by fire," I shouted over the loud sound of water spraying against plastic. Then I began to feel strangely calm. I was not naive enough to think that a new puppy wouldn't puke, but I had worried about how I would handle it when Athena vomited. Now that I had faced the situation, my fear dissipated, and I was more concerned that my new baby, wet from the hose, might be cold in the spring sun. I wanted her to feel clean and warm and to have a spotless crate to sleep in when it was time to go to bed. I left the crate to dry out in the sun, and then I wiped it with a light disinfectant. Later, I found out that I needn't have bothered.

I knew Athena had recovered from her ordeal when I heard Robin exclaim, "Ouch! Wait . . . Okay, just a minute! God! Brat!" as Athena wiggled out of the towel. Mr. Hyde was back. I was prepared with some toys this time, and Athena set upon each one with the savagery of a one-puppy wolf pack, picking it up, carrying it, dropping it in favor of the next one, and running around the yard the whole time like she was being pursued by demons. I clicked at her to get her attention, and she ran to me enthusiastically, practically bowling me over when she jumped on me. I caught her up in my arms and snuggled my face to hers, expecting some cute submissive puppy kisses and getting instead a sharp bite on the chin followed by a swipe on the face with a fat, damp paw. She gazed at me joyfully the whole time, with a manic expression of happiness, and I could see that she wasn't mean-spirited in the least, just a little clumsy and, well, violent when it came to expressing affection.

Throughout all this, Robin laughed and shook her head and took photos of me and Athena.

"Enjoying your new puppy?" she called, watching me try once more to cradle the squirming, spastic Athena in my arms.

I let her go and picked up a tennis ball from the pile of toys and held it out to her balanced on my palm. She was suddenly riveted, standing perfectly still. She gazed at that ball with a level of intensity spooky to see in such a young dog. A chorus of angels seemed to sing, and she looked at the ball as though it were surrounded by an aura of sparkling gold, as though she were King Arthur and I were showing her the Holy Grail. I rolled the ball for her, and for fifteen minutes, she batted it around like she was a cat, before holding it in her mouth or between her front paws. She didn't want to let it out of her sight. I had unwittingly discovered the only other thing besides a bone that would calm Athena down long enough for me to pet her.

6. Who Needs Sleep?

By the time Robin went home, Athena seemed to have tired herself out, so I brought her and her crate into my kitchen, which was to be her room. The baby gate was still propped across the doorway (I still hadn't figured out how to install it), and for the time being, Athena seemed to believe it was a secure boundary.

Kashka came tentatively into the living room and stared across the baby gate at Athena with his round green eyes, and Athena stood on the other side of the gate staring back.

"Kashka," I said, "this is Athena, and she—" I took a step toward Athena and accidentally stepped on her paw, and she let out a wall-rattling screech. Kashka dropped low and scrambled like a roach out of the room. I lamely comforted the still-screaming Athena and alternately called after Kashka, but neither of them would be placated. Kashka went under my bed, where he stayed for the majority of the next six months, and Athena continued to wail halfheartedly even after I suspected her paw had stopped hurting that much.

"That went well," I said to myself and stepped over the baby gate to talk to Kashka. He lay in the very center of the floor underneath my bed with his back to me, and when I called his name, he refused to turn his head toward me. Instead he flicked the end of his tail before laying his chin down as though he couldn't bear to hold it up anymore. I called him again. He ignored me. I went to the other side of the bed and lay down on the floor so I could see his face. I said his name again. He slowly and deliberately turned his head so that it was facing the other direction and then put his head down again, as if he had resigned himself to just die there on the spot. When I reached under the bed to touch him, he lay perfectly still and allowed me to stroke him with the very tips of my fingers, but he had gone completely limp. I poked him gently, and he just slightly rolled back and forth like a lump of furry dough. He often used deadweight as a strategy when he didn't want to do something, like leave my bedroom at night. There were only one or two things that Kashka ever did that irritated me, and then only slightly, but deadweight was one of them. As though to dilute my irritation, he would always begin purring when I lugged his lifeless carcass away from wherever he had inconveniently planted himself. This current protest was dead-weight times ten. And there would be no purring.

I heard Athena scrabbling around in the kitchen, and it sounded like she was trying to get into the cabinets, so I quickly returned to check on her. She was just batting some toy around contentedly, so I sat down and thought, "Now what do I do?"

I had this fluffy terror who would not sit still when awake, unless she had something in her mouth. Although she preferred fingers, I tried to dissuade her from biting by giving her stuffed animals and rubber squeaky toys. The lure of the tennis ball seemed to fade unless there was a hand nearby, so even though the ball was rolling around on the kitchen floor, she now gave it no more attention than any other toy. And I still hadn't figured out how to work the damn baby gate.

Nevertheless, I decided it was time for bed. I let Athena outside one more time, and she promptly peed. I waited for her to poop. And waited. And waited. She came back inside. She played with her toys. I coaxed her outside again. She came back in. Finally, figuring it had all come out on the way home, I put her in her crate with a few toys. I had read all about crates. They shouldn't be too roomy, the books said, but just large enough that the puppy could shift comfortably. "Your puppy will consider it a safe place, like a den," I'd read. Supposedly puppies knew instinctively not to "eliminate" in their dens. I had friends who told me their puppies went several hours and *never* went potty in their crates. I'd also read that if my puppy whined in her crate, I was to ignore it, since I did not want to reinforce the connection between whining and human attention.

No one, however, had told Athena these important facts. Inside her crate, she yelped and howled, and I partially shut my bedroom door and checked on Kashka, who looked practically comatose splayed out under the bed, the perfect picture of dejection and misery. I tried to feed him some leftover turkey hamburger. He turned his head away. I checked his litter box in the second bedroom, where I kept all his things. There was no sign he had used it. Fearing he was going to sulk his way into hurting himself, I moved his litter box and food dishes into my bedroom and lay down fully clothed, suddenly exhausted. I fell asleep in spite of Athena's yipping and carrying on, which finally stopped, but I'd only been asleep for an hour when I was awoken by the screeching of what sounded like an enraged chimpanzee.

I went into the kitchen, where Athena, not having read the puppy manual, had crapped in her crate, and, panicked, was clawing at the sides of the enclosure, alternately sitting in and stamping on her own crap, which was everywhere in there. I let her outside into the yard again, and she stood there, looking confused. I threw her towels and toys in the washing machine and got my back-up towels, scrubbed her crate clean, and tried to wash her off as best I could. I figured she had pooped already, so I put her back in her crate, with new towels and new toys. I lay back down in my bedroom. Kashka's food bowl sat untouched, but as I drifted off, I heard him urinating in his litter box, which made me ridiculously happy. I smiled and sighed, thinking everything was improving by the second.

I had just drifted off when Athena started her screaming-monkey noises again. This time she was thrashing around, tromping un-daintily in her own urine. So I took her out again into the yard, and again she stood there, confused. She had already used her outhouse prison that I had trapped her in and calmly came into the kitchen and lay down on the floor in an exhausted, smelly heap. Having had so little sleep and being now convinced that I had already failed as a dog owner made me agitated. I sat next to Athena and stroked her fur while she lay there finally quiet and sound asleep. I silently cursed her, listening to the churning washing machine that contained the latest set of towels. The stench coming off her and her stubborn refusal to be a normal quiet puppy who could be crated suddenly disgusted me, and I had a sudden urge to take her back to Megan. That feeling was coupled with the feverish notion that I had hastened Kaskha's death. Kashka had been my constant—my only constant—for twelve years, and he had never wavered or shown me anything but affection and calm acceptance of all my flaws. And how had I repaid him? By bringing this uncivilized, reeking dog into our home.

I choked on a sob and moved away from Athena. I had spent a fortune on a pedigreed dog, supposedly a member of the third most intelligent breed in dogdom, and it turned out that her personality was a mixture of feverish howler monkey, troublesome ferret, and soulless shark. My fingers were cut up, and I had tiny tooth marks on my chin and cheek from where she had bitten me.

"What's *wrong* with you?" I hissed at her, but she just kept sleeping. I thought of all the puppies I had played with over the years—affectionate, snuggling, soft-tongued Labrador puppies; gentle beagle mixes with velvet ears; snuffly, silken toy breeds. None of them that I could recall had ever shown affection by jumping wildly on me and lacerating my skin. None I could remember had responded to a firm "No!" with even greater frenzy, biting joyfully harder. None I saw had responded to my claps and coos with blank stares. None had ever raced around a room like mad only to turn into Rain Man when a bone or ball appeared. Our first hours at home together had been spent with me prying Athena's jaws off tender digits or trying to maintain eye contact with her—a next to impossible feat while she tore around in circles in the garden or violently shook her toys.

I lay on the floor beside my dog and leaned on my elbows, my sore chin in my hand, and looked at her as she sprawled there like a fur rug. Just then, she sighed in her sleep and wiggled closer to lie against me, her staticky little back pressed up tight to my body. Her face was wrinkled into a worried expression, and I stroked her brow with two fingers. With uncharacteristic tenderness, she moved her muzzle with her eyes still shut and took my fingers into her mouth and held them there. I winced, waiting for the painful bite, but she just held my fingers there gently and continued to sleep uninterrupted. Then I realized that as rough and weird and unruly as my puppy was, she was my puppy, and I clasped her stinky, solid bear-cub body to me with as strong a wave of protective love as I'd ever felt for another creature.

"You're just a baby," I whispered. "You don't know you're not supposed to crap in your crate or bite people's hands." I thought how frightening this all must be, being away from her mother, her litter mates, Megan, her former life. All this time, I had thought of her as something that was just happening to me, assuming that she would magically turn into something else once she calmed down. That we'd automatically bond. I didn't want to admit that maybe she'd always be a little disconnected and strange, but lying on the floor in the dark holding her I decided to love her no matter what. I nuzzled her puppy fur, which ordinarily would probably smell pretty good, and whispered that I loved her.

Like a guilty boyfriend, I edged myself out of our spoon and glided to the sliding glass door to open it and air out the public bathroom stench of my kitchen. I moved her giant stuffed seal to nestle against her and crept back into my bedroom. Checking on Kashka, who was still prone under the bed, I told him that I still loved him, too, and got two blissful hours of quiet sleep.

7. A Visit from Gamma

On Athena's and my first morning together I was awoken at dawn by her headlong rush into my room, where instead of jumping onto the bed and saying, "Hi, New Mommy!" with affectionate licks, she hurled herself at the window next to my bed, shrieking and standing on her hind legs and staring urgently out the window into the yard she'd visited at least eight times during the night. I realized that she had breached the propped-up baby gate and had been roaming the rest of the house unattended, possibly for hours. I mentally prepared myself for the destruction as I leaned over to look under the bed to check on Kashka, who was still lying in the same spot under there, glaring out balefully at the world, while Athena keened at the window, oblivious of his presence.

"Well, hello there," I said, laughing, and got out of bed. Athena seemed to suddenly remember that I came with the house. She leaped on me, allowing me to pet her for a full ten seconds before the encounter escalated into frantic hand chewing. When I ventured cautiously out of my bedroom, I found that the only things out of place were Athena's stuffed seal, which she had dragged into the living room, and one of Kashka's cat toys, which she had stolen from my bedroom and taken out to the yard while I was asleep. It miffed me a little that she had bothered to creep into my bedroom to take one of Kashka's toys but wouldn't even jump onto my bed for a joyful reunion with her mommy.

Since her eruption in the crate on the way home, Athena had refused to touch the leftover K-9 Kraving Megan had given me, so I fed her some dry puppy kibble. Then we went out together into the back yard. She went behind one of the bushes and pooped. "What a little lady," I said. It was another of my assumptions that Athena would prove utterly, embarrassingly wrong.

Our first full day at home together, I learned Athena had a sense of humor. I invented a game where I threw the tennis ball from the yard into the house through the open sliding glass door, and she ran to get it. This seemed to channel her crazy energy, and she got very excited and smiley when she returned with the ball and I praised her. On one occasion, I threw her ball inside, and she returned with one of her stuffed animals. She stared up at me with the stuffed animal in her mouth, wearing an expectant look, as though she knew it was funny. I gave her an astonished laugh and said, "*What*? What is *that*, Athena? *That's* not your ball!" She dropped the stuffed toy at my feet, and I threw it back into the house. She was in the house a beat too long, and when she came back through the door, she had her ball again. This time she was practically quivering with anticipation, looking up at me. "Silly girl!" I mock-yelled at her, and I swear, if a puppy could giggle, she would have done so. She didn't do the switch again that day, but every so often, even now, she pulls a fast one on me, fetching something other than what I've thrown, staring up at me, wagging her bushy tail, her lips pulled back in a smile.

Later in the day, my mother came to visit. An avowed cat person, my mom was curious about the new puppy but was mostly being polite. When she came into Athena's kitchen, the first thing she did was look at the elaborate setup I'd rigged to keep the baby gate in place, gave me an exasperated but affectionate eye roll, promptly lifted the gate, and firmly snapped it correctly across the doorway. "You had it upside down, first of all," she said, and we both started to laugh. She gazed down at Athena and said, "Hi there, little girl!" and Athena sat and stared at her with displeasure and uncertainty, glancing at her, then at me, then back at her again, then back to me with a wary expression. "Who is this?" she seemed to say. "And who is she to us?"

"It's okay, Athena," I said, putting my arm around my mom's shoulders. "This is my mom." My mom reached down toward Athena, who broke into what I can only describe as a relieved grin before jumping up to say hello. My mom averted her head and turned her body away, ignoring Athena, just as I had instructed her to, and Athena politely replaced all four feet on the ground. She sat like a perfect little angel while my mom petted her, never once even attempting to nip her fingers. "She's so cute," my mom said. "Bless her little heart!"

I don't know if she was channeling the love she'd been saving up for her nonexistent grandchildren, but after meeting Athena, Mom softened towards dogs. Athena took to my mother with a delicacy and respectful manner she rarely displays with others, and my mom adored her wholeheartedly from the beginning.

My mother took in the scene in one quick sweep. The living room was a disaster, and the kitchen was strewn with Athena's toys and other accessories. I was shivering and haggard; the house was cold from leaving the kitchen door open, so I was wearing my coat inside.

"Have you eaten?" Mom asked me, frowning.

"Um, no. I didn't plan very well, and I've been afraid to leave her to go to the store. I haven't slept much, either," I admitted, without saying that whenever Athena was out of sight, my imagination was prone to wander:

She's too quiet; what's she doing?

What if the neighbors throw chicken bones into my yard?

What if she eats a poisonous plant I didn't know I had in my yard?

If Kashka dies from heartbreak, will I be able to forgive Athena?

What if she chokes on one of her toys?

I couldn't say these things to my mother, who had, with immense skill and organization, raised three kids while keeping the house immaculate, cooking homemade dinners every night, and listening to our stories from school with interest and patience. I was a grown woman who could barely care for a puppy and a cat at the same time. It was very embarrassing.

"I'll go to the store and get you some groceries," Mom announced, eyeing my cluttered living room.

"I don't have any cash in the house," I said reluctantly. The truth was, Athena had cost a lot of money, and my budget would be exceedingly tight until my next paycheck. I could live with that knowledge, but I hadn't anticipated telling anyone about it.

"I can get the groceries," my mother said, and gratitude, lack of sleep, embarrassment, and anxiety about Kashka converged, and tears spilled over my eyelids.

"Thanks." I said.

"Um, okay," my mom said. "I'll be right back." Of course, she knew just what to get and supplied me with a week's worth of easy-to-prepare, healthy food.

"So why were you crying?" she asked when she came back. I told her how inept I felt, not being able to handle a stupid dog without worrying that everything I did was wrong. Cats I understood. Cats I related to. Dogs, for all my research and knowing friends' dogs, were an alien species to me. I knew that, as pack leader, I had a tremendous responsibility to raise a good dog. A dog I could trust. I hadn't expected such a loopy, demented little girl. If I didn't raise her right, I would end up with a seventy-five-pound time bomb. My mom never suggested that I was overreacting (which in hindsight I was) or that there was anything wrong with wanting to do the right thing, even if Athena was "just a dog." Instead, she listened, nodding her head, and then said with a rueful smile, "Now you can get a small taste of what I went through with all you guys." It made me marvel all over again how people could have kids without wanting to send them out the door dressed in a helmet and bubble-wrap suit.

Then I told her how Kashka wouldn't come out from under the bed. "If he goes into some kind of decline over this, I'll never forgive myself," I sniffled dramatically, the tears threatening again. "I mean, he *is* twelve; two of my friends' cats died at that age."

"Okay you have to be sensible," my mom said softly but firmly. "It's only been *two days*. Give it some time. Here, why don't you take this ginger ale and go lie down and rest for a little while. I'll watch Athena." She looked at my living room again, longingly, wanting me out of the way so she could tidy everything up. I nodded and went to lie down. I fell into a deep nap, and although when I awoke I immediately wondered what Athena was doing, I came out to find my living room completely straightened, my mom reading a magazine.

"You know, I saw some unpaid bills in that stack. Some are a few days past due." My mom indicated my newly neat pile of bills.

"Yeah, I know." I said. "Where's the puppy? Did she bother you? Did she cry?"

"No," my mom said casually. "She took that bone you gave her outside and chewed it. I sat out there with her for a while and she chewed her bone. It's very relaxing, that noise, actually." My mom imitated the grinding noise of Athena's gnawing. "We had quite a nice visit."

I glanced through the kitchen and saw Athena lying placidly in the yard. I was in awe of how comfortable and calm my mom was. She came and stood in the doorway with me, and we both watched Athena doing nothing. I gave my mom the Haus Juris windbreaker, and she put it on and said, "Wow, I feel like a real dog person now." She looked at me thoughtfully. "You know," she said, "you've always made your life work and have been very independent. So I don't think I'll worry about it. You just as easily could have spent that money on . . . I don't know

. . . a trip or something and gotten behind on a bill or two. But instead you've gotten yourself a nice new little friend, and I think that's better in the long run."

I felt a surge of optimism overwhelm my doubts. "Yeah, I think everything's going to be okay." I said and decided right then that it was true.

8. Can We Close the Door?

I never crated Athena after that first night. Many dog experts I'm sure would tsk and purse lips and wag fingers over that, but Athena loathed her crate with a singular burning hatred that threatened to bring on a grand mal seizure. When I wasn't home, I left her in the kitchen and used her crate as a makeshift storage shed for toys and bones. Although I left the door to the crate open, not once did she lie down, sit, or sleep in it. She would go in, retrieve a toy, and then back out again quickly.

Her kitchen den was a small space, and the back door opened onto my equally small yard, so it was like she had her own private kennel. The only problem was that the door was a sliding glass door, so she didn't have constant access to the outside. I dutifully took her out every few hours, because according to my sources, puppies can't hold it in for more than a few hours, but she never seemed to get the timing right and go *before* the door was shut for the night, and instead would use her time in the yard before bedtime to play for long stretches at a time. I consistently assumed (incorrectly) that she didn't have to go again, but once we were back inside with the door closed, after a varying number of minutes, she would go on the floor and then announce her displeasure by producing the sound of a thousand untuned violins. Here again, her timing was off, since if she had bawled ahead of time, I could have let her out rather than getting up merely to clean up the mess.

To her credit, she always left whatever it was inches from the door, as if to show me she knew she was supposed to go outside. After a day or so, I began leaving the back door open just enough that she could fit through the gap, and this arrangement kept her quiet and relaxed and kept my floors clean. The problem was that the temperatures were in the thirties at night, so my house became a freezer. I slept in my coat, and I think several times I saw my breath when I woke up in the morning. To get five hours of undisturbed sleep, however, it was worth it.

With all that extra sleep, I was wakeful one morning at four a.m. I decided to peek into the kitchen at Athena to see if she was awake. I crept out of my room, through the living room, and over to the baby gate. I didn't see Athena's crow-black body in the dark at first, but she saw me. I had the hood of my coat up, so she must not have recognized me, and my nine-week-old, one-floppy-eared puppy let out a long staccato growl. It would have been scary if it weren't a high-pitched puppy growl. As it was, I burst out laughing. When Athena realized it was me, her skinny tail began to whip around and around like a fan blade. She ran to get her seal and drag it to the gate. To this day, whenever she's excited to see someone, the first thing she does is run away and retrieve a stuffed animal, wiggling her way back, ears pressed down in greeting.

"Good watch, Athena!" I praised her.

I wanted to call everyone I knew and brag about my baby watchdog, but seeing that it was four in the morning, I wisely refrained. "You're going to be a badass, Athena!" I said as I went back to bed.

Robin and her husband Bob came over that evening to meet the dog and watch a movie. They eyed me with dismay when they saw that I had a fire going and that I was wearing my coat. I had neglected to tell them my back door was permanently open, since by then it was merely a fact of my life, and I was used to it. I had developed my own version of the Stockholm Syndrome, where the demands of a foot-tall puppy dominated my life.

"Why is it so cold in here?" Robin asked me.

"Oh. Because Athena panics and screams if she doesn't have access to the outside," I explained, as if it were perfectly normal. They looked at each other and back at me for a long time without saying anything. Then the three of us, wearing our coats, went into the kitchen, and Robin and Bob were treated to Athena's piranha hand attack. I diverted her attention by showing her the tennis ball, and she happily batted it around long enough for them to pet her.

"Hey, buddy," Bob said, bending so that his face was near Athena's. Her eyes lit up, and she leaped towards him with manic joy.

"Ow! She bit my chin!" Bob complained. Athena stared up at him adoringly, mouth open.

"Yeah, we're working on that. Sorry," I said. Athena had stopped biting my face, or at least she no longer did it every time my face was within range. She still forgot occasionally and would lash out in a burst of random enthusiasm. I was adept at recognizing the rapturous gaze that preceded one of her launches by now and was able to tell her "No!"

or at least avert my face before she followed through. Instead, she would settle for my hands.

"How does she fit in the crate, with all that stuff in there?" Bob asked.

"Do you just take it all out when she's ready for bed?" Robin asked.

I looked at Athena's crate crammed with bones, her various toys, and her stuffed seal, which was larger than she was. I said, casually, "Oh, I decided not to crate her after all."

"Why not?" they asked in unison, perplexed.

"Oh, well, because she panics and claws at the sides and screams like a monkey when she's in it."

"Didn't Megan say it was normal that she'd cry?" Robin said.

"Yes. But these noises are…" I was at a loss for words to describe them. "Anyway, she also poops in it."

"She *poops* in her *crate*?" Bob asked, incredulous. He had a meek little Shetland sheepdog named Logan that loved its crate and would explode before soiling it.

"Yes. And pees."

Robin and Bob looked at Athena doubtfully. I felt oddly bad for her, like she was suddenly the slow, stupid kid on the playground. I quickly told them the story of how Athena had growled at me in the dark when I'd had my hood up. They both thought that, at least, was pretty cool.

Athena was furiously batting her ball around the kitchen, glancing up periodically to make sure we were watching her. She wasn't a clingy dog; as long as people were around to be her audience, she was happy. But when we settled in in the living room to watch the movie, Athena hovered by the baby gate like a specter, wondering why we weren't watching her play anymore. She started to whine, standing up on her hind legs, her face barely making it over top of the gate. I ignored her.

"Be quiet, dog!" Bob said.

"Don't pay any attention to her," I said a little shrilly. I knew that if you so much as glanced at her when she wanted attention, she would keep going. "Once she realizes she won't get anywhere by making noise, she'll settle down."

"It's thirty degrees in here. Can we shut the door?" Robin asked.

"No!" I snapped, feeling my eardrums wince at the very idea.

"I'm sorry," I softened. "She really freaks out when the door is shut. Can I get you some blankets?"

As Megan had said, Athena was smart, and she learned very quickly that whimpering got her nowhere. She slumped to the floor, pressed up against the baby gate, and patches of her fur poked through the holes as she slept there peacefully. However, as soon as someone said something in a normal voice or there was a loud scene in the movie, she stirred, uncurled herself from the floor, and began whining again.

"We have to whisper, or she'll do that whenever she wakes up," I whispered. I could see her alert outline through the holes of the gate, and I knew she was fixing all of us with her unrelenting stare. Out here, there were so many tantalizing hands to bite and eyes to watch her play she wanted to get at. The dark, short silhouette didn't move. It was a little unnerving. I threw a blanket over the gate so she couldn't see us, like putting a bird to bed. It worked. Athena settled down, and besides the meat-locker temperature of the house, the rest of the movie passed nicely. Sometime near the end of the movie, we heard Athena drag her seal out of the crate and try to run with it out the sliding glass door. It was too big, and I could hear her struggle to pull it outside.

"Aw, she's been so good," Robin said. "Can she come in here and play?"

"Are you sure?" I asked skeptically.

"Yeah. Cool. Bring her in here." Bob agreed.

Both had developed amnesia, I figured. I opened the gate and called to Athena, who whirled into the room, beyond ecstatic at this unheard-of treat. She had apparently been planning what she might do if she ever entered the forbidden room, because it was with laser-like precision that she attacked her various targets.

First she mauled several throw pillows, pausing only long enough to grab one and sail through the room with it full tilt, knocking everything off the coffee table onto the floor. "Athena!" I clapped. She dropped the pillow and dove greedily into the planter I had filled with decorative dried grass. She snatched a tuft and shook it. I darted over, pulled it out of her mouth, and put it back into the pot, but by then she had already pulled out another mouthful. Then she galloped to the other corner of the room, where she dropped the grass in clumps and began biting the leg of my antique desk, carving long scratches into it. I went to shoo her away, as Robin took over the regrassing. At my first footfall toward her, however, Athena spun away from chewing the desk and skittered to my bookshelf. In mid-run she pulled a book off one of the shelves and tossed it up into the air, putting the force of her whole body behind it. Then she pounced on the book and lay down on top of it, ripping the pages to shreds, her head swinging back and forth like a metronome.

All of this had taken approximately thirty-five seconds.

I ran and got the tennis ball from the kitchen, Megan's voice echoing in my brain (*Give her something else to play with if you take something away!*). When I showed the ball to Athena, she ignored it and grabbed a second book from the shelf and dropped it, suddenly intent on bringing down yet a third. She had it in her mouth already as I grabbed her around her strong little chest and pulled her away from the bookshelf. "No!" I said as she bucked and strained against my hold.

She made an excited grunt, gave the book a good ripping shake before dropping it, and sank her sharp little teeth into my hand. "Eh!" I yelled and threw her away from me. She rolled right back up and, thoroughly enjoying this new game, made another flying pass at my bleeding hand, and bit it again, making it bleed harder. I pushed her away, and like some horrible robot, she recovered again and launched, trying for a better grip on my hand this time. "No!" I said, and without thinking, I fluidly gripped the nape of her neck and flopped her onto her back, pinning her.

Don't ever pin this dog! I heard Megan's voice say. I ignored it.

Athena let out a squeal and struggled to get up. "Nope," I said calmly. She looked at me with embryonic understanding and lay still for a few moments.

"You really need to calm down," I said, staring into her upside down eyes. She averted her eyes, and although she still rolled them around crazily, she stayed prone and didn't struggle.

"What a brat!" Robin said, laughing as we surveyed the damage. It looked like the living room had been hit with a small yet efficient tornado. I let Athena up, kissed the top of her head, and carried her back into the kitchen.

"Your dog's insane." Bob concluded sourly. Logan, his Shetland sheepdog, was afraid of its own shadow, and I couldn't imagine him wreaking such havoc. I had never even gotten close enough to Logan to pet him. One night when I was sitting on Robin and Bob's couch, I felt something wet on the bare skin between my jeans and where my shirt had ridden up in the back. It felt like someone was tentatively using a Sharpie to write letters on my waist, and when I turned to see what it was, I realized it was Logan being inquisitive. By the time I could say, "Hi, Logan!" he had already darted away, looking like a shy little dik-dik. If someone's defenseless muffin top had been hanging out around my new puppy, it would have ended up resembling the aftermath of a shark attack.

"I mean, look at this room. Look at your hand!" Bob added.

"She's a German shepherd," I said, shrugging grimly, but I had to admit I said it with a hint of unmistakable pride.

9. Private in Public

After three days of being cooped up with Athena and the comatose Kashka, it was time to brave the outside world and start Athena's socialization. I wanted her to be used to people, other animals, and new situations.

First I took her to the vet's office so that she wouldn't associate it with being stressed or ill. She charged through the door, tugging on her cat leash fervently, ready to see what this new place had to offer. The staff welcomed her warmly. The receptionist offered her a cookie, which she promptly spat out onto the floor, where it landed with a decisive *click*. The techs and doctors admired her in all the appropriate ways. She has since always been thrilled to go to the vet. The patients in the waiting room were not as thrilled, however. Athena bounced up to an elderly miniature poodle head-on, staring intently into his face. The poodle startled and shrank against its owner. "He doesn't want to play, honey," I said, pulling Athena back. We stayed long enough that the waiting room filled up, and when it was as full as I'd ever seen it and Athena had as large an audience as possible, she squatted and crapped on the floor. Up until that point, I was under the impression that she was shy about going to the bathroom. I was unprepared for this kind of public display and asked for paper towels. I wasn't too embarrassed; I figured at the vet's office it was a common occurrence. "Every puppy has accidents," I reasoned.

Next we drove to a nearby park. I had read that I should keep car rides short initially to acclimate the puppy to being in the car, and this ride was only slightly longer than three minutes. Athena was fine for the first couple of minutes. When I glanced at her in the rearview mirror, she was looking around, wearing her usual happy expression. But then she became still and began to look serious and contemplative. I recognized that look of hard focus. It was the same expression I could feel on my own face when I'd had too much to drink and was trying to fixate on a point in space to quell the nausea. No sooner did I make this connection than Athena threw up all over the back seat. The strategy had never worked for me, either.

Aborting the trip to the park, I took Athena home instead, and we went for a walk around the neighborhood; rather, I went for a walk, and she went for a lurch/drag. For being a herding dog bred to effortlessly lope great distances, Athena's first attempts on a leash were more stop/start than anything. She kept her stubby nose to the ground, and the more disgusting an item looked to me, the more important it was to her that she pick up and carry with us on our walk/drag/lurch. Ignoring smooth sticks, she instead pounced on sodden Kleenex, a limp gray sweat sock, a jagged beer can, and a half-smashed cigarette with the tobacco sticking out in a fuzzy bouquet. I patiently pried each one of these things out of her mouth, shuddering. I picked up a clean, dry pinecone and tapped it against my thigh as I walked along, and she craned her neck, staying in a heel for about four paces, until she saw something in the gutter and gleefully zigzagged away and attempted to mouth it. It turned out to be a discarded condom—and I nearly swooned when I had to pull it from between her tiny jaws. I'm sure nothing would have capped our walk off more nicely than a used hypodermic needle, not unheard-of in the neighborhoods next to ours.

A couple of weeks later, I decided to take her to Petco, which was about six minutes up the street by car. Athena had built up her tolerance and could last about that long until she got sick. The whole six minutes, I talked to her in a peppy, happy voice I suspected I'd been overusing since I'd brought her home. "We're going to Petco!" I said. "It'll be so fun! You're so good! You're a good girl, Athena!" In the rearview, I saw her contemplative, serious, drunk-person-trying-not-to-puke face.

She had recovered by the time the sliding doors of Petco parted before us. Apart from her joyous destruction of my living room during Robin and Bob's visit, I don't think I'd ever seen her so stimulated. She couldn't decide what to look at or sniff first. She also got her first chance to interact with other young dogs, or at least dogs not hiding behind their owners' legs. She seemed to have no inkling of the rules that govern doggie interaction. As she greeted all things in life, she lunged pell-mell into the faces of other dogs, staring at them. I pulled her back, apologizing, because the gesture sometimes unnerved even the calmest dogs. I didn't want her to associate meeting other dogs with the jerking of her cat leash, so I began asking people if my puppy could say hi to their dogs. Most everyone agreed with smiles, which froze on their faces in confusion when Athena did nothing a normal puppy would do when greeting another dog. There were no submissive muzzle licks or adorable play bows with her fat rump in the air. Instead she would push her face up to the other dog's face and stare into its eyes as if she were trying to understand a foreign language. Her body language said, "What? What does that *mean*? Tell me! Tell me!" She wanted to skip all the niceties and go right to wrestling. She terrified a small terrier by bounding up at him and staring into his face so intently for so long ("Tell me! *Tell me!*") that he retreated, shivering, behind his owner's knees. Confident dogs quickly taught her that it's not polite for a dog—a puppy no less—to greet another dog so directly and used their paws or larger mouths to gently subdue her

Athena was in love with every life form she came across at Petco and seemed convinced that everyone should love her back with equal enthusiasm. She looked genuinely hurt when she would trot toward a new person and that person would not even look down at her. It made me a little sad to watch. I couldn't understand how they could breeze by an eager smiling puppy who was rushing to greet them, who stood wagging her tail and looking up at them with adoration. Often a stranger would look down, smile at her, and say hello, and Athena would shimmy and waggle her whole body in delight. If someone bent down to pet her, she was beside herself with ecstasy and jumped around at the end of her leash like a marlin.

When we reached the middle of the store, Athena hunched down for her grand finale. Aghast, I watched her crap on the floor, and it dawned on me that she wasn't so shy about going potty after all. She actually seemed to *like* doing it when there were a lot of people around, watching. To make matters worse, she wound up her rear end before going. It was never a simple stop and drop. She swayed her fluffy-panted bottom around like a magician's hands over a hat as if to say, "Will she go folks? Oh, I don't know! Oh yes! It looks like she's now going!"

The passersby in Petco either grimaced or laughed, and Athena gazed at all of them as though they were in on it. Afterward, she grandly and with great ceremony stepped away from her pile and kicked backward at it, first one foot then the other, like a giant chicken. This motion I later dubbed her "poo kick." She then pranced around at my feet, seemingly proud of her great accomplishment. A nice Petco worker offered to clean it up; I protested, trying to take the roll of towels from him, but he gallantly insisted.

On the way out of the store, Athena encountered a first in her short life: a dog who hated puppies. She did her hulking gnu impression, dancing toward the dog to stare in its face, and it snarled and lunged at her. Athena stared incredulously, looking extremely offended, and backed up to my legs. "I'm sorry," the owner said, yanking his dog back. The dog gave one last growl at Athena, and they turned to leave. Still wearing an expression of astonishment and disapproval, Athena launched into an indignant volley of barks after the dog, her hackles raised. It reminded me of someone who has been saved from fighting a bigger, tougher opponent but who yells, "Oh yeah?! Let me at him! I'll show him who's boss!"

After that, I took Athena outside, where we could watch the rest of the dogs from a safe distance. It was adoption day for a rescue group, and all was peaceful until a friendly lady from the rescue asked us to leave, joking that Athena had gotten three application requests. As we left, I saw an adorable fuzzy German shepherd puppy inside the store, and I pointed at it and exclaimed, "Oh wow! I love *that* one!" before realizing I had in fact been looking at Athena's reflection in the window. She really was meant to be my dog, in so many ways. I looked around to make sure no one had heard me.

Athena was in buoyant spirits for the rest of the day, and I was pleased to see how much being around people and other dogs energized her. The next day we went to Milwaukee Frozen Custard. I wanted her to get used to outdoor cafés, because it was my intention to take her as many dog friendly places as I could. I didn't think much about it when she jumped into a two-foot tall decorative planter, but then her rear end began to sway, and soon she was letting loose on the mulch, demonstrating her prowess up on her own personal stage and no doubt ruining many patrons' enjoyment of their frozen custard. I stood there holding Athena's leash like some toady stage hand. A lady walking by took pity on me and passed me a plastic bag. "I have dogs," she whispered.

What a recognizable phase, I'm sure you're thinking. *My puppy had accidents in public, too.* Well, there have been too many instances for them to all be accidents, and the behavior didn't stop as Athena got older. The higher the density of the crowd, the greater the likelihood she would poop.

When she was around six months old, I took her into Home Depot with me one day with my friend Lauren and her Rhodesian ridgeback mix, Carman. The dogs weren't technically allowed in Home Depot. They had at some point allowed dogs but had changed the policy. The greeter took pity on us when we showed up, though, and said, "Well, just this one more time, it'll be okay."

We were there for ten minutes before I began to sweat. The store was a perfect setting for Athena's demonstration. There were plenty of people around, and the aisles were vast and concrete.

"We need to get out of here ASAP," I muttered to Lauren, who just looked at me strangely. She and I hadn't known each other that long, and she didn't know Athena's propensity to defile any public place she entered.

Then as we crossed the center of the busy main thoroughfare, I felt Athena's leash pull taut. I turned and saw her squatted down, swaying back and forth like she was riding a camel. Lauren immediately ducked down a side aisle with perfectly non-crapping Carman and knelt in the aisle, beet-faced and laughing. "Help me!" I hissed at her, and she went silent with mirth and shook her head. "I don't know you," she mouthed, and watched along with me as Athena lay a set of gigantic turds for everyone to see. People pushing their shopping carts past dropped their eyes to Athena's straining form and then glared at me, their mouths tight with disapproval and repulsion. Athena performed her poo kick, and wagged her tail at the store manager who came to tell me my dog should be removed. Now, please.

She was full grown, three years old, when she pooped at the *Super Pet Expo!* Again, she waited until we were walking the most crowded aisle possible. When we reached the center, she dipped, as the stream of people parted around her like water around a rock.

10. Good Dog!

By the time Athena was three months old, I had taught her how to sit. That was, so far, our only accomplishment. She was still a whirling dervish who bit me regularly and didn't know how to walk on a leash. I knew we needed puppy training. Still, when Megan called and left a message to remind me about her training class, I avoided calling her back, dreading both the vomit-soaked car ride and the inevitable reprimands for my incompetence. I looked online and found a website that featured two photos of a Weimaraner, the first with the caption "from this . . . " that showed the dog standing on a picnic table, and the second with the caption " . . . to this," of the dog sitting placidly in the grass with a halo over its head. It was the site for Good Dog Obedience, a company that would send a trainer to my house. I spoke to the owner of Good Dog, Victoria Schade, who was also a trainer, and she penciled me in for her only opening—Saturday mornings at eight a.m. First, she came by for a consultation, and I let Athena into the living room from her kitchen kennel to meet her. Athena jumped on Victoria, trying to bite her hands, and Victoria looked away and pretended Athena didn't exist. Cowed and confused, Athena dutifully trotted next to Victoria, fascinated. Victoria pulled from her bag a Bully Stick—a dried bull's penis—and said, "Just so we don't have any distractions." She gave it to Athena, and it was as if my dog had suddenly morphed into " . . . to this." She left us to chew the stick in the kitchen, and Victoria went over the details of her program unmolested. Athena had run away from a perfectly good set of new hands to bite. It was unprecedented.

I liked Victoria immediately. She smiled easily and didn't make me feel stupid. The basic training would take six weeks, she told me. When she had finished describing the training schedule and strategies, she looked at me carefully. "You seem a bit afraid of your own dog," she said.

I was astounded by how obvious it was, and I admitted with some shame that I was still slightly nervous around dogs in general. I told her, blushing, that Athena bit me almost daily, and I was worried how she was going to turn out, given that she had very little—in fact an almost sociopathic lack of—awareness or natural remorse when I disciplined her.

I also kept a secret from Victoria; I had had two extreme experiences with the German shepherd breed growing up. I was completely at ease with my aunt's dog, Gina, who followed me all around the horse farm, quietly nudging me for a pat every so often. She was the perfect friend—unobtrusive but fully engaged. She was what I compared all dogs to after we met, and most were found wanting.

The other German shepherd I knew as a child was Maxel, who was owned by the German family that lived next door to my grandparents. I was around seven when the family first brought the dog over from Germany. Maxel was a lean, enormous black-and-red male with an all-black face, amber eyes, and white, white teeth, which he showed frequently when standing on his hind legs at the end of his chain, roaring mere feet from my face as I walked past him to get to the front door to see if my friend Britta wanted to play. Maxel seemed to hate everyone, regardless of how long you had known him. No one could control Maxel but Franz, the father.

One day Britta and her older brother had Maxel, who was around nine months old, off leash next door. I saw them and went out to my grandparents' back yard and waved to them. Within seconds, Maxel had run into my grandparents' yard and tackled me. As I was going down, I rolled instinctively onto my stomach to protect my vital organs. Maxel stood on my back and growled against the base of my skull while I lay petrified, completely still. I can to this day remember what his hot breath felt like vibrating against my head. Britta came over, and I begged her as calmly as I could to get Maxel off me.

"He's just playing," she said, but I knew it wasn't true. I didn't protest; I was just glad he hadn't ripped a hole in my neck. Back then, in 1970s Pennsylvania, if a dog stood on you and tore your nape open, well, that kind of thing just happened sometimes. There were no police reports or lawsuits. My grandparents' neighbors down the street had a lion cub in their back yard, and no one seemed to think it odd.

"That's the house with the lion," Britta pointed out as I helped her deliver newspapers one day.

Maxel bit me only once, and it's a testament to my own dumb luck and Franz's control over him that it happened only once. The single time he bit me was one night where at dusk, Britta, her bothers and I were playing "Spotlight" where you ran around hopefully undetected by the person who had a flashlight, reaching "home" where you were "safe". "Home" in our game was their car in the driveway. Britta's parents were on lawn chairs sipping drinks, and Maxel was off-leash. Not a single person considered it a bad idea to skulk and dart frantically in very low light like an intruder with a hyper-vigilant guard dog loose, and on one of my passes towards the car, Maxel snarled and jumped up, sinking his teeth in between my shoulder blades. "Tsk tsk, Maxel was just excited. He couldn't see very well." Britta's mom calmly explained while treating my puncture wounds with iodine. Again, it never occurred to me to "tell on" Britta's family; it made perfect sense to me that the dog had bitten someone he didn't recognize in the dark, even though he had recognized me fine not even an hour earlier when I was throwing leftover steak fat to him. With Franz, Maxel off leash was, while never nice, at least obedient. My grandmother loved to tell us, shuddering, that Maxel would "give her his paw" on Franz's command. "There he will sit in front of you, and he hands you this big *mallet* of a paw into your palm! He's terrifying even with Franz there." Another "fun" activity I was invited next door to do with Britta and her brothers was to play keep-away from Maxel with a ball; they thought it entertaining to have him in the middle, running from person to person, leaping to try to grab the ball. I always let the ball go sailing by me, much to everyone's annoyance, because even though Maxel was intent on the ball and never really looked at me, I had a phobia that he would suddenly remember that when he was chained up he wanted to kill me and realize that the chain was a hindrance no longer and that he could finally take his opportunity.

The most foolish thing I did in regard to Maxel (and perhaps the most foolish thing I ever did in my life) occurred one day when Britta and her brothers and I were playing hide-and-seek. Maxel was nowhere to be seen, which was why I didn't hesitate to run freely around the yard. I don't know where I thought Maxel had gone, but I was sure he wasn't home. So sure, that I decided the most ingenious hiding place was in his dog house, which was carved into the side of the garage, the doorway shielded with a heavy clear plastic tarp. I crawled in and sat in the very back corner of the dog house, giggling silently and congratulating myself until I heard the terrifying metallic ring of a chain dragging along concrete.

Maxel had been home the whole time; he had just been napping around the back of the garage, and I hadn't seen him. I didn't have time to get out of the dog house before I saw his dark silhouette in front of the plastic door flap, through which he appeared wavy and nondescript and somehow even more horrific. "This is how I'm going to die," I said to myself. "I can't believe Maxel is home, and because of this stupid idea, I'm now going to die." Somehow I became very calm, and as Maxel pushed into his house, I said, "Hi, Maxel," and squeezed past him, running my hands along his side, slowly somersaulting out the door and rolling halfway across the yard where I lay without moving for several minutes.

I don't know why Maxel didn't attack me for invading his inner sanctum. Was he so lonely that it was a nice surprise to have company? Was he half asleep and not really registering my presence? Whatever the reason, I feel fortunate to be able as an adult to chew solid foods.

My grandmother, although scared of him, always felt that Maxel was heartbroken and love-starved. She would sneak out and throw meat scraps to him from dinner, watching from a safe distance in awe as he crushed up massive stew bones with no more effort than a biscuit, and she reported more than once that she could hear him on frigid nights howling. "That poor dog," she said, "all by himself in the cold, always on that chain, howling away."

Even though as a kid I thought that Maxel was crazy and evil, I think of my grandmother's words now and feel sad for him. He was a beautiful animal who didn't deserve that life of being on a chain all the time.

The bottom line was that Athena's daily rumble-tumble psychotic episodes reminded me more of Maxel than Gina, and I worried that her biting and seemingly blank incomprehension that it hurt would turn her into a dog like him. She never had an angry demeanor when she bit; she didn't growl or look hostile. If anything, she looked thoroughly contented when she was doing it. Knowing next to nothing about puppy behavior, I had taken to pinning her every time she bit me, and it just couldn't go on. There had to be other strategies that would work for me. She had no aggression for anything else; from our first days together, I reached in routinely and took food out of her bowl, pulled her away from the bowl, and tugged on her while she was eating, and she never seemed annoyed, never demonstrated any dominant food-aggression.

Victoria assured me that with training, Athena would have a structured outlet for her energy, and it would help give me some boundaries, a framework, within which to work with her.

"I think we both need this," I said, sighing in relief. She looked at me kindly and said the fact that I was even worried about it showed that I wanted to become a responsible dog owner. I nodded vigorously, a bobble-head.

It rained for five of the next six Saturdays, so we had to improvise and train inside exclusively. Our lessons consisted of learning the click-treat method. I received from Victoria two small plastic clickers and an official apron to hold treats. I was instructed to give Athena a command, and if she complied, press the clicker and quickly give her a small treat—we settled on small pieces of turkey hot dog. The idea of clicker-training was to "mark" or reward good behavior rather than punish bad behavior, and the clicker was a method to tell the dog exactly when it had done something correct with a unique uniform sound, followed closely with a tasty treat to reinforce the good behavior. My mother was so enamored of the idea of clicking as praise that I eventually gave her a clicker of her own, which she attached to her keychain. She liked to tell me that she clicked herself when she did something she was proud of, such as fitting into a difficult parallel parking spot on a busy road or putting together a desk. "Clicka, clicka!" my mom sang if she was praising one of us kids on the phone, and within seconds, we would hear the click. Pressing the clicker joined biting into an apple as an empowering trick she learned to do whenever she faced something daunting. "You can't doubt yourself when you're biting into a crisp apple," my mother said one day. I heard the clicker in the background, and she started to laugh; she was clicking her own good advice.

Victoria was a great teacher. If I made a mistake, she corrected me without scorn, and she encouraged me constantly. I got the hang of click-treating fairly rapidly, and having goals finally gave me some confidence that I was on the right path with my puppy.

Athena loved training and went all out to learn each new command. We practiced every day between lessons.

"You're doing your homework!" Victoria said during our third lesson, clapping her hands after Athena and I executed a more or less perfect "down."

I pressed the clicker, and Athena barreled in for the piece of hot dog in my hand. "Ow!" I winced as her sharp puppy teeth reopened my freshly healed cuts. Overly eager to get her reward, she usually scraped her teeth along my fingers in the process. I looked like I had been feeding a tank of baby alligators by hand.

In addition to "down," we worked on "sit," although Athena had been doing that one since she lived at Megan's, "bed," and her two hardest commands, paradoxically, "come" and "stay." Since our practices took place in the kitchen, she could see me at all times, so the command "Come!" had little to no meaning for her.

"We have to let her into the living room to practice this," Victoria said, eyeing me. "Is that okay?"

I almost broke into a sweat, remembering Athena's rapturous destruction of every corner of the room. I hadn't let her in there unleashed since that episode, other than to meet Victoria for the first time.

"Oh," I said, "well, she's a little crazy when she goes in there."

"Does she *ever* go in there?" Victoria asked.

I had to admit, that no, she didn't.

"Well, that's a problem—it's forbidden fruit. She's a shepherd, and it's a very curious breed. She has all this pent-up curiosity."

Thinking of the manic glee with which she had ransacked the room, I had to agree that she had acted as if all the treasures she wrecked had been haunting her for years.

We opened the baby gate, and the Tasmanian devil spun forth, making a beeline for Victoria. She jumped up and pawed the air next to Victoria. Since we'd begun our training, Athena had learned it was unacceptable to jump up on people, but she could never quite resist the urge to jump, so she made this modification, which she practices to this day.

She then whirled around, not looking either me or Victoria in the eye, and disappeared into the kitchen again. We heard rustling, and then she reemerged, dragging her stuffed seal. Victoria broke into a broad grin, raising her eyebrows at me, and I knew that she now got how weird my puppy was. Athena was enthralled by Victoria for mere seconds, and then she dropped her seal and went behind the couch. When

I peeked back there, I saw that she was winding up to ride the camel. I clapped and said, "NO!", picked her up, and practically threw her outside. Allowing her to go there would effectively have given her permission to go on that same spot throughout the rest of her puppyhood, no matter how well I cleaned it. Outside in the rain, because there were only two people to watch her, she crept behind a bush.

Back inside, we had to get creative to work on the command "Come!" Victoria held Athena around the chest in the kitchen while I stood out of sight in the living room. Athena squirmed and reared but didn't squeal or whine—a good sign, Victoria said.

"Come!" I shouted, and Athena ran sideways into the room toward me and skidded to a halt, sat down at my feet, and waited for her click, her hot dog, and three fingers' worth of skin.

She was, I found out, a quick study. Her hyperactivity was simply a manifestation of her desperate desire to learn new things. She learned every command in a maximum of three attempts, panting anxiously if she went through her known repertoire with no reward. Even now I sometimes have to sharply correct her, because in her frenzy to do the right thing, she has a tendency to not hear what I've actually asked her to do. So when I tell her to "Roll over and give prayers," she will sometimes sit, lie down, sit again, lift each paw in turn for a high five, and bark before what I've actually said penetrates, and then she'll hurl herself to the floor, roll over onto her back, and put a paw on either side of her nose, moving them up and down. As a puppy, she lived for the click and the treat. As an adult, she lives for whichever stuffed animal I'm holding hostage until she does her trick correctly.

She also learned a sizeable vocabulary around this time. When I asked, she could identify and bring Seal, Moo-Cow, ball, key, and Tiger. When she got older, she could distinguish between the basketball and the football and recognized the words for ten stuffed animals, including those she hadn't played with for months.

"Athena?" I'll ask, and she will tilt her head sideways to get her orders, her ears at five o'clock and her muzzle at ten o'clock. "Where is bone rope?" and she will run to her basket and pull out various toys, searching for her soft toy featuring a long tube with two squeaky bones on either end. Occasionally in her excitement she will pick up another toy, and I'll have to remind her, "No... That's Goosey Goose. Where's bone rope?" I can actually *see* her thinking sometimes: she'll stop and concentrate for a second, brighten, and then trot to a different room from which most often, she will emerge carrying the correct toy (sometimes I know she has the right one already, because I hear its unique squeal or honk coming from the other room).

One of her favorite toys is a stuffed grizzly bear, and since she also has teddy bear, she knows that grizzly bear is the brown one with a hump. I was watching a television special on Animal Planet about grizzly bears one night, and the announcer talked about the grizzly bear diet, the grizzly bear habitat, and the protective nature of the mother grizzly bear with cubs. Athena left the couch, which surprised me, because she likes animal shows, and disappeared into the kitchen. I understood when she emerged with her stuffed grizzly bear and brought it with her back up onto the couch.

Within five weeks with Victoria training us, Athena had learned "come," "stay" (for a record of thirty seconds), "down," and, most adorably, "bed," which was a command for her to go to her bed and lie down on it. Once she understood what "bed" meant, when given the order, she hunched her shoulders in delight, took three jumps, and belly-flopped onto her monogrammed dog pillow, landing with a decisive poof. The first time Victoria saw Athena respond to the "bed" command, she gave an abrupt burst of laughter. I praised Athena, and she looked up at us with vacuous, open-mouthed pride and then rose and trotted away. Athena's follow-through never lasted long. She was excited to show off that she *knew* a command but seemed bored by holding it and waiting for the next command.

Athena treated "come" as a negotiable command when we went outside to practice. I liked to show off how good she was, and often I put on my apron and put her through her paces out in the grassy common area between my condo and my neighbors'. Virginia, a pleasant young woman with a toddler, came outside one day to talk and to watch me train. Athena executed everything perfectly. Then I recognized the obsessive gleam in her eyes and, a second too late, tracked where she was looking: through Virginia's open back door. I watched as she turned and galloped toward Virginia's house. Virginia moved in front of her and tried to cut her off before she could reach the door, but Athena successfully dodged her.

"Athena, no!" Virginia cried.

"Athena, come!" I said to her retreating hind end, but she did not obey.

Virginia ran inside after her, and I heard her faint cry: "No! Athena! No!" Then Athena emerged from the house, running full tilt, and I was able to grab her collar. Virginia followed, panting heavily, and told me that Athena had run first to her daughter's room, picked up a stuffed toy, and then run into every other room with the toy in her mouth. Fortunately she hadn't damaged anything, even the toy, which she'd dropped on the floor before making her getaway.

The common area in which we worked was about the length of a football field and ended at the main road that runs through our development. I thought that the road was too far away to pose any real danger, but one day, Athena spotted someone she thought she recognized far in the distance, across the street. She began a headlong dash in that direction.

"Athena!" I gasped, ripping off my sandals and running barefoot after her. "Come! Athena!" Again, she did not obey. She made it to the edge of the street but stopped, distracted by some smell in the grass along the curb. I grabbed the back of her neck and hoisted her into my arms, carried her to a safe distance, and then plopped her down on the ground. I grabbed her muzzle and made her look into my eyes. "*Athena!*" I screamed. "*You come when you're called!*" I was shaking, and I felt as if I might faint. "*You could have been killed!*" I continued, pointing at the street, as if she would have any possible clue as to what I was angry about. I culminated her punishment by holding the scruff of her neck, pointing her at the street, and yelling, "*No!*"

Athena winced and soberly trotted back to our yard as I held her collar. She looked crestfallen. She knew she had done something wrong, but she couldn't, I thought, possibly know what it was. One thing was true: in the common area she never ran down that far to the street ever again. I kept her on a long lead for several lessons as a precaution, only letting her off when I deemed her trustworthy. She made one last dash toward the street a few weeks later, but when I yelled, "Athena, come!" she froze and then wheeled around and came back to me. It may have been for the hot dog, but I think it was something else. She was showing the awareness of a dog with a good memory and a dawning sense of self-control; she was growing up. I also believed then that she really did want to do the right thing, and I realized that I would have to show her that doing the right thing meant doing whatever I deemed the right thing. It was up to me.

And she tested me constantly. At around nine months, she went through what I think of as her version of the terrible twos, a short period during which she defied me almost every time I used the recall command. "Come!" I said and watched her ears move back toward me as she loped in the opposite direction, seemingly suddenly *mesmerized* by a branch or leaf on the ground. So every single time, I would march over to where she was, grip her collar, and walk her into my yard. "Too bad," I'd say and shut the gate, leaving her inside the yard and me outside. She would yip and howl on the other side of the fence, and inevitably I'd see her long black snout poke out imploringly from underneath the fence. I ignored her. And then the next day we'd start all over again.

Usually her banishment to the yard meant that the next day she listened especially well, but she would push her luck the following day or the next. Her most flagrant act of defiance was to evade me when I grabbed for her collar to take her inside. She would see me coming and quickly trot in the other direction. But I was relentless, and soon she would drop to her belly and look at me for mercy. I gave her no mercy and walked her to the yard for the usual isolation behind the fence. Our test of wills lasted two weeks. After that, she came when I called her. Most of the time, anyway.

Athena's dominance came naturally. Even in the whelping room, she had pushed her brothers and sisters aside to stand up against the gate when I said goodbye to her the first time we met. When she play-wrestled with other puppies, she always went over the top of the neck. Throughout her life, whenever greeting another dog, she carries her tail at a crooked high angle, almost over her back.

When our training sessions were complete, Victoria sponsored a happy hour for her puppy clients at Dogma, a dog bakery in Arlington. I watched the other female puppies Athena's age skip daintily around one another with toys or quietly play with each other on the rug in a closed-off area in the middle of the store. If something scared one of them, she ran back for reassurance to her owner sitting on one of the sofas. I coaxed Robin to come with me to the play group ("There'll be free food!"), and as we watched all the reserved little females play the equivalent of dolls with each other, Robin asked, "Where's yours?"

I squinted. "There," I said, pointing at a rowdy throng of large males who were running nonstop as one unit around the perimeter of the store, as if they were in a car race, nipping and shoving each other. Athena was in the center of the pack, the only female, tackling and pushing with the best of them. She wore a ridiculously blissful expression and seemed unfazed when a bulkier friend knocked her aside; in fact, she merely sped up so she could reenter the rollicking flock teeming with teeth, paws and ears. It was hard to tell individual puppies apart, and I only was able to pick her out by looking for the puppy who was sweeping its head back and forth. It was mine, moving to better bite the boys on either side of her. My little tomboy only left her group of roughhousing males once, to poop on the carpet in the makeshift living room—"coincidentally" where most of the invitees were sitting, talking, and eating their hors d'oeuvres—and twice to take a sudden detour and plunge out through the front door of the bakery. The first time, I tried to chase after her, but two ladies of considerable girth stood in the doorway with the door open, talking to each other, half in and half out the store, as if deciding if they wanted to enter or not. They dully watched as Athena skirted by them.

"One got out," one of them told me, as they stood still as statues and continued to block the doorway. I bobbed and danced, trying to get around them, as they then turned their attention back to each other and resumed their conversation. With the door still open.

"Yeah," I said, on the verge of hysteria, "*can you move?*"

They stared at me a beat longer and then, in slow motion, apologized and came fully into the store, still blocking my exit. I edged uncharacteristically smoothly around them, although honestly I had been prepared to drive through them like a linebacker, so sudden and overwhelming was my adrenaline rush. The bakery was in a busy strip mall with a parking lot out front. Making sure no other puppies had been tempted to follow me, I ran into the parking lot in a complete panic, which dissolved into a combination of relief, exasperation, and ruefulness as I caught sight of my girl visiting people next door at Starbucks. It was a warm summer night, and the outdoor patio was crowded. She was in mid-jump when I caught up with her, her front paws landing on an unsuspecting patron's lap. The man flinched dramatically, almost spilling hot coffee on his hand.

"Athena!" I said and hauled her into my arms and apologized. Not cowed in the least, she looked cheerily at all the Starbucks customers, smiling like an idiot, and if she could have, I think she would have waved at them and yelled, "Bye! Bye!" as we walked away.

Robin shook her head when I stomped back into the bakery, a completely unrepentant Athena panting happily, her paws on my shoulder.

"She's such a *brat*!" Robin reminded me, for the fiftieth time.

11. She's a Bomb!

I hung Athena's certificate from puppy obedience on the refrigerator next to her pedigree, which read *Athena Justagirl Haus Juris*. I had ordered the official pedigree when I registered with the American Kennel Club. There were only a certain number of spaces on the form for the name, and Megan had already filled in "Haus Juris" at the end of the line, as that part was mandatory. "Justagirl" came from the song "Athena" by The Who. Whenever I sang along with that song, when no one else was in my car, I replaced "She's just a girl! She's a bomb!" with "She's just a girl! She's a *dog*!"

Pedigree and certificate aside, I was very puffed up over the achievements of my "daughter," and I waxed ecstatic about my smart, good German shepherd girl, giving my friends and coworkers frequent updates on how quickly she learned her commands, how big she was getting, and how much better behaved she was becoming. Everyone who saw the pictures plastered all over my office at work agreed she was an adorable puppy, with "such a pretty face!" "Oh she's *so cute!*" they'd say, as Athena stared innocently into the camera lens, often with a slight cock to her head.

Then someone would ask, "What happened to your fingers?"

"She misses sometimes when she goes for her hot dog," I mumbled, defeated. Didn't they care about the monumental strides Athena and I had taken together? Then Athena and I reached the moment of perfect balance between pet and owner. We had had a full week of flawless behavior, during which Athena followed my commands; walked with grace on her leash; and resisted the urge to poop in a crowd, bite me in the face, and destroy the objects in my home. Could it be that she had finally relaxed her tremendous will, reformed and become easy?

I came home from work at the end of the week, walked through the front door, and passed the kitchen, where Athena was standing as usual behind the baby gate, wagging her tail. As I walked by, I noticed an abundance of evidence leading to conclusions that I didn't want to be true, so I averted my eyes and began to hum, going into my bedroom to change into some raggedy clothes. I sat on the bed an extra minute, still humming softly.

When I returned to the living room and looked into the kitchen, the full horror penetrated.

There was mud everywhere.

The pattern on the vinyl tile was barely visible, as the floor was covered in mud. Mud was caked to the baby gate, which looked as though someone had tried, sloppily, to frost it. Mud was smeared on the walls in great long stripes and speckles spattered higher up than my head and on the ceiling. Athena's stuffed seal was unrecognizable, as were her blanket and "Athena" pillow; they more closely resembled oversized bon-bons.

Finally I looked at her. She was wet, completely brown, and her fur spiked up in all different directions in a porcupine full-body Mohawk. The only black parts of her left were her two eyes and part of her nose. She was *extremely* happy to see me. I watched as mud flew off her wagging tail, adorning the walls nearby with tiny splats. In shock, I climbed over the baby gate and watched in stupefied detachment as she jumped up on me and left long brown streaks down my gym clothes.

"What . . . did . . . you . . . do . . . Athena?" My kitchen looked like a crime scene—as if some horrible savage butchery had taken place in it of a family filled with Yoo-hoo.

Unbeknownst to me, Athena had learned how to dig in the garden. She obviously enjoyed digging. She enjoyed it very much.

After staring stupidly at the kitchen and then at her and then at the kitchen again, not knowing where to start, I gathered my pitiful collection of cleaning supplies and just dove in. Her seal, blanket, and pillow cover I tossed gingerly into the washing machine, where they left mud on the rim. I pushed all the towels I had and a mop along the floor in a daze, and then washed the suicide walls with sponges, pushing Athena out of the way every time she tried to drink from the bucket of warm soapy water.

With the calmness of a cow, I patiently re-wiped the walls when she jumped up on the areas where I had just cleaned; she found the sponges hilarious. The whole cleaning experience, for her, was an adventure, and she followed every aspect with a bounce in her step and her mouth open, relaxed and smiling. Luckily, her tail had dried to the degree that when she wagged it, just little crumbles of mud the consistency of Feta cheese dropped off.

Most of the mud was cleaned up before I was able to acknowledge her, and when I sat on the floor, she clambered onto my lap and rolled onto her back. I sighed with resignation, knowing I could not get much more dirty anyway, and hugged her. Athena was beside herself with joy and wiggled like a damp salamander in my embrace.

After about an hour, I brushed the dried mud out of her coat and she looked as good as new. I worried the whole next day at work that I was going to find another kitchen abattoir when I got home, but she had seemingly exhausted her interest in digging in one dramatic explosion.

I figured Athena's desecration of my kitchen was my karmic punishment for being obsessed when I was a child with *Mary Ann's Mud Day,* a book about a little girl who played in mud one day and got filthy making an elaborate mud city. It became a blueprint for both my lazy indifference towards housekeeping as well as my love of playing a song I like over and over again while driving, as I used to pester any literate adult to read me *Mary Ann's Mud Day* cover to cover and then start over until they were hoarse. My mother didn't forget this childhood appreciation; when I told her how my kitchen looked, my mom practically clapped her hands and told me in a delighted voice what a naughty but clever girl our Athena was. "Isn't it funny that your favorite book was *Mary Ann's Mud Day?*" my mother snickered. She had the typical grandmother syndrome where everything her "grandchild" did was adorable and blameless.

12. Kashka's Bête Noir:
"Why Can't We Be Friends?"

Athena tried for a whole year to make friends with Kashka. Any time she was allowed into my bedroom, she ran to the bed with renewed optimism, seeming to forget that she would be as welcome as the plague. It took Kashka six months after Athena arrived to venture into the living room, and he would stay only until she shifted in the kitchen behind her baby gate. When he heard her, he would scurry back into my bedroom, his belly a centimeter off the ground, his hindquarters stretched back, tail puffed. It was a major breakthrough when he didn't run under my bed, but instead waited for me in my room, his tail lashing, glaring at me.

"Kashka," I'd explain for the thousandth time, "she's a very nice dog, I swear. She loves you." I'd edge up to him, a sycophant, trying to pet him. But he dipped just out of reach, too disgusted to let my foul hand soil his back, and walked away, pointedly turning his face from me and flicking the end of his tail.

"Kashiiii," I'd implore. If I prostrated myself long enough on the floor, eventually his kind-hearted feelings would stir, and he'd come back over to me, burbling quietly like a turkey. We had made significant progress by now; I had moved his litter box out of my bedroom into the attached bathroom approximately twelve feet away from the comforting position of a foot-flip proximity to my sleeping form where I had groggily gotten up and kicked it more than once by accident. I was still forced to feed him in my bedroom, however, since any closer to the monster two rooms away was enough to completely stifle his appetite. I think he got a wee bit of satisfaction bearing his cross. He always had an air of injured dignity when things didn't go completely his way, even as a kitten, but he always responded with happy gurgling if you showed him the proper respect—in other words, if you groveled like a serf begging his pardon.

I tried a flooding exercise, thinking if he met Athena face to face, she'd lose some of her unknown terror for him. It went poorly. Kashka scrunched himself to his usual bunker, the very center of under the bed, and Athena lay on her side, swimming along the ground until she fit her whole head and some of her shoulder sideways, keening and moaning to say hello, her tail tapping and swishing on the carpet. From his safe position, Kashka stared at her in silent rage. If Athena tried the head-on approach, deeply huffing and pawing blindly at him, Kashka growled. It was the first time in his life I had ever heard him growl, and when he did it, Athena shrieked even louder in misery and beseechingly turned on her side, flailing in place. I lay next to her, stretching my hand to him, talking the whole time, praising both of them.

I even tried introducing Kashka's favorite, Gerber meat sticks, into the process. I tossed pieces to him, hoping he'd associate Athena with them. He'd glance at the pieces in revulsion, turning his back on both of us and the food, feigning sleep—or death. Later I would retrieve desiccated pieces of meat stick, untouched. This went on almost every day. It is perhaps a testament to Kashka's class and basically sweet nature that never once, no matter how close Athena's nose or paw got to him, did he scratch her. He seemed to instinctively know that this loud, smelly abomination was, nevertheless, a baby. Once he swatted her face mightily, hissing. Athena recoiled, crying, and I expected to see furrows. There were none. Kashka had just batted Athena with his large pickle-chip paw but had kept his claws sheathed. It gave me a slight feeling of hope. Kashi, for all his wounded pride and anger, deep down was still a very nice cat.

After eight months, he came into the living room and stayed even if Athena stirred in the kitchen. I doled out affection and attention on a strict schedule during these months. Athena had the morning before work, my lunch hour, and evening until about nine p.m. Kashka had from nine p.m. through the night, as he slept next to me on the bed. He got to wake me up at five a.m. to be fed. He couldn't have been happier with that arrangement, but he was thawing in infinitesimal ways, invisible to probably anyone but me. I caught him one night, lurking near the baby gate, sniffing into the black silent kitchen. He seemed particularly interested in Athena's dog door. He was aware that it led to the outside. I watched him peer into the kitchen, and I stood frozen and silent. I knew that if he knew I saw him, he'd arrange himself into his usual disdainful posture and act like he hated me.

Kashka had always had a panache for theatrics. When he was around five years old, he limped up to me in the back yard, his front paw swollen. I made a big fuss over him, petting him and exclaiming how poor he was. I took him to the vet, and she told me he had just gotten a bee sting and that the swelling should go down in a day or two. But Kashka milked my sympathy. Whenever he caught sight of me, he exaggeratedly limped up to me, looking tragic, and I petted him and told him how sorry I was. This went on for nearly four days before I caught on. I stood at a window and watched him pad completely normally through the back yard; he looked jauntily happy, and if he could have, I think he would have been whistling. I went to the back door and opened it. When he saw me, he froze and then arranged his face into a pitiful expression. He limped over to me like Quasimodo, his disability even more pronounced than it had been originally. He held his paw up and blinked at me, waiting for the shower of sympathy.

"Nice one, Kashka," I said, and petted him vigorously. After that, he knew the jig was up, and the limp disappeared for good.

I gazed longingly at the photos in my cat calendar of cats and dogs nestled together, but I resigned myself to the possibility that such cuddling may never happen between my two friends. I would have settled for them coexisting in the same room. There were more setbacks, however, than triumphs. One lazy afternoon Athena was sound asleep next to me on the couch. Kashka plodded out of my bedroom towards us, chattering to himself, asking, "Ehh, ehh, *ehh?*" which was his standard quiet hoot. He got all the way to the couch, squinting at me drowsily, before the dawn of comprehension lit his gray pointy features: Athena was next to me sleeping. Kashka's eyes hardened, and a long hiss erupted from him. He stared at me with righteous horror at the indignity I had forced him to suffer. That I hadn't somehow transferred telepathically the knowledge that Athena was lying next to me was my crime, and down he dipped, scuttling out of the room like he was being chased.

Athena looked up, sighed, and allowed her head to thud back down. She seemed by that point, at nearly a year old, to be over Kashka. She had tried, she figured, and had apparently reached her limit of begging. I didn't follow Kashka; it was, after all, still technically Athena's shift, and I had had enough of his drama, too. Later in the evening, I could tell he didn't hold it against me, because when I got into bed he still gurgled and meowed his daily news to me, curling up against my thigh.

13. Common in German Shepherds

Thanks to a vet handbook I casually picked up at a bookstore when Athena was a puppy, I was convinced at various times during her first two years that she had cancerous lumps, anal fistulas, hip dysplasia, bloat, and Cauda Equina Sydrome, all horrible conditions common in German shepherds.

"Oh, hi, Ms. Needham!" the vet tech chirped when I brought Athena in one day. They all knew Athena by this point. I took Athena to the vet so often that I insisted jokingly that I didn't have the dog-parent form of Munchausen by Proxy.

This time, Kashka had tipped over the garbage can, which contained a discarded bucket of chicken bones. Athena was the beneficiary of his largesse; by the time I discovered what had happened, the inside of the bucket was gleaming white, like it had never had anything in it. Athena didn't act sick afterward, but I was sure that one of the sharp bones would perforate her colon.

My calm, sweet vet, Dr. Tohill, took an X-ray and saw a bunch of bones in her stomach, but nothing was at that moment penetrating her digestive tract. He recommended that I leave her overnight for observation, to see if everything came out all right.

I had only left Athena there twice before. The first time was for her spay operation, the second, for her official hip exam at age two. Each time, she had done the same thing she did to me now: She gamely trotted alongside the vet technician, looking up at her, wagging and smiling, until they made the first turn around the reception desk, when it suddenly occurred to her that she was being "taken in the back" and that I wasn't coming with her. She looked back at me, her eyes widening, her expression saying, "Hey . . . *Hey* . . . *Heeey*!" She walked backward into the holding area, not breaking eye contact with me until the door closed. I almost burst into tears.

Fortunately, she didn't go batty crazy the way my friend Jim's Lab, cocker spaniel, Chow Chow mix Mindi did if Jim so much as left the room. Mindi had almost removed paint from a door as she dug and cheeped in panic. And that's just when Jim went to the bathroom. Athena's attitude was far calmer, both deeply sad and resigned, as in, "Oh. I always knew you were going to leave me." It rattled me more for some reason.

When I returned for her the next day, it turned out that there had been no perforations; everything had passed without incident. I thought later that I should have taken her to a crowded store; she would have eliminated the bones instantly.

When I first bought Athena, the only hereditary disease I knew about in relation to German shepherds was hip dysplasia, and I knew at age two I was supposed to get her hips X-rayed. Her parents, Romeo and Iris, were of sound German stock, so I was moderately confident that Athena's hips would be okay, but you never know. It wasn't until I began studying the seemingly endless list of afflictions German shepherds can get that I realized her hips were the least of my worries.

My advice to first-time dog owners is never buy a vet handbook, because every symptom you might notice in your dog, however slight, could be caused by some horrible disease that is usually fatal. You will be certain that your dog has whatever it is you're reading about. For example, anal fistulas.

Athena's anal glands regularly stopped up when she was a puppy. I didn't know what was wrong with her; I just knew she stank. I read about anal glands in my vet book and then learned about anal fistulas, a mysterious condition characterized by microscopic fissures in the anus that go deep into the skin and cause painful open sores. No one has discovered what causes them, and there is no known cure. I read heartbreaking web rings where people talked about having to keep their dog's rear ends shaved, and in some extreme cases, remove the tail. The dogs had to soak their butts in cooling baths daily to relieve the discomfort the condition caused. The disorder was most common in German shepherds. "Common in German Shepherd Dogs" was a sentence I saw regularly in my vet guide.

I took Athena to Dr. Tohill to have her anal glands expressed, which meant he squeezed the foul-smelling goop out of them. It was disgusting. She had to get them done every few months. I could tell it was time when that telltale sharp fishy smell began emanating from her back end.

"Can you check to see if she has any fistulas?" I asked Dr. Tohill, who tolerated my frantic diagnoses with no outward sign of annoyance.

"I don't see any evidence of those developing," he said soothingly, shining a bright flashlight on her butt.

I watched Athena diligently for the next few months, but as she got older, her anal glands presented fewer problems. Dr. Tohill offered to show me how to express them myself, should the problem reoccur. I declined.

At around two years old, Athena started running with a stiff-legged gait at the dog park (I disobeyed Megan and had been taking her ever since she was 4 months old). She kept her back legs together and bunny-hopped. Several people in the dog park commented that she didn't look right. One especially helpful gentleman mentioned that his dog, also a German shepherd, had gotten hip dysplasia. His dog, he said, looked a lot like Athena several months before it couldn't walk anymore and had lost control over its bowels.

Back to Dr. Tohill we went to get X-rays. He was convinced she had just jumped up too high to retrieve a catch and jammed her back. "But she should be checked for CES." CES, or Cauda Equina Syndrome, is a narrowing of the vertebrae above the tail, which presses on the nerve endings of the spine, causing pain and, eventually, lameness. According to my book, it is common in German shepherds. The X-rays came back inconclusive, and after a week of rest, Athena was ready to return to running and jumping. Ultimately, her hips proved to be sound. Another emergency health crisis resolved.

One night I was positive she had bloat (common in German Shepherd Dogs). Bloat is the entrapment of gas in the stomach and the twisting of the organ that is fatal if left untreated. Normally a result of swallowed air, it can come on suddenly after a meal consumed too fast or a large intake of water. I was always careful to not let Athena play too vigorously after a meal, but one night she gagged with no result. I immediately felt her sides and belly for any signs of distension and checked her gums for signs of paleness, a symptom of shock or pain. She gagged twice more, and I called the emergency vet. We had never been to that one, so they didn't recognize me as the crazy woman who let hcr dog eat cooked chicken bones or made her vet shine a flashlight on her dog's ass. The vet tech sounded concerned and told me to watch Athena for the next few hours for rapid panting or pacing and whining.

I sat and stared at her like I was waiting for a bag of popcorn to finish in the microwave, but no more symptoms appeared.

One day I found a lump on Athena's left front leg I was sure was cancer. I made another appointment.

"And we're seeing . . . Athena today?" the receptionist asked me. I heard "again" in there; I had just been in for her back problem.

"Yes, she has a lump on her leg," I told her. The lump turned out to be a benign cyst, also common in German shepherds.

I accidentally slammed my car door on her tail one day before we left to go to our agility practice. Her tail when it grew in was a voluminous, puffy anteater tail, and the fur at the tip dragged along the ground, it was so long. Usually she was very good about tucking it away from the car door, but Athena was distracted because Jim, on whom she has an all-consuming crush, was coming with us to agility, and at the last second she swept her tail into the path of the door. I wasn't sure I had actually caught her tail, until I saw her buck and gyrate in the seat, looking like she was being electrocuted; even with the door shut you could have heard her screams down the block. I opened the car door, feeling thoroughly terrible, and apologized over and over to her gibbering face.

She seemed well enough to go to agility, and afterward I noticed that her tail looked swollen. I made an appointment first thing the next morning at Dr. Tohill's. As mentioned, I had just been in for Athena's back problem, and I was convinced the vet's staff was going to call dog social services on me.

The X-rays showed a hairline fracture and a lot of bruising. I felt completely guilty. Oddly, the only time I had ever hurt Kashka was when I had inadvertently shut his tail fringe in the bathroom door. He panicked and ran, leaving a large hunk of fur behind. Both Kashka and Athena have abnormally long tails, and being that I am occasionally absent-minded and a bit clumsy, it's a hazardous combination.

14. "Have you seen mah base-ball?"

While we were at Dr. Tohill's office for yet another phantom malady I frightfully suspected Athena had, he told me that she did have an honest-to-goodness problem, something I'd never even thought of. Her canine teeth were worn down dramatically, and the tan pulp was visible. "She should see a dental specialist," Dr. Tohill told me.

"They actually have those?" I asked, laughing.

"There's a very good one in Vienna," he told me, not laughing along. "She should definitely see him."

So I made an appointment. The dog dentist's office looked just like a human dentist's office. The receptionist asked if Athena liked tennis balls. I had to restrain myself from snorting. Did Athena like tennis balls? She "liked" tennis balls the same way crackheads "like" cocaine. They once did a study with rats where one would press a lever and get drugs. The rat neglected sleep, food, and water to press that lever. That's how Athena was when it came to tennis balls. At home, she had invented something I called "the couch game." She brought a tennis ball to the couch, set it down next to me and stared at it like she was a cobra and the ball a charmer, before sensing my hand moving .000013 of an inch and lunging forward to grab it again in her mouth. Then she chewed the ball lustily as if to confirm it was indeed in her mouth, safe and sound, and the process would begin again. I knew that Athena could have played the couch game from sunup until sundown and resumed playing it as soon as my feet hit the living room floor the next morning. For the sake of both our sanities, I banned tennis balls from our home and gave them to her only when we visited the dog park.

I had been told by numerous people that Athena would excel in flyball, being so "ball-motivated." Flyball features a box containing tennis balls that fly out when a dog slams a lever with its paw. The dog presses the lever, catches the ball, and runs back to its owner. I imagined Athena standing in front of the box, pawing the lever until her pads bled, staring transfixed at the tennis balls shooting out. She would keep one in her mouth all the while, because it never mattered if she had one already. She could easily live with a ball welded to her palate if I would let her.

So I was sheepish when the receptionist asked about tennis balls. "Heh, heh, yeah," I said. "She loves tennis balls."

"You know those are about the worst toy you can give a dog. And so many people make that mistake," she said.

"Oh. Yeah. I can see that." I couldn't, actually. Was she talking about the addiction factor? "Well I don't let her play with them at home, just at the dog park."

At the dog park, Athena had created her own version of the couch game, called "the bench game." While other dogs frolicked and chased each other and play-bowed and wrestled, Athena played the bench game. She preferred to play with a person whose hand moved toward her ball, and she startled more than one person sitting minding his or her own business by popping her head through the back opening of the bench like some crazy jack-in-the-box, so that they were abruptly sitting next to a large disembodied German shepherd head. She set the trap then by putting her dirty, soggy ball next to the unsuspecting dog park patron and waiting, quivering, for the person to reach down and pick up the ball to throw for her. Then, when the person did, Athena would snatch the ball out from under the reaching hand.

"Oh!" the person said, flinching, when Athena snapped up the ball again. "I can't throw it if you don't drop it!" the victim would laugh, before he or she realized that Athena had no intention of ever giving up her tennis ball.

If she found a willing participant who took it as a personal challenge to try and beat her to the ball or pull it out of her teeth, she bothered the poor patsy for the duration of time he or she sat on that bench, or until I dragged her away by her collar.

She didn't, however, need human intervention to play the bench game. She could play all by herself and often did; the foes taking her ball were wind and gravity. She would lay the ball on the bench and stare at it. Sensing an air current, she'd spring forward and grab the ball. Sometimes she did it so spastically that the ball slipped off the bench and rolled away, which was a cause for a dirt kicking, racing frenzy after it.

"Oh, isn't that funny!" I heard someone say as we watched Athena playing the bench game all alone, away from the other dogs and people, like some autistic child in her own little world. Sometimes she would just stand in front of the bench with her ball in her mouth, resting her chin on the seat.

It occurred to me then, while standing in the dog dentist office, that the ground at the dog park was sandy. Athena's ball was always covered with a generous coarse dusting of sand. I may as well have pried her mouth open daily and filed her teeth with a rasp like the ones used for floating horses' teeth.

"Tennis ball attrition is one of the most common problems we see," the receptionist said, interrupting my mental close-up of Athena's mouth chewing the gritty ball.

Tennis ball attrition. It actually had a name. I wondered if I would find it in my vet guide. If not, I was sure it would be there in a future edition, along with a note that German shepherds commonly suffer from it.

The dog dentist turned out to be an affable man who proclaimed Athena "a pretty sweetheart." On the wall of his office, he had a picture of a cow hoof on a plaque with a big red slash through it. Cow hooves and tennis balls were two items strictly forbidden according to the dentist and two items I naively allowed Athena to have. In fact, the very first time I let her choose a special treat at Petco, she chose a cow hoof. She was always allowed to pick out one thing whenever we went there, a concept she inexplicably seemed to understand.

The dentist examined her teeth and said that she did indeed have a classic case of tennis ball attrition and gave me two options. The first was to simply give Athena a different kind of ball to play with. The dentist suggested a baseball.

I didn't get it. "Isn't a baseball even harder than a tennis ball?" I asked.

"Yes," the dentist said, "and because it's so hard, she won't be able to chew it."

The second option was to put stainless steel caps on Athena's canines. The caps wouldn't be pointy replacement teeth; they'd just cover her existing teeth so they wouldn't wear down more. The dentist told me that he had many police dogs as patients, due to the strenuous bite work they did.

I left the office thinking about my options. I had to decide if I was buying my dog a grill. When I told my friends, they were amused. At various times in various conversations about it, someone would inevitably mock me. To wit:

"She'll need a three knuckle paw ring,"

"Will she be wearing a gold, jewel-encrusted goblet strapped to her collar?"

One leaned over her saying, "Yo, yo, yo, Athena!" doing rap star jab-hands.

And of course, more than one called her Jaws.

Given the expense of putting metal caps on my dog's teeth as well as the terror and/or derision she would inspire, I opted for the baseball. I had a period of having to retrain her away from tennis balls. "Eh! No *ma'am!*" I scolded her every time she put a tennis ball in her mouth. It had taken her an admirably short time for her to realize and accept that she wasn't allowed to have them anymore. As a precaution, for the first few days at the dog park after our dentist appointment, I scooped up every ball in the park prior to letting her in, putting them in a plastic bin. More than one person stared at me curiously, the crazy lady with an armload of tennis balls and no dog in sight. I had to leave Athena in the car while I gathered the balls; if she saw me stow them in the bin, I was convinced she would have stood frozen, staring at it for the duration of her visit. Athena made the transition relatively easily after a few trips, and began carrying her beloved baseball around constantly in her mouth. She looked, truthfully, a little stupid with her mouth that wide open all the time, and I occasionally began to call her Warren, after the mentally challenged brother of the title character in *There's Something about Mary.* "Have you seen ma base-ball?" I asked her, and the question usually motivated her to jump on me, deservedly scratching me in the process. Her devotion to her baseball and her overall deportment were quite similar to Warren's, actually. She only liked her ears touched by people she trusted, and she was quite adamant that other dogs should never try and remove her precious baseball from her mouth or steal it when she dropped it for two nanoseconds to get a drink of water. "Athena! Stop it!" I had to remind her whenever she started growling at any dog who came within a four-foot radius of her muzzle. Because her baseball was her most prized possession, she assumed that every dog was conspiring to take it from her. This peccadillo was one of the things that set her apart from other normal dogs.

"Oh, there's that dog with his baseball! He never drops it," I heard a man at the dog park say. "Is that like her binky?" a woman asked me once. I had to laugh and say, "Yes, I think so."

Athena abandoned the bench game once she got her baseball. I don't know why, but it could be that with her mouth so wide open, it was more difficult to squeeze her head through the back opening of the bench. She did like me to throw the ball for her, and like the bench game, fetch was something she seemed capable of doing all day. One sunny day at the dog park, I commanded Athena to sit and drop her ball, which I picked up. Just at that moment, a boy who looked to be around eleven came over and started asking questions.

"She's cool. Is she a German shepherd? Did it take long to train her?"

"What does she eat? Do you feed her special food?"

"She likes her ball. Does she play with other things too?"

"Wow. She really is from Germany?"

I was impressed with his interested questions and tried to answer each one thoroughly, forgetting I still had Athena's baseball in my hand. Athena remained in a sit, but she wiggled like she itched, moving her paws back and forth. Without thinking, I had violated the Athena-owner pact, the rules of which stipulate that I have a specific window of time in which to throw her ball. Once that window has closed, anything goes. I was adding insult to injury by waving my hands around a lot, as I tend to talk with my hands.

Finally overcome, Athena jumped up onto her hind legs and lunged for the ball. I was just expounding on the stockier build of the German lines of shepherd dogs versus the American line as well as the color differences I noticed in the working shepherd dog lines from Eastern Europe, when Athena missed the ball completely and fell toward me, her paws level with my chest. It should be noted that on this warm day I was wearing a tank top with spaghetti straps. Athena's paws, large as catcher's mitts, landed on my chest and slid, catching the tank top and pulling it down. Out popped both of my boobs.

"Athena!" I gasped, dropping the ball.

Athena zoomed in to reclaim it as I sidestepped and simultaneously attempted to stuff my boobs back under my shirt. However, the tank had a built-in shelf bra, and the elastic had bunched up underneath my boobs, so I had to dig excruciatingly long before I could straighten out the top to cover myself as the elastic also made them wantonly appear like I was pushing them up from below on purpose with cupped hands into his face.

"Oh, God, sorry!" I said to the boy. With the help of my obsessive dog, I had turned a G-rated dog park into a park not suitable for anyone under thirteen. To his credit, the boy tried to look away, but not before he stared, wide-eyed, his expression reflecting shock, hilarity, and absolute amazement at the good luck that had befallen him.

I finally was able to tuck myself back into my tank top, and then I began scanning the park to find the boy's parents and apologize to them for including their son in my unplanned Bourbon Street moment. Heedless to the display she had caused, Athena kept insistently placing the baseball at my feet, backing away, glancing from the ball to me and back again. Then I spotted the boy's dad not far away, and when our eyes met, his lips puffed out in a helpless snort of laughter. Red-faced, I looked around, realizing from the strained grimaces and the way people were turning abruptly away from me with shaking shoulders that no less than ten people had witnessed the most embarrassing moment of my life. In subsequent visits to the dog park, I made sure to throw Athena's baseball in a timely manner and to wear shirts with sleeves. And a bra.

15. The WHAT Diet?

Since so many diseases and conditions were common in German shepherds, when she was just under three years old I decided to stop feeding Athena dog food and instead put her on the BARF, or bones and raw food diet. Many dog and cat owners reported that their pets responded to the diet with improved coats, digestion, and overall health and that it was closer to the optimum nutrition they needed. Vets were and continue to be split on the wisdom of this diet, but I decided to give it a try. I bought her chicken drumsticks, thighs, and backs. I read that vegetables were good, and I got a food processor with the ambitious thought of buying sweet potatoes and carrots to puree. Then I remembered how lazy I am and instead bought jars of baby food. The vegetable variety pack was the best; it had carrots, sweet potatoes, squash and peas. I assumed Athena would hate peas, because I hate peas, but she liked them well enough. I also fed her raw eggs, cottage cheese, and canned sardines. She got a glucosamine and then later, a flax seed supplement. The maiden feeding was an immense success. She easily chewed up her drumstick, ate a whole egg, shell and all, and licked clean the sweet potatoes and cottage cheese.

One of her favorite delicacies turned out to be chicken feet with their delicious little bones and cartilage. She loved them as a snack and treated the four or five I gingerly dropped into her bowl by the toenails, almost gagging, like they were potato chips. After a few weeks on the diet, her coat shone. She was always a very enthusiastic eater. If I had to substitute her meals for a day or two between supermarket visits with mere dog food after we'd started the BARF diet, she stared at it, stared at me, and walked away, deigning to eat it only after leaving it for a few minutes until she figured out that she wasn't getting anything else.

I sent a picture of her to Megan, and Megan called me. "She's *gorgeous*!" Megan yelled. It was the first time I ever felt like I was doing okay with my dog. "What are you feeding her?"

"I have her on the BARF diet," I admitted.

When Megan didn't yell, "Why are you doing *that*?" I considered it a major victory. In fact, she didn't criticize me at all, like I thought she would; she only mentioned that BARF was basically the same thing as K-9 Kraving.

"If someone wants to see what a long-coated Shepherd looks like as an adult, I'm going to show them her picture," Megan concluded, and I felt like I could have floated away, I was so happy.

After that, I became the annoying BARF evangelist people everywhere want to escape.

"You give her chicken bones?" almost every person I told about it asked.

"Yes," I said. "Raw chicken bones are fine for dogs to eat. They're flexible and don't splinter. It's the cooked chicken bones that are dangerous. They're brittle."

"Aren't you afraid of salmonella?" was the next inevitable question, to which I responded authoritatively that dog's stomachs tolerate the bacteria, assuming they are not puppies, elderly, or sick.

When I went to the grocery store and put bulk packages of chicken parts, stew bones, beef liver, chicken feet, twenty cans of sardines, and cases of baby food on the conveyer belt, I always felt I had to explain myself.

"You must have a big dog at home," one clerk guessed correctly before I could say anything.

"Yes, a German shepherd! And she's on the raw foods diet." I had learned that calling it the BARF diet caused most people to recoil. That's hers, that's hers, that's hers," I crowed, pointing at 85 percent of the contents of my cart.

"I wish I was your dog; she eats better than I do," the clerk said.

"She eats better than I do, too," I laughed.

He didn't laugh, and I suddenly felt so much like Marie Antoinette— "Ha, ha, ha! Let them eat cake!"—that I gave a cash donation to a local food bank.

I didn't feed the BARF diet to Kashka (he'd sooner have performed kicks in a chorus line than eat anything raw), and although my new dog-owning friends were intrigued, most stuck with dog food with occasional departures when I would give their dogs leftover chicken parts to show them how much their dogs liked them. "Your dog eats better than you do!" they all agreed, echoing the disapproving grocery clerk.

16. Schutzhund

When Athena got a little older, and we had finished basic obedience with Victoria, I looked for productive ways for her to channel her energy. I remembered that both her parents had passed the highest level of Schutzhund training, so it seemed the logical activity to try. Schutzhund, German for "protection dog" is a sport combining bite work, tracking, and obedience. German shepherds are the most common Schutzhund breed, although Belgian Malinois, Rottweilers, and Dobermans are among the many other breeds also represented. The training does not focus on aggression, despite the inclusion of bite work, but instead encourages mental toughness and discipline. A well-trained Schutzhund dog is stable and confident and thus far less likely to bite out of fear or insecurity. Successful training also strengthens the bond between the handler and the dog, but like everything dog related, the sport isn't for everyone—human or canine.

Conveniently, Megan ran a Schutzhund club at her breeding facility, where she had a beautifully maintained field set up for the training. She invited me to bring Athena to be evaluated by Pedro Jimenez, one of the top Schutzhund Helpers in the area. "Helper" is the official title of the person training Schutzhund dogs in bite work. Athena was to be tested on her willingness to bite and hold. Megan told me to bring a long lead.

When I arrived, the parking area was full of SUVs with their tailgates down, revealing dogs in crates. After our early disastrous experience with her crate, Athena always rode in my back seat, the seat belt looped through the back of a special harness.

The first person I met was Meg, the Vice President of the Schutzhund Club. She was a tall, slender soft-spoken Patrician woman with a frosty manner that intimidated me. I felt like a loud, slovenly dwarf whenever I talked to her. She was the kind of woman I would likely accidentally spit on while talking.

"Your dog should be in a crate," Meg informed me. I was too nervous to explain how Athena reacted whenever she was in a crate, and I didn't get the impression that Meg would understand "monkey screams."

"I don't have one," I said. It was true; I had given away Athena's crate to a deserving home and now kept her toys in a large wicker basket in my living room.

It was an excuse that worked for me as well with Meg as it had in junior high school when I forgot my textbook and was asked by the teacher to read aloud.

Meg said, "Megan has an extra one. Athena can use it until you get your own."

Damn it! I thought.

"Okay, great, thanks!" I said.

Meg brought me a collapsed metal crate, and recalling with a sense of dread my upside-down baby gate, I knew that I'd pick and stare at the crate helplessly for hours without understanding how to assemble it. I chuckled, flushing, and admitted I didn't know how to put it together.

Meg gave me a flinty smile and said, "It's easy. You lift this up here and it snaps together here . . . " With great efficiency and economy of movement, Meg snapped the crate together in 2.43 seconds as I watched, nodding, squinting, and frowning like I was absorbing the process. I understood myself very well, however, and knew without a doubt that until I practiced putting the crate together myself four to six times, I would never be able to mimic how she'd done it.

After Meg uncollapsed the crate, I got Athena out of the car and took her to potty. She threw a suspicious glance at the crate but walked along with me, anyway. We passed another club member walking her German shepherd, and Athena flailed around on her hind legs as per usual, barking at the other dog. Then she caught sight of Pedro working with one of his own dogs, a large black male German shepherd, under the glare of the floodlights. He was teasing the dog with a dumbbell to get its attention. Before I knew it, I was on the pavement, and Athena was dragging me like a Malamute with a sled of goods toward the field, yipping and gabbling with excitement.

"Athena!" I gasped, and she gave me a look of surprise, turned back, and licked my face. She at least had the decency to wait for me to get up before springing to the end of her lead again, jumping up and down as I struggled to stay upright.

Just then Megan came out of the main house. She clapped her hands in delight, exclaiming, "Look how much drive she has! Look at her pull!" She laughed at my attempts to hold Athena and said, "You just need to develop your leg and butt muscles, girl!" Megan said Athena looked great but needed to drop some weight. "All of Romeo's puppies turned out to be *monsters*! They are all on the large side!" she shouted. She reminded me that I needed to get a crate by the next lesson before she disappeared back into her house.

I opened the door to the borrowed crate and told Athena, "In!" Athena favored me with a puzzled, affronted look and went in halfway, her head and shoulders inside, and then froze. "In, Athena!" I said and pushed her puffy rump in all the way. Athena pulled up her shoulders and gingerly turned around to face me, but she didn't sit or lie down. She was tense and bunchy in there, as if she were afraid to let any of the walls touch her. I ignored the accusatory look she gave me and went to introduce myself to the rest of the club members and to Pedro. As is common when groups of people know each other already, after the pleasantries had been exchanged, they pretty much ignored me, and I stood among them like a different-colored toadstool.

I listened shyly to them talk about their German shepherds and "Club" (If you were cool, you didn't call it Schutzhund, you called it "Club") and offered a few timid facts about Athena. Then a car pulled up, and a young college-aged woman named Liz got out, jabbering a mile a minute about the traffic, and greeted the circle of regulars. Liz's mom was with her, and everyone greeted them warmly.

Liz had the supreme self-confidence I had never had at that age, and still don't, and she joined the conversation easily. She talked about her horse, and soon I learned that she lived in McLean, a wealthy town, and I thought, *Oh no, it's one of those spoiled rich brats who go to private school and have a horse and everything handed to them and a ton of friends.* She was essentially everything I'd ever wanted to be growing up but wasn't.

We eyed each other and said hello, but it was not what I would call a friendly greeting. Then she brought Kiera, her German shepherd, out of her crate. Kiera jumped around with all four feet off the ground, like she was in her own moon bounce, and then she jumped up on Liz. "*Yeeeah!*" Liz squealed. She caught Kiera's front paws, and they jittered around together in a mad, joyous pas de deux. I was already on edge, feeling like Athena and I were the new kids wearing floods, so I went back to my car to stand next to her, the stiff humpbacked silhouette in the crate.

Liz's mom followed me over to meet Athena. "Aw, she's so fluffy," she said. "She looks like a little bear." I was struck at how genuinely sweet and open her expression was. It didn't have a hint of condescension or forced politeness. I gave a relieved smile, grateful that finally there was a bit of conversation in which I could actually participate with confidence. I thanked her and answered her questions while Athena and I waited for the class to start.

The training itself was astounding. Athena's evaluation would be last, so I had the chance to watch everyone else work. Pedro stood in the middle of the field, one arm in a huge padded sleeve. With his other hand, he performed various functions, from shooting a gun loaded with blanks to cracking a whip in the air next to him, all meant to help the dogs focus despite distractions. The dogs varied in ferocity in their responses, but all barked and growled and showed their teeth. Each owner held the dog's lead as the dog leaped at Pedro, and Pedro would taunt the dog with his padded arm several times until he got close enough for the dog to latch on with a decisive chomp.

Standing on its hind legs, the dog would cling to the sleeve as Pedro walked along or used the handle of the whip to stroke the dog's sides. When he was satisfied that the dog was biting correctly and sufficiently, Pedro slipped his arm out of the sleeve and the dog trotted around in a giant circle, triumphantly holding the sleeve in its mouth.

"That's so cool," I said aloud, glancing over at Athena in her crate. The other dogs waiting all carried on mournfully in their crates, beyond hyper to get out and have their turn. Athena stood with her ears tilted towards the noise but didn't seem too interested. When it was time for Athena's evaluation, Pedro explained that we would be using a jute tug, a two-foot-long burlap tube with two leather handles on either side, rather than the sleeve. I was a bit disappointed but understood that it was necessary since she was a novice.

"Okay, bring her out," Pedro ordered. I had the urge to say, "Yes sir," and salute. Pedro had an aura of authority that made me want to begin executing the command before it had even finished leaving his mouth.

Athena seemed relieved to be out of her death cage and did a fast trot out to the field. She made a beeline for Pedro, and since she had an instant crush on almost every man she saw, she put her ears back, made her high pitched whines, and tried to jump on him.

"That's Pedro," I said.

Pedro grinned, and then he said, not unkindly, but still with a sense of authority that made me want to hide in my car, "I'm supposed to be the bad guy, not her friend."

I guess I looked so abashed that he added, "But she's a nice dog, isn't she? Friendly."

I agreed that she was pretty friendly toward people.

My job was to hold Athena while Pedro teased her with the jute tug. It was almost impossible. She wanted to bite it very badly. When she wasn't rearing and lunging, she barked in a whiny pitch that, with dismay, I recognized as her play bark. When that didn't work, she went into a crouch, stalking Pedro like he had turned into a sheep and she a Border collie, giving him a hard stare, cautiously lifting her paws forward just so, belly inches off the ground. The other club members giggled.

"She looks like a lion," one called out to me, albeit good naturedly.

When she finally sprang and got hold of the jute tug, I felt the impact all the way down the lead to my shoulder. I watched silly play-barking Athena turn into a deadly Great White, shaking her head back and forth, her front paws entirely off the ground.

"Good!" Pedro said, stroking the sides of her face and body. He explained later that he wasn't petting her to praise her; he was trying to make sure she used "both sides of her bite equally," as well as get her used to being touched during training. No matter which way Pedro tugged or pulled, Athena kept her grip on the tug, pausing here and there to shake it, using her whole body.

"Okay, now when she drops it, kick it back to me," he ordered, and I clicked my mouth like I had seen other people do as if at a horse and turned a prancing Athena in a circle, the tug still in her mouth. I reeled her in and then lifted her slightly by her collar. She spat out the toy, but as I kicked it, she lurched forward, her new version of the couch/bench game, and picked it back up. The next time, I kicked it further, and she pulled me forward all the way to the ground. Miraculously, I rolled to my feet and then stood with my feet apart, as if I were water skiing. Pedro picked the tug up, and I was again pulled along as Athena whipped around at the end of her lead. She bit the jute tug again and held on as tenaciously as before.

"Good!" Pedro said. "Now take her home."

From watching the others, I knew that when Pedro said, "Go home," it meant run back to your car with your dog as it held the sleeve in its mouth. When we reached my car, I had to jerk Athena up by her collar several times with both hands to get her to let go of her trophy, and since I was closer to the back seat than to her borrowed crate, I opened the back door and hip checked her so she would hop in. I brought the tug back to Pedro and waited for his verdict.

"Well, your dog did great," he said. "You? Mmmm . . . " he made a so-so gesture with his hand and laughed. "But you're new, so it's okay. You have a lot of enthusiasm, which is good."

I grinned.

"Your dog? She has the most natural talent of almost any puppy I've ever evaluated," he said decisively. "Her bite is solid, and she's very motivated."

I resisted the urge to bounce up and down and clap, but I couldn't resist turning around and looking at my classmates, who were watching open-mouthed and wide-eyed.

When I went back to my car to tell Athena the good news, I found her sound asleep on the seat.

For the next four months, in skin-aching cold and wind, I took Athena to Club. I never did get a crate, and fortunately everyone seemed to forget about it. Except Megan. Every time she came out, she told me Athena *must* be in a crate, because she had seen dogs at Schutzhund injure themselves; one broke through the window of its owner's car in its excitement to get to the field. I nodded, and looked into the car at Athena, who was snoozing in a tight-eyed lump.

Athena liked to sleep in between her turns, and most of the time, I had to wake up my very groggy dog and tell her, "It's time!" It took her a few paces after exiting the car to perk up, and then it was time to water ski again. After our third lesson, Athena had graduated to the sleeve and also to her seatbelt harness instead of just a collar, because we all were a little afraid she was going to snap her own neck in her frenzy to get to Pedro.

She never properly learned how to turn on the fierce "hard" side of her personality during bite work, however. She still smiled and yipped at Pedro like, "I love ya, you big lug! Now, give me that sleeve!"

Pedro told me that Athena had a high "play and prey drive," which meant that she never really took Pedro's role as the "bad guy" seriously but still had a burning obsessive desire to get the sleeve in her mouth and hang onto it, which was considered a good sign. Dogs that had weak bites or were fearful of the helper were seen as undesirable for the sport. Pedro thought it was best to tie her long lead to a post on the field and let the post keep her back, because half the time when I held her lead, it was like "Oh, hi, Pedro!" as I skidded to within feet of him, Athena latching onto the sleeve prematurely. I still had to pick up the slack in the lead and try to run her around in a circle even while the very end of the lead was tied to the post, and it often went poorly, resulting in me turning around in place like I was in a music box and Athena not running along behind me but instead paused, flipping the sleeve up into the air and pouncing on it like it was a toy (a Schutzhund no-no). "You're doing it again," Pedro would call from the field.

My favorite part of bite work was when Athena and I got to do a backup bite. A backup bite consisted of Pedro, the bad guy, running away from us while I held Athena by the collar and revved her up to go chase him. It reminded me of the Evel Knievel motorcycle toy I had when I was a kid, where the cycle sat on a base, and I would crazily turn and turn and turn a crank and then hit a button to release the bike. The noise when you turned the crank was a satisfying escalating scream, and the power that was built up by cranking made the motorcycle pop wheelies when you let it go.

I held Athena's collar and patted her sides rapidly, urgently whispering, "You going to go get that bad guy?"

Athena, with her play bark, always sounded like she was answering, "*Yyyep!*" as she strained against my hold.

"*Packen!*" I'd command sharply, the German command for "bite," as I let go of her collar. Athena would zoom after Pedro, jump with all the force of weight and forward momentum, and bite the sleeve.

Pedro was an expert at "catching" dogs who ran at him, and several times Athena swung around with all four feet off the ground as he whirled in a circle, her mouth firmly gripping the sleeve.

Once I practiced the official warning before letting Athena go: "If you don't stop, I'm going to release my dog!"

When I shouted it, Pedro pantomimed running away even more crazily, flailing his arms around. Playing or not, it was an awesome sight watching the aerodynamic Athena, ears back, body low to the ground, speeding single-mindedly toward her target. I imagined what it would look like to someone who didn't know her and decided it would look pretty damn scary.

Our Schutzhund training also included obedience, which is to regular obedience what dancing around your bedroom is to being a principal in the Bolshoi Ballet Company. There are no clickers in Schutzhund obedience, and your dog is expected to obey without fail. It was here that I was told by Barbara, the Schutzhund obedience trainer, to buy a tool to help me finally obtain control of Athena, particularly during walks: the prong collar. Walks, until I put a prong on her, were a hazardous exercise for my lower back because I just didn't have the strength to walk over half my body weight that had its own mind and opinion of where we should go. After the prong collar, I would give Athena a fast tug on her leash if she started to pull, and she wouldn't pull anymore. What I didn't know at the time is that prong collars are universally despised by the positive-reinforcement trainers like Victoria, Athena's puppy trainer; they find them cruel. The collar has metal "teeth" (e.g., prongs) that when the leash is popped produces a quick pinch to the neck, an attention-getting technique to get the dog's focus and correct an unwanted behavior. The action is supposed to recall a mother dog's disciplining neck-bite. Trainers who specialize in strong-willed breeds like German shepherds or Rotties espouse their efficacy, but eventually I stopped using a prong collar, preferring more positive-based methods. For Athena's early-adult years, however, I admit she wore a prong.

Barbara was a genial, even-tempered lady with adult braces, something that instantly endears someone to me. Barbara's calm attitude masked an iron will on the training field, where she trained her two Rottweilers for competition. They were lovable muscled teddy bears outside their crates, but I almost had an accident the first time I walked by Barbara's tailgate and they barked at me.

Barbara noticed instantly that Athena was a "friendly girl." Also noticing that Athena's owner was mechanically inept, Barbara unsnapped Athena's prong collar. "This is too loose," she said, and expertly removed several links. "It goes up here," she said and fastened it high on Athena's neck, just under her chin and behind her ears. Athena flashed me a look of outrage and Barbara a confused expression as I clipped her leash to the repositioned collar. I passed her a few pieces of hot dog to bribe her into thinking it was all great fun. I waited until Barbara's back was turned to do this, because I was pretty sure food rewards were seen as soft in Schutzhund obedience.

Barbara taught me German commands, and I preferred them to the English commands right away. Athena seemed much more amenable to obeying me when I spoke in German, and I sounded more authoritative when I said them. Thus we were introduced to "platz" (lie down), "zeet" (sit), "fuss" (heel at the left side), "hier" (come and sit right in front of me), "aus" (let go of what's in your mouth), and "come" (come in the general area). Later, Liz would teach Athena "gib laut" (speak), which I loved and whispered to Athena to get her to wish happy birthday to someone on the phone.

Athena wasn't too crazy about several of her four-legged obedience classmates, a fact she let them know by barking loudly at them whenever they stared at her. Now that she was wearing the prong collar in the correct position, a quick pop of her leash usually got her attention. But sometimes a quick jerk wasn't enough. Barbara was standing with us one lesson, and she said, "Put her in a platz."

"Platz!" I said to Athena. Athena paid not a smidgeon of attention to me.

"Here, let me," Barbara said and took Athena's leash. "Platz," Barbara said mildly. Athena was far too interested in making sure the other dogs across the way didn't look at her wrong to care that I and now Barbara had told her to lie down. Barbara gently, but with unmistakable determination, grasped Athena's prong collar and pulled it towards the ground, mimicking the bite on the back of the neck Athena had employed on her fellow canine playmates on numerous occasions. Athena wailed to the volume one would hear standing inside a fire engine as she went to the ground. My first impulse was to dart forward to comfort my grievously injured pet, but Barbara put her hand up, palm out and said, "Stop. Don't." I stopped.

"That was a protest. That did *not* hurt her the way she's carrying on. The truth is, your dog is very manipulative. She manipulates you."

I stared at Barbara. Nobody wants to hear that about her dog.

"She does?" I asked.

"She's a female, for one, and I think they tend to think about things more than males. That, and she's a very dominant female. I'm not saying she's a mean dog or that she's playing you in a mean way, but if she can get away with stuff, she will try. She's also very smart. Smarter than she lets on."

I looked down at Athena, who was now resting comfortably on the ground.

"Release her from the command," Barbara said.

"Free," I told Athena, and she stood up to continue her vigilant surveillance of the dogs who were potentially talking about her behind her back.

"Now watch," Barbara said. "Platz," she said. Athena looked up at Barbara and instantly dropped to her belly. She didn't cower or tremble when she did it. She merely respected Barbara's authority and amiably lay down, ears alert, with no change in her expression.

17. Athena the Puppet Master

Of course, I doubted the truth of Barbara's comment. Athena didn't manipulate me! She respected me. She listened to me. Most of the time, anyway. Okay, some of the time, when she felt like it.

It was a hard truth to face. Athena was a master at playing to my sympathetic side. When I felt she was mature enough, I took down the baby gate and let her out of the kitchen during the day, but there were times when I would come home for my lunch hour and find unpleasant surprises. They weren't technically surprises, because Athena always greeted me at the door, and I could gauge by her body language if she had done something.

I didn't need to look over her shoulder at the ripped-up pages of magazines flung all over the living room floor or the garbage tipped over to know those events had occurred. When she had done something naughty, she became an earless German shepherd, all forehead, her ears drawn so far back that it really looked as if they had been amputated. Her eyes would be the circumference of poker chips. Her tail would be low, just the very tip swishing back and forth. For added sympathy, she licked her lips, a gesture that produced a dry, nervous sound. The overall effect called to mind one of those forlorn huge-eyed children in a Walter Keane painting.

If I so much as raised my voice above a floating whisper to ask, "What is that?" she would urinate submissively, so I stopped chastising her. Instead I walked by her as if nothing had happened, opened the sliding glass door, and wordlessly pointed like Scrooge's final spirit to the yard, and when she went outside, I closed her dog door with a flat cover. Outside, her ears magically regenerated, and I'd hear the dog door flap impotently and see her peering in through the glass door. If, however, she caught sight of me looking at her, her ears would disappear again and her eyes would swim with tears.

I would clean up the mess and let her back in. She would always try to act nonchalant, trotting into the house as if nothing happened, but when she looked at me and saw that the incident was *not* forgotten, she deflated and found one of her stuffed animals to clutch in her mouth. Lying on her blanket, she would cast sullen pouty looks at me, her long eyelashes and mobile eyebrows giving away every glance in my direction. I would leave her in emotional time out for usually only five minutes. When I finally talked to her, calling her name, she brightened considerably and acted so relieved that I figured the trauma of our spat would motivate her to turn over a new leaf. It didn't.

But she made herself so miserable with her own actions that I felt bad scolding her on top of it. Liz, my Schutzhund nemesis, had thawed towards me after we had exchanged funny emails and realized we had a lot in common, ruled Kiera with a Stalinesque iron fist and decreed my inability to *really* punish Athena "letting her get away with it." I had to agree that to a certain extent I did. Fortunately, Athena's defiant tendencies disappeared as she grew up—in all areas save two.

Kashka's soft food and his litter box proved irresistible when she could get at either. I used a stack of paper plates to feed him, and removed the top plate to reveal a clean one when he was finished.

Sometimes the used plate on the top of the stack would turn up missing. I could usually find it on Athena's blanket in the living room or out in the yard. And if I turned quickly enough as I reached down to pick up the remnants of the cleanly-tongued plate, there Athena would be, standing penguin-toed, wagging, with no ears and watery eye saucers, holding one of her more absurd stuffed toys (like her two-foot-long wooly bowling pin) in her mouth. That, or I would catch her tiptoeing away.

She reacted the same way when I caught her emerging from the bathroom, casting guilty looks up at me as she subtly chewed. Athena was a veritable glutton for Kashka's poop. If I yelled at her mid-chew, she was likely to dutifully spit out what she was chewing, so I had no choice but to allow her to finish. I then pointed into the kitchen and said, "Trinken!" (drink of water in German). After the rhythmic plashing, she would come back into the living room and stare at me, pinning back her triangular ears and hesitantly oscillating her tail tip. Her only punishment after a delicious enjoyable cat turd was that she wasn't allowed on the couch next to me afterwards, but she still lay dejected on her Athena pillow like I had ruined her life.

She couldn't get to Kashka's food or litter box as easily after I had a baby gate installed across the hallway entrance to my bedrooms and bathroom. The baby gate is the kind that swings open, and if one doesn't latch it properly, it will come loose fairly easily. I normally heard her pushing it with her nose, trying to open it without success before I yelled, "Knock it off!" and I heard the tick of her nails as she padded away. Sometimes, however, she could open it quietly so I didn't hear or even better, wait until she was alone in the house.

I always had to pick my battles with her.

One of her more endearing manipulations was her head tilt. Whenever she wanted something, she tilted her head. She instinctively knew it was adorable. Even now, years later when she's sitting next to me on the couch, if I just glance at her, she tilts her head. When meeting new people, she gazes at them rapturously and pulls out her secret weapon. It gets people every single time, and it gets me most of the time. Athena, however, also uses her head tilt for out-and-out evil, such as when she does it right after she's shoved a stuffed animal onto my legs to throw for her when I'm sitting on the couch.

"No," I will tell her, and down to the right her ears go, her nose up to the left. She'll even pull her lips back into a smile, staring at me with "but I looove youuuuu" eyes. She backs up a few steps, still staring at me, and adds a swishy, happy tail wag for good measure. "No, Athena," I will say. "I'm not throwing it when you decide I should throw it." Her eyes register slight panic when I start speaking to her in complete sentences. It's the only thing that momentarily disrupts her wheedling as she tilts her head entirely in the other direction, leaning forward in her effort to understand what I have said, straining to discern if I have possibly mentioned "outside," "bone," or "baseball." When I don't move after saying no, she feels, apparently, that we have had a horrible failure to communicate and I'm not understanding what she wants, so with an exasperated screech she picks the toy up from my lap and throws it down even more adamantly, backing up again.

"Stop it!" I tell her. Her response is to pick the toy up and stomp over to her dog pillow where she then flops down, heaving a loud martyred sigh, holding the toy in her mouth.

Athena is one of the most prolific sighers I've ever encountered. A fourteen-year-old girl being embarrassed by her parents at the mall sighs less. After I have denied her simple request to throw her stuffed animal and she's huffed over to her pillow, she makes sure to look to see if I'm watching her. If she catches me watching her, she readjusts the animal in her mouth by moving it with her paw, just so she can put her head down and sigh again, in case I didn't get the message the first time that I'm a horrible, dull owner and that Athena merely puts up with me.

When she's very bored and wants to go out and play, she doesn't do anything cute like bring me her leash. Instead, she will jump on the couch next to me, settle into a perfect sit, and stare at me. I can feel her doing it, and I can see her with my peripheral vision. If I look over at her, she will languorously set her head down on the back of the couch, batting her eyelashes at me slowly, and then wind up with a lazy inhale before exhaling the longest, the breathiest sigh, the sigh of all sighs, indicating how difficult it is for her sometimes to even be alive. She even knows to time her sighs for maximum effect. I have denied her some *perfectly reasonable* request when I have had company, and she will deliberately wait until there is a lull in the conversation before she will treat my guest and me to the extended hiss of air being released from a tire.

When she is merry, on the other hand, she wants the universe to know. She has stayed with my friend Lauren and Lauren's dogs Carman and Cody on occasion. The thrill of being with them and playing sometimes makes her forget that the dog door is all the way downstairs and that it is difficult for her to fit through. As a result, she has had a few accidents in Lauren's house. Lauren is merciless when it comes to breaking house rules, and she punished Athena severely (according to Athena), once locking her outside in the yard for a full half hour. Athena is hyper-attentive now about following the rules at Lauren's house and goes into exaggerated cowering whenever Lauren's dogs are corrected. Lauren always has to reassure her that she wasn't the one who did anything wrong.

"I've never seen a dog look so tragic, for no reason," Lauren informed me one day.

"I know," I said. "Athena is a bit of a drama queen."

"Just a bit," Lauren joked.

Whenever we were at Lauren's, I knew that an intense, frantic stare from Athena meant that she would like to go out and go potty, please. One night, however, she followed Cody downstairs out the dog door and went potty all by herself, without my having to take her. She bounded back upstairs, a precarious feat in of itself with her clumsy paws, and found Lauren, who was in the bathroom washing her hands. Lauren said Athena walked to the open door and peeked around the doorjamb at her several times, wearing a bright, anticipatory expression. Lauren said, "It finally occurred to me that she wanted me to praise her for using the dog door, so I said 'Good girl, Athena! You used the door!'" Athena broke into a wide, addlebrained grin, and still grinning to herself, walked away.

That's the thing about Athena. Was Barbara right and Athena is manipulative? Yes. Do I find Athena's behavior irritating when she's trying to get her way? Yes. Do I also find her behavior adorable when she's trying to get her way? I'd like to be able to say no. But I can't.

18. Athena's Friends

Kiera

I only have to start the sentence, "Athena?" (Head tilt: ears down to the right, nose up to the left.) "Would you like to—?" Whatever "it" is, she would like to. I could ask her if she would like to walk on burning coals or take a trip to be given away at the pound, and she would still jump and shriek "Yep!" and then gambol around the living room like the winner of a new car on *The Price is Right*. Since she always interrupted my question, I could only get out a name.

"Athena? Would you like to—"

"Yep! Yep! Yep!"

"—Kiera?"

"Yep! Yep! Yep!"

Kiera, Liz's German shepherd, was one of Athena's best friends. Like Athena, Kiera was born at the Haus Juris kennels, but her parents and bloodline were not the same as Athena's. She was a slight, well-proportioned shepherd, thin and angular, and she possessed the most fluid gait I've ever seen. Next to Kiera, Athena plodded along like a mammoth. Nimble and clever as a squirrel, Kiera never met a fence or crate that she couldn't figure out how to breach or open.

They had a strange history together in that Athena pinned Kiera to the ground the first time Liz brought her to my house, but eventually Athena, with a combination of annoyance and enjoyment, allowed Kiera to mount her in very disturbing, graphic ways whenever they played.

My first impression of Kiera was that she was hyper, and that impression never changed. All along, I thought Athena was a major busybody. When I met Kiera, I realized that as German shepherds go, Kiera was at the quivering type-A end of the spectrum, and Athena was more at the type-B relaxed end. I nicknamed Kiera Samara, after the little girl in *The Ring*. Footage of the evil little girl shows her being interviewed by a psychiatrist. The movie wants you to pay attention to the fact that the clock rotates a full twenty-four hours and Samara *never sleeps*. I was convinced that Kiera bounced around and brought humans toys in a never-ending stream of activity that would continue into infinity. Then I babysat Kiera for a week and discovered that her frenzied pace was balanced by her ability to sleep. As with all wicks that burn hotly, when she finally crashed, Kiera slept in a virtual hibernation state. She was not stirred by noise and snored loudly.

While Athena was a slouchy leaner who enjoyed lying next to you being cuddled, Kiera short-circuited if you so much as looked at her. She was exceptionally friendly, but her happy mania overflowed, and before you knew it, she was jumping on you, clawing at your torso, and trying to nibble your earlobe.

Unlike Athena, who looked merrily empty-headed at times, Kiera had an air of anxiety, as if she constantly was trying to understand the world around her and failing. Liz and I once joked that if Athena and Kiera were human college students, Athena would be the outgoing but slightly vacuous C-student who filmed herself on a webcam for boys, and Kiera would read Sylvia Plath, be a straight-A student, and cut herself to deal with her pain. Their e-mails to one another would consist of Athena bragging about the clothes and jewelry her online suitors bought her and Kiera's would contain angst-ridden poetry and an opinion on a newly discovered theory of physics that Athena wouldn't understand.

Of the two of them, Athena got over being scolded relatively quickly. I just didn't know that she really thought about things very long. From her earliest puppyhood, Athena was blithely impervious to common scolding, and even when I had to punish her severely for destroying my living room, she got over her misery quickly, even if at the time she urinated or looked at me with no ears and tearful saucer eyes. As she got older, her remorseful periods grew shorter and shorter, until it took only about twenty seconds for her to perk up and look congenially around the room, panting with her customary brio. She'd put on a good show if you gave her a glare, but as soon as you looked away, her ears grew back, and she grinned again.

Kiera, on the other hand, responded to scolding with the canine equivalent of a Victorian-fainting-couch swoon that might last for three hours. Because she was intact, it got even worse when she was on her period. She was the picture of suicidal despondency if she had been chastised, lying down across the room, away from all other people and animals, staring with her usual agitated wide eyes at something in thin air. Even cajoling her with her jolly ball or her tug toy made from the leg of a pair of jeans could not revive her joie de vivre. She would look at you as if all the existential questions of the universe were troubling her brain, before resetting her gaze on nothing visible to the human eye. The only reaction she would give when you tried to revive her good spirits was to climb into a chair and turn into a dainty ball.

The amusing thing about both dogs was that Athena got over being severely yelled at, but Kiera could go into one of her sulks if you spoke to her in a normal voice. She sometimes went into a self-imposed shame spiral that neither Liz nor I could ever decipher.

I was subject to one of Kiera's extended mopes when I babysat her while Liz and her family were away in Europe. I didn't even yell at her.

I left both girls loose in the house while I was away at work, and both were at the age where most things they did were benign—playing with one another or sleeping. I was reasonably secure that nothing would be molested because I had latched the swinging baby gate before leaving. Of course, I had forgotten that Kiera could jump over the baby gate from a standing position with nary a tummy hair brushing the top when no one was there to watch her. She was smart enough to let Athena do her dirty work when I was home because then one or both of them would nose-push the gate open. When I was in the bathroom, which is directly in front of it, I'd hear "Click. Creeeeeaaaak" and look out to see two sets of inquiring pointy ears and four lined-up legs, as they would stand at the threshold of baby gate and hallway waiting to be invited across like a pair of vampires. Lauren or Liz would have doubtless punished them for opening the gate in the first place, but I had to most often clamp a hand over my mouth to stop myself from laughing. Both of them always looked so hopeful, and I did find it polite that they knew where the boundary was. I never gave them permission to enter, and they never took advantage, except once. I was in the bathroom with the door closed one night, and I could by now almost count down the number of seconds I knew I'd hear "Click. Creeeeeaaaak," from the baby gate outside the door. Sure enough, after about five seconds they pushed, and I crouched down and peeped out the crack underneath the bathroom door. I was just in time to see first a very small set of ladylike paws silently tip toe by the door, heading for Kashka's room, followed by louder fat round paws that slapped the ground lazily.

"Hey!" I said through the door crack, muffling my laughter. The small antelope-hoof feet quietly but with a definite sense of urgency trotted back past the door and out into the living room where they belonged. The fat round paws, on the other hand, did not move at first, until I noticed that they were getting larger. My view then became completely dark as, with a broomlike noise, Athena pressed against the bathroom door and slid down to loll comfortably against it, brazenly acting unperturbed that both of them had gotten caught sneaking where they shouldn't have been. When I opened the door, Athena had rolled onto her back for good measure, peering at me upside down, her feet curled sideways, tail brushing back and forth across the floor (this was her latest manipulation to avoid getting punished, and it worked). Kiera was back standing at the invisible line between baby gate and living room, smiling and wagging her tail.

The day I inadvertently set Kiera off on her bender of melancholy had been a particularly draining day at work, but I came home to find the baby gate locked and in place. After Athena and Kiera had gotten their fill of jumping and delivering most if not all of the toys from the floor or Athena's basket and slapping them onto my lap, both dogs settled into a calm routine. For them calm meant that they stood in front of me gazing up with adoration, waiting for me to do something interesting with any of the seven or more toys with which they had covered me. They both seemed to believe that bringing me a variety of toys was good and that the key to making me play a ten-hour round of fetch or tug was just the next toy away. When one or both realized that I wasn't interested in playing fetch or tug for more than twenty minutes, tops, one would pick up a toy from my stockpiled lap and they would, to my relief, play with one another. Periodically, they would stop as if it had been prearranged and stare at me again, wagging.

It was during one of these breaks that I happened to brush my hand over something on the couch. Mystified, I picked up a red hair elastic decorated with a ball of rabbit fur, that I had neither seen nor worn in months. The spiky separated fur indicated that it had been in a dog's mouth. I suddenly remembered the last time I had seen it, in a small basket on top of my dresser.

"What the hell?" I wondered aloud, surprised and confused as to how my bunny-ball hair tie had managed to get to the couch. My reverie was disturbed by a small pitter, and I looked up in time to see Kiera standing after having crouched and urinated submissively on the floor.

Athena looked exactly the same as always, smiling obliviously, but Kiera slunk away as if I had hit her with a baseball bat, leaving no doubt as to whom, at least, had moved my hair elastic to the sofa. I cleaned up Kiera's pee, marveling at not only her ingenuity at being able to even find the hair tie, but the dexterity it must have taken to pluck it from the basket. When I looked in my bedroom, I noticed nothing to indicate that Kiera had disturbed anything else in the process.

Although I didn't punish Kiera at all, she seemed to take my "What the hell?" as a severe blow and spent the next hour and a half wallowing in self-pity that no amount of happy talk or encouragement to play could alleviate. After a suitable duration of suffering, known only to her, she was frenetically, unpettably happy once again.

Mindi

Mindi is Jim's black Labrador, cocker spaniel and Chow Chow mix. She is a medium-sized black dog with a semi wavy coat and a curled up tail. Mindi to Athena is the little kid next door you're best friends with, but with whom, when you grow up, you don't have much in common anymore. Conversely, it's the same friend you can be completely yourself around; with that friend, you find yourself regressing to childhood.

Mindi and Athena met as puppies. As a baby, Mindi resembled a black Labrador with a purple spotted tongue. Athena looked like a wildebeest next to her, as she did next to most other puppies. When Jim came to visit, we put the girls in the kitchen to play together so we could have uninterrupted conversation. Mindi, every time, would promptly scramble up the baby gate like a spider, climb over the top, jump down, and leave Athena to stare at us from the other side with her large wildebeest head and puzzled wildebeest eyes, whining that her friend got to be in the living room and she didn't. Athena could have copied Mindi and climbed the gate herself, but she never once tried.

Mindi was the first dog with whom Athena got into numerous scuffles. Although Mindi fashioned herself as the dominant female of the pair, Athena put an end to such delusions.

Mindi was unequivocally a Daddy's girl, and there was no doubt who ran that household. Things got even worse when Mindi visited "Camp Grandma," because Jim's mother was even more besotted with his dog than my mother was with mine. My mother, for example, has never left a voicemail specifically and exclusively for Athena. At Camp Grandma, Mindi was allowed to do all the things she was forbidden to do normally, which actually was a short list. My house was a Gulag compared to Jim's.

Growing up, despite their occasional clashes, both girls were smitten with each other and went bonkers if the other's name was mentioned. Mindi even got ecstatic when I sent Jim a picture of Athena and it popped up on his computer screen. Both liked to wrestle, and they took turns flopping on their backs or chasing each other. Chasing each other at Jim's house was always much more fun than at my house, because he had a fireplace in the center of his living room, so the girls could stalk each other and peek around the corner at one another. Athena liked the fireplace at Jim's house; Mindi liked the graveyard at mine.

For a while, I left Athena's old bones in her toy basket, figuring that she might like to take a different one out and chew it. Over time, the bone pile grew to an alarming height, and for a while I procrastinated and just kept putting her newly chewed bones on top of the old ones. My friends said I had enough bones to build myself a brand new cow, albeit one with seventy-seven legs, and they also told me it was pretty disgusting. I never argued.

Mindi, however, was a fan of my laziness, and saw the bone pile as an Eden of choice, where she could dip her head into the basket and remove four or five bones at a time, surrounding herself with bones as she lay on Athena's blanket. She could move in increments like the pointer of a sundial, chewing one and then another. The fact that the bones were long clean of any meat never bothered Mindi. Just the gnawing seemed to satisfy her. If you stepped within a two-foot radius of her pile, however, she would give an unnerving snarl and stare at you as if she'd never met you in her life. If Jim went to move one of the bones, she snapped at his hand—not very close to his hand, but not very far away from it, either. It was normally the start of a bad evening between the dogs when Mindi did that; Athena, no matter where she was or what she was doing, disapproved heartily of such behavior and pounced on Mindi, yelling and pinning. Bone-time would then have to end prematurely.

Mindi is devoutly enamored of people she met when she was little; seeing me sends her into a whole-body shimmy, as she weaves through and around my legs, emitting grunting piglet noises. She does not care for the rest of the human population, however, and lets those less fortunate individuals know by howl-barking at them and then walking away, casting angry looks over her shoulder. She also has a nagging case of separation anxiety and when Jim leaves, she squeaks in terror and convulsively paws at the window. When she stayed with me for a few days, I was the beneficiary of her unhealthy devotion, and when I got home, the blinds that covered the window of my front door were slashed and bent, some of them lying in pieces on the floor.

Mindi was also the very first dog to whom I ever saw Athena play bow. She was a late bloomer in this regard and didn't learn the maneuver until she and Mindi were both around age three, a late start for any dog. Typical of Athena, her initial play bow was unlike any normal play bow I had ever seen. Most dogs naturally and fluidly drop to their elbows, raising their rumps in the air in an easily recognizable invitation: "Come on! Let's go! Yippee!" The movement is usually precise and quick. Athena's play bow had neither of those qualities. Her head began to wobble as though she had vertigo, and then she dove with her front end into an ungainly splay, her front legs out to the sides like a giraffe bending down to get a drink. Open-mouthed, Athena continued to swing her head back and forth like Axel Rose. Her hind legs stayed rigidly straight, and she pushed her rear end out. It looked as if her back feet were crazy-glued to the carpet. Her tail whirled around like a sail that had come undone in a squall. Mindi stared at her like Athena had lost her mind.

In turn, Jim turned and stared at me. "What. Was. That?" he asked me, before busting out into gales of laughter.

"That was, I think, her very first play bow," I said, laughing also. Fortunately, Athena never reacted badly to being laughed at, and in fact seemed delighted to provoke it. This contrasted to Kiera, who would go into an angst-ridden sulk if you laughed at her, glancing at you with hurt and embarrassment before finding a corner where she could curl up glumly. Kashka was even worse. He would glare right into your eyes like you were a bad smell and then turn and exit the room, shaking his hind leg behind him in a catchall gesture of disgust. Athena often acted like she was in on the joke, too, and would run and get a noisy toy, chewing it spastically so it would squeal its own laughter.

Athena didn't just limit her newly discovered skill to Mindi. Because I suppose she felt so free to be her and me with her childhood pal, when she spotted one of Mindi's large stuffed animals on the floor, before she could control herself, she awkwardly play bowed to the silent, inanimate toy.

"Did she just play-bow to Mindi's moose?" Jim crowed, delight turning his voice into a high pitched-lady's voice, his face wrinkled in anticipatory laughter.

"Yes," I sighed.

"Your dog's retarded," Jim sang, guffawing loudly.

I muttered, "I know."

Carman

When Athena met Carman for the first time, she was only a waddling toddler, and Carman was an adult with a frightening lack of gaiety. Carman was three at the time but already had the air of a dog who had seen it all and wasn't duly impressed. A Rhodesian ridgeback, German shepherd, Rottweiler mix, she had Ridgeback coloring and appearance, a thickly ticked shepherd pelt, and a Rottweiler's strong wide jaw. Carman did not suffer fools gladly, and a more dominant dog, male or female, I have yet to meet. She did not bow to any dog, and all the dogs in the neighborhood gave her a wide berth or slavered over her with the quavering of the conquered.

She even put the fear of God in Kaiser, an intact handsome brindle pit bull who also lived in the neighborhood. Kaiser was indisputably the emperor of the development. Full of powerful menace, one glance from him, and any other male dogs would look the other way, anxiously licking their lips. They knew that had there been a brawl, they'd likely end up dead. Females, on the other hand, treated him like a dictator or mob boss—a bad boy who was hypnotically attractive.

Kaiser was Athena's first dog-crush, and it was the first time I ever saw her flop down and roll around on the ground, submissively showing off her half-bald puppy tummy to anyone. Kaiser tolerated Athena, but as she grew older and started getting close to her first heat, he stopped looking at her as the annoying little brat down the block and started instead to view her as the preteen Lolita of his dreams. Whenever they met, he stiffened his cinderblock of a body and made halfway aggressive feints at her with his head, like he was going to snatch her into his wide jaws and shake her like a chipmunk. He raised his rapier-like tail straight up into the air to emphasize his jurisdiction over any stretch of land he was standing on.

Apparently, Athena thought this was sexy as all get-out. Shrugging her shoulders so much that her neck disappeared, she giddily danced and capered just out of his reach, sometimes hurtling herself onto the grass in front of him before getting up and scampering away. This could go on for several minutes. Sometimes she would perform a whole routine of spins, somersaults, and crawls before his impassive gaze, like she was a court jester, and Kaiser would merely stand there.

"Athena, you're embarrassing me," I would tell her. "Have some dignity. Boys don't like girls that are so obvious." When she saw Kaiser for the first time after being spayed, she ran up to him as usual. It took all of Kaiser's owner's strength to hold him back, because he almost savagely attacked Athena, not recognizing her scent anymore. Athena shrank back, terrified, and it took Kaiser a few more meetings to treat her like he used to. Presumably, it took him that long to get over the fact that his young girlfriend was off the market. Athena still maintains her fluttery devotion to him; she is like one of those women who sees her aged teen idol crush in concert and throws her panties at him onstage.

The only dog who did not bend to Kaiser's considerable male charms was Carman. When meeting Carman, it was Kaiser who did the equivalent of grinning and shuffling his feet. It was like watching a Mastodon come a' courtin'. Kaiser was not designed to flirt, but he tried with Carman. Her exquisite tan tail raised and curved almost to her shoulder blades, Carman would silently stare at him, with a slightly disdainful air. If he got too mushy, she'd favor him with a barely audible yet unyielding growl.

I was not comfortable around Carman or her owner Lauren when I first met them. Quietly fierce if they didn't know you, they acted as if you hardly existed. Neither was obtrusive or loud; their intimidation was in the confident way a leader expresses herself. Both ladies met anyone they met with a level, searching look that said, "Yeah, who the hell are you?" We walked by them one day while Carman was off-lead and Athena on her cat leash. Athena yanked away as she tried to keep up with Carman, who decided instantly that she liked this new puppy and wanted to play with her.

While I wasn't instantly enthralled by Carman, Athena had no such reservations; from the moment she met her, she was a devoted follower. It came as a pleasant surprise to me that, although they appeared impenetrable fortresses, both Lauren and Carman when they got to know you revealed a warm, steadfast nature that was also unswervingly courageous and protective.

Carman took to Athena like a benevolent older sister, or even perhaps a mother figure, and Athena was her besotted second banana. Carman took it upon herself to protect her new charge, and woe to any creature that upset Athena. Mark, a genial neighbor who loved and was loved by Carman in return once made the mistake of picking up baby Athena without supporting her hind end correctly. Athena screeched as only Athena could, and Mark quickly put her back down, but Carman marched in, blocked Athena with her body and clasped Mark's arm in a brief, soft, yet emphatic hold with her teeth. If Athena was playing in the common area with Dante, my neighbor Virginia's goofy Lab/Dalmatian mix, and Dante accidentally got too rough, Carman disciplined him severely.

Similarly, Lauren became my close friend, and just like her queenly mutt, she was fiercely protective. No man or beast would ever hurt me while Lauren was around—if they knew what was good for them, that is. Eventually, Carman became quite fond of me as well, and I her. Aloof and intimidating around strangers, she was a cuddly love-bug to those in her inner circle. Her sensitivity to Lauren's moods spilled over to me, and during the tearful conversations Lauren and I had about the guys who had broken our hearts, it was always Carman who came over to burrow her head against whichever one of us was crying, or sometimes she just put her paw out so you could hold it. If she was feeling especially sympathetic, she reared up gracefully and put both paws on your shoulders for a hug. Athena, meanwhile, showed no change in behavior when someone was upset. I'd love to say that she could instinctively tell when someone needed comfort, but despite her gentleness with children, she didn't much concern herself with people's moods. I hugged Carman more for consolation during teary episodes than I ever did my own dog. It wasn't that Athena ever minded being hugged, it's just that in contrast to Carman, who lowered her head and seemed to weep along with you, Athena merely panted and smiled, impatient to be released so she could resume playing.

As Athena grew, Carman loosened up and let her playful silly side come out more often. Seeming satisfied that she had raised Athena properly—for there was little doubt that Carman considered herself Athena's guardian—she allowed Athena all kinds of liberties that would have caused an ordinary dog to have its jugular torn out. Growling like Harleys, Carman and Athena mouth dueled, sometimes clicking teeth together loudly and alternating rolling the other onto her back for a faux pin. It all looked mildly frightening, as if real fighting were occurring, but each dog understood exactly her place in the relationship, so it was perfectly safe. Lauren and I would laugh and have to reassure people who saw Carman and Athena play fighting for the first time.

One night, however, I was convinced that things had gone too far and that Athena had killed Carman. Lauren and I were good friends in addition to neighbors by then, and we babysat each other's dogs, watched movies together, and took turns making each other dinner. I was watching Carman at my house one frigidly cold evening after a heavy snow. Athena and Carman both loved snow (the first snowfall Athena felt as a puppy caused her to race around the edge of my yard as if possessed). They loved to shovel it, scoop it, eat it, run in it, roll in it, catch snowballs, you name it. Everything about snow was A-OK in their books.

That night, I stood outside in the silent common area with them, holding a cup of tomato soup, watching them run after each other as I smiled tranquilly. After one of their crunchy passes, I noticed that Carman lay on her side, not moving. Athena plopped herself on top of Carman's neck, mock-growling. Athena then stood up, grabbed Carman's loose neck skin and started dragging the prone Carman along the snow. Limp and floppy, Carman bounced along the uneven ground, as lifeless as a ventriloquist's dummy.

"Carman?" I called. "Athena!" I yelled, almost dropping my soup cup, ready to extricate Carman's neck from Athena's teeth. I was convinced that one of two horrid scenarios had come true: either Carman had fallen over from too much exertion or frostbite, and Athena was dragging her friend to safety, or Athena had accidentally choked

Carman's air supply off and was dragging her as a defeated trophy. Both scenarios threw me into a panic. What the hell was I going to tell Lauren?

Suddenly, Carman sprang up with a decidedly happy, stupid look on her face, bounded toward Athena and then turned and ran away, and Athena took up chase. Carman had not hurt herself in the least; she had been "playing dead" and in fact seemed delighted to be hauled like a corpse across the snow. I imagined how mutilated a different dog would be who *ever* dared pull Carman anywhere by her neck skin, and I felt very glad that she trusted Athena so much.

There was another time I got nervous about an interaction between Carman and Athena, and this time, they weren't playing. As Athena matured, she became larger and heavier than Carman. This did not stop her from keeping her submissive role in their friendship. Carman had every privilege to take Athena's spot on the pillow, remove a bone right from Athena's mouth, and basically do anything she pleased. Carman asserted herself infrequently, however.

One night when Carman and Lauren were visiting, I went to feed Athena her dinner. She had exerted a lot of energy that day and was obviously starving. Normally Carman left Athena alone when she ate. That night, however, Carman decided that she was hungry, too, and as Athena dipped her face into her bowl to begin eating, Carman stood next to her and leaned towards Athena's food bowl, waiting for Athena to step aside. Being the dominant female, Carman was well within her right, as unfair as it may seem, to eat Athena's food. Athena decided she didn't agree. To my utter shock, and I think to Carman's, Athena lowered her head and bared her teeth at Carman.

"Carman, let Athena eat; I'll feed you something else," I began. Carman wasn't looking at me, however, she was looking at Athena. She let out a warning growl, indicating to Athena that it was not acceptable for her to flout Carman's authority. At that growl, which Athena may have mistakenly interpreted as being directed at me, my dog whirled her head sideways, hackles raised, and the two began a terrifying fight up on their hind legs in my kitchen. I shouted at them and inserted a foolish knee into the middle of the fight, as Lauren, who had an injured ankle, struggled to get up from the couch and hobble into the kitchen. We managed to pull them apart, after I had pushed Carman away from Athena several times. Carman in a dog fight was not a casual combatant. She had come up underneath and temporarily choked the air out of many a rival, which stopped any fight instantly, and I didn't want Athena to meet the same fate.

Both dogs ceased simultaneously, but both wore an expression of downtrodden confusion afterwards; both were cowering and nervous. One of the two dogs had nicked my hand, and I was bleeding. Carman was especially shaken by the startling turn of events, and she went into the living room, where she crouched sadly away from us and gagged. When I walked over to her, she rolled onto her back, presenting her belly to me. Athena didn't touch her food until Carman had gone home; instead she lay timidly on the floor far away from us, clutching a stuffed animal in her mouth, her ears back, looking miserable.

After that night, Athena's and Carman's relationship changed. They never played as freely or roughly and instead treated each other with a restrained politeness. It was disheartening to witness. It took the introduction of Carman's incorrigible baby brother, Cody, to save the day.

Cody

Cody, also known as Athena's love child, was a puppy taken in by the rescue group for which Lauren worked. Of all the puppies that came through her house, Cody was the one who stood out and the only one Lauren adopted herself. Half shepherd, half something we don't know, Cody possessed preternatural self-confidence mixed with an easy-going personality that made him instantly appealing to both humans and other dogs. Leggy and lithe in body, he resembled a "blanket" German shepherd, almost all black with tan markings. His ears were, comically, somewhere in between erect and floppy, and his eyes were an unusual yellow-gold. If a person, Cody would be the friend who never minds being the butt of any joke and takes everything in stride with unfailing good humor. Cody also had moments of supreme dumb oafishness, smiling empty-headedly at things. Naturally, we couldn't help but see a lot of Athena in him.

Athena and Cody formed an instant bond when they met and had a lot of alarming similarities. Like Athena, Cody was melodramatic and wailed to air raid siren decibels when the slightest thing went wrong. Carman, in contrast, could slice her paw pad open and stoically lift it up for Lauren to examine, never uttering a peep. A similar injury to Cody or Athena would have resulted in cries loud enough to reach the next county. Cody was also dismayingly clumsy. If he accidentally stepped on one of his own toys, he reacted as if he had gotten an electric shock. He would fling himself up in the air, screaming, usually bumping himself harder on something else and surpassing the original scare. And while both Athena and Cody possessed moments of admirable intelligence, ersatz mother and son would stand side by side, panting, looking out onto the world with exactly the same contented, dopey look on their faces. Like mother, like son, both of them splashed in an undignified way in Lauren's plastic baby pool, and Cody likewise dribbled water from his muzzle after a drink as if he had a hole in the bottom of his mouth. Cody was a frequent recipient of Athena's giraffe-like play bow, and Lauren's reaction when she saw it was no more charitable than Jim's had been. Cody and Athena were both lounging snugglers, and they leaned against each other shoulder to back whenever they had down time.

Cody was happily the beta of the three when Carman, Athena, and he would play together. He spent so much time on his back that Lauren had to admonish the two ladies to give him some relief and let him up. Cody gave as good as he got, however, and the clack of his mandibles was audible as he tried to bite Athena's cheeks as she jerked her head away, yowling playfully. While Athena and Carman never regained their easy camaraderie with one another, they certainly shared a love for Cody, and his presence served to ease the tension between them. Cody was the only dog I had ever seen who could march up to Carman and remove something she was chewing. Carman gave Cody a scary face and snarl when he approached her, but he didn't care. He pawed and licked her muzzle, fawning over her until his submissive tactics softened her, whereupon he'd smartly pull whatever she had from her jaws, happily trotting away without a care in the world. Carman looked flabbergasted whenever he pulled that maneuver. He had no fear whatsoever of his sister. Similarly, Cody was impervious to Athena's warning gums and fangs. The expression that would have sent most dogs reeling had no more effect on Cody than if she had given him her bone or toy herself. Seeing both Carman and Athena, two indisputably dominant bitches, stare after him with such confusion was very humorous.

Cody was also the only male that never once tried any shenanigans with Athena, or any female. He was fixed but he still never mounted or indulged in any typical boy behaviors that even neutered dogs sometimes do; it took him almost a year to figure out how to lift his leg.

Cody was so good with other dogs in any situation that Lauren used him to help ease the transition when she had to take in other foster dogs for her rescue. Even scared and undersocialized dogs that had come in with nervous tucked-up tails would soon be playing happily with Cody. Cody also had a natural affinity for and love of cats. He adored them, and every single one that ever met him felt inexplicably comfortable with him. Fireball, a Grinch-faced female Persian Lauren adopted, became Cody's best pal. If she was ever scared, she knew right where to go: underneath Cody's belly. Once when Lauren and her animals were out in the common area together, some teenage boys started chasing Fireball. Fireball ran up and dove underneath Cody, who stood barking at the kids menacingly. When Lauren rescued a feral Maine Coon kitten, Cody took over as foster mother and gave the kitten her first baths, never letting her out of his sight. Soon the kitten followed him everywhere, lying on him and kneading his belly. Even the most skeptical feline around didn't have a chance of resisting Cody's charms.

19. Athena the Protector

Athena's protective nature made itself apparent around five months of age. She was still relatively small, but when I walked her, many people still went to the other side of the street when they saw her dark mask, alert ears, and confident walk. She walked with her head up and her chest forward. She also had the unnerving habit of staring up at passersby, into their eyes if they happened to look at her. If someone smiled and said hello, and I seemed relaxed about the person, Athena broke into a smile and favored the person with a benevolent look, her ears first up at attention and then pulled slightly back. If, however, I did not say anything and the person seemed at all ill at ease, Athena stared at him or her intently as we passed, craning her neck, even, and never breaking eye contact. If the person made the mistake of staring directly back at her, maybe thinking to avoid being bitten, Athena would erupt in a series of sharp barks that seemed to fill her front end with helium; she rose off the ground, twitching and shaking with the force of the barks.

"Okaaay, Athena," I'd say, yanking her leash. Sometimes I had to scream, "*Enough*!" and pop her leash before she got the message. It was hard to decide whether to let her continue this behavior. On the one hand it was annoying, and on the other it gave me a feeling of security when walking around my poorly lit neighborhood.

I was strolling with a Mindi-less Jim one night, and Athena focused her attention on two cars parallel parked along the dark street. She let out a very grown-up-girl, deep growl and stopped, staring in that direction.

"Athena, no," Jim said, and I told him politely but with no room for argument that *never* should he tell my dog to be quiet. That was my job, and furthermore, I was happy to let her nighttime senses, which were much keener than mine, help me out. We crossed the street, Athena prancing sideways, not removing her eyes from the cars. When we got a little further out, we realized that two men were crouched down in the dark, next to the cars, whispering. We could see that they were not doing something innocent, and I was glad I hadn't been walking alone. I stopped and let Athena stare at them. She stood stiff-legged, never averting her eyes. The men decided it would be better to do whatever they were doing somewhere else, and they slunk off.

"Wow. I'll never tell her to be quiet again," Jim said.

Another evening, Jim and I were sitting in the grass, talking, and Athena was panting loudly next to me, lolling against me with her back. All of a sudden, she became alert, rolled into a more rigid down, and watched a nearby road. Fifteen seconds later, a man walked by on his way somewhere. Athena didn't react with any kind of bark or growl; she just watched the man walk down the sidewalk. After he was out of sight, she resumed her loud panting, and I realized that from the instant she had noticed the stranger, she had closed her mouth and had remained silent. Silent and watching. The man didn't even have any idea she was there.

I was getting money out of an ATM at dusk, and Athena was with me. A large, muscular man stood behind me waiting for his turn. His expression was friendly, and I could tell he was just waiting in line, but Athena rounded the back of my legs and positioned herself broadside, standing between him and me. She stood there staring at him but didn't growl or bark. She seemed to know instinctively that my senses were weaker at night, because it was usually dark when she went into full-alert.

"Wow. Um. I guess no one will ever bother you," the guy joked, and I turned, looked down, and laughed. "No. Probably not," I said as I patted Athena's side. She wagged her tail briefly, but despite the easygoing banter, she didn't move from her spot or stop watching him.

My girlfriends were all very impressed with these stories. "Your dog's a badass," Diana said.

Her overprotectiveness could be truly embarrassing, however, as it was one Halloween when I took her to Petco in her angel costume: a halo that bobbed around on a wire over her head and a pair of white sparkly wings that fit over her shoulders. Several of my "friends" had asked if all the devil costumes had already sold out, and others had asked why I hadn't gotten her a clown costume. "She wouldn't even need shoes!" one of them said. It was true that Athena had never grown into her large feet—feet she tripped over in slaphappy moments. My dog, on the surface, was a gorgeous, elegant, imposing animal, but in her heart of hearts, she really was a bozo. Once I watched her run gracefully through the woods on a rare off-lead walk, looking like a wild predator, and my heart thrilled at the sight. Then, just as I felt my chest tighten with awe and pride, she jumped over a log, caught one of her huge paws, and rolled end over end. I also saw her trip over her own foot, slip on leaves, and splay onto her chest. During both scenarios all the woodland creatures in the vicinity took flight, driven far away by Athena's piercing screeches, something she hadn't outgrown. It didn't matter that she had fallen into a cushioning pile of brush; she still reacted as though the forest floor were covered in pieces of stinging coral.

Regardless of my dog's clumsiness and her occasional evil intentions, I frowned and told my misguided friends that the only reason Athena had an angel costume was because the princess one was gone already. I described the pink cone hat with the gauze hankie attached to it and the glittery collar and elicited more uncharitable laughter.

"That *angel* costume is bad enough for Attila! Angels are supposed to be nice!" Robin said. She had called Athena "Attila" ever since witnessing the more unsavory of Athena's early puppyhood antics of ripping my hand-flesh and trying to bite my face.

The only person who thought it perfectly appropriate that Athena wear an angel costume was her grandmother, who recognized the pure goodness in my dog. "Teeny! Pretty girrrl! She *is* an angel!" my mother reassured me so we could be delusional together.

Athena's angel costume was a hit at Petco, and she was immediately surrounded by children, whom she loves times the heat of ten suns. She will stand, immobile, with the most placid, contented, nearly cross-eyed expression when children (many of whom are no taller than her back) pet her. She is happiest when swarmed with kids who are stroking her, hugging her, leaning on her, patting her—the more of them the better. I've watched my big scary shepherd roll onto her back and present her stomach, not caring a whit if her tail gets tugged or her fur pulled. If a child passes by her head, however, before I can block her, she stretches out and gives a quick lick to the face. She has caused more than one child to burst into sobs when she does that; mainly because she has a tendency to lick their mouths or around their eyes. "The dog licked meeee!" the child will wail. This often causes her to try and lick more, as if to explain, "I'm nice! I'm nice!" as the child runs away bawling.

She also loves babies and has given some parents an instant coronary by veering toward them, intent on sticking her giant timber-wolf head into the stroller to kiss the baby.

So the children at Petco petted and hugged Athena, who was smiling dimly, and then we made our way to the back of the store to get Kashka's food. That week he only liked Fancy Feast chicken slices in gravy and refused to eat anything else. "Just leave it; he'll get hungry enough and eat it!" never worked with Kashka. He was as determined as a political prisoner on a hunger strike if he didn't like his food.

Athena, who was always bright eyed and smug after being the center of attention, trotted beside me, her halo dancing on its wire. We rounded the corner and came upon another customer, a man with hunched posture and angry eyes who walked towards us. I didn't take his attitude personally. Maybe he didn't like dogs in costumes or maybe he'd just had a bad day and just wanted to go home, I didn't know. But Athena decided she didn't like him and started barking wildly, the effort making her bounce and jump in place. It was an incongruous sight, a dog dressed in fey glittery wings, her halo swaying to and fro while she maniacally barked like an awful Nazi guard dog. The guy froze in his tracks, and I firmly commanded her to stop, mortified. She must have felt my urgency, because she stopped immediately.

"I'm sorry," I said to the man.

He walked by us, and Athena did her unblinking shark stare, all business in her white sparkles and quivering halo. I remember thinking that perhaps my friends had been right about the angel costume.

I'm ashamed to admit this about my dog, but for about a month when she was one and half years old, she barked almost exclusively at African American people. Perfectly nice men, women, and children with kind eyes, bothering not a soul were treated to an Athena-launch at Starbucks, on walks in our neighborhood, at Milwaukee Frozen Custard.

To this day I don't know what triggered her outbursts. Was I unconsciously cueing her, tensing up because I was afraid she *would* bark and thus giving her the idea *to* bark? Did the African American people I encountered feel especially nervous around Athena, and if so, was it because they associated her with the German shepherds that were historically used as weapons of brutal racial prejudice? I don't know. But it horrified and embarrassed me. Some people looked at me like I had deliberately trained her to behave that way, and I wanted it to stop. I made a concerted effort to relax and not assume she was going to bark, and if she did, I punished her soundly. She seemed to finally get the message that what she was doing was wrong.

Once her racist phase passed, Athena stopped barking at innocuous strangers altogether and became approachable and friendly in public. A true example of the German shepherd breed, she didn't solicit physical affection from strangers, but she certainly allowed people to approach her, and she seemed to revel in pats and compliments. People of every race petted her without her batting an eyelash.

She is still protective of my home, which she should be. We got home one day to find that my cleaning ladies had not come at their regularly scheduled time and were instead in the house just then. I had Athena on a lead, but it was loose. She backed one of the poor women into a corner and stood a few feet away barking until she knew they were supposed to be there. When I reassured her that they were, in fact, sanctioned, she acted as if nothing had happened and tried to bring them one of her toys. The ladies were not enthused about playing tug and were petrified of her, so I took her over to Jim's house until they were finished.

Jim, probably Athena's favorite person on earth, liked to test her defensive skills. One day he pulled a hat down low and snuck up to the car while Athena and I were inside it. When she saw him, Athena barked and growled, until she recognized him, and then her attitude changed completely—her ears disappeared and she began to whine and waggle. Jim also bravely ran at me one day from behind a bush in the common area next to my house to see how Athena would react. Athena and I were playing with her Jolly Ball on the grass. She was gripping the handle in her mouth and methodically swaying her head back and forth, dancing along like a circus elephant. Jim emerged abruptly from the bushes and ran at us. He had prepared for the experiment by dressing in a thick leather winter jacket and layers of clothing in case anything went awry. When she saw him, Athena charged forward, already growling, ready to defend. When she caught Jim's scent, however, she began wiggling, letting out excited monkey yips, and jumping into the air. Jim and I were both impressed by the ease and speed with which she turned from a goofy idiot to a fierce warrior and back to a dork again.

20. Athena the Hero

For all her protective skills, the one time Athena really saved my life, she did so unwittingly. It was a fall night, and I decided to run a couple of errands. I hesitated to bring Athena along, since she would have to wait in the car. But she had already run to the door and was spinning in anticipatory circles, mouth open, eyes shining, so I told her okay. Athena had outgrown her early carsickness and was uncharacteristically agreeable about staying in the back seat. She lay down during trips and waited patiently for me if I had to run inside a shop. We had a ritual greeting whenever I returned: I gave her an enthusiastic hello, and she put her muzzle up to the gap where I'd left the window down and give me a few quick kisses.

First we went to the video store, where I bought a DVD. Then I went to pick up some dinner at a takeout restaurant located at the very end of one of the strip malls clustered off one main road. I found a parking spot on the side of the building, next to a few other cars. I told Athena to stay, and she curled up on her side on the back seat. When I looked back at the car after getting out, the only indication of her presence was the barely distinguishable tips of her pointed ears. It was very quiet in the parking lot. During the day I hadn't noticed how desolate the area was and how little foot traffic the strip mall attracted.

As I walked around the corner of the building to the entrance of the restaurant, which faced the road and not the parking lot. I noticed a guy walking rapidly in my direction from across the parking lot—a young white guy wearing a sideways baseball cap and the typical baggy clothes popular with young men emulating their hip-hop idols. None of that bothered me, but there was something about him, I couldn't put my finger on what, that made alarm bells go off in my mind. I felt the hairs on my neck and arms prickle as he entered the restaurant behind me. He seemed casual enough, and he never really looked directly at me, but I got the distinct impression that I was part of his focus somehow.

I stood in line to order, and he stood directly behind me. After my order came out, I picked it up, got my drink from the self-serve dispenser, and turned to leave. As I moved toward the door, the young man spun on his heel and left the restaurant ahead of me. It felt like he had been waiting for me, and I realized that *he had not said a word to the clerk or ordered any food.* He had just been standing silently behind me the whole time. My first impulse was that I didn't want to blow something out of proportion, so I rationalized that he wasn't hungry or had forgotten something. I couldn't ignore, however, the nagging instinctive fear, and mentally I was calculating how far it was from the exit to my parked car. I wanted to get to my dog. I had never felt such an overwhelming urge to be near her.

When I left the restaurant, I went quickly to my car door and put the key in the lock, watching the young guy over the top of my roof. He had gone over to an old beat-up pickup truck that was idling in a parking spot a few down from mine, and he stood talking inaudibly to the driver, an older man, through the open driver's-side window. The man with whom he was conversing could have been right out of central casting for an ex-convict. He was disheveled, unshaven, and leaning out the open window, staring intently at me. The stare wasn't harmless ogling, either. He was appraising me in such a way that I felt cold in the middle. I didn't even want to know what he was thinking about doing to me.

Subtly, he pointed to me with his chin. The younger guy nodded, turned around, and started walking toward my car. I tried to catch his eye, but he focused his gaze just to the right of my head and refused to look at me. I still had the hypnotized, tugging sensation you get when you feel yourself being examined, and I momentarily froze in shock. He acted nonchalant, but there was a tension I sensed in his body language that belied his surface attitude. He was still coming toward me, fast. No one else was in the dark parking lot, and the glassed front entrance to the store was facing the other direction. Not a single bystander was able to see me from any angle. Realizing I was completely alone snapped me out of my inertia, and with suddenly icy fingers I turned my car key in the lock and opened the door with my other hand.

"Hey girl!" I said cheerily, and Athena uncoiled herself from the back seat and stood up, placing her front paws on the center console of my car, excitedly sniffing at the bag of food I had with me. Standing thusly on the center console, Athena looked enormous, even larger than normal, and I knew her looming body would take up all the window space if someone were looking into my car. Over the roof of my car, I saw the young man's eyes widen briefly in surprise, and then he

130

stopped dead in his tracks. He took one more hesitant step toward me but seemed to think better of it, pivoted, and jogged back to the pickup. Before I could obtain a license plate number, he and the older guy sped off. I closed my door, locked it, and sat breathing deeply in the driver's seat.

The sequence of events in the parking lot had happened so fast, perhaps only taking seven to ten seconds, but I replayed the scene in my head and went over it more slowly. Incredulously, I realized that something bad had really been about to happen. "Oh my God," I said to myself, recounting every detail. It hit me then that I had known somehow in my gut that the younger guy had been sent over to either rob me or, based on the way the older man's staring had made me feel, more likely abduct me for a sexual assault. They must have either followed me around the strip mall when they saw what they thought was a lone female driver, or they had been opportunistically parked near the isolated lot and had watched me go into the restaurant. The younger man had most likely been sent in to see what I ordered. Was I picking up food for a large group who would notice my absence? Was I meeting someone at the restaurant? My small to-go order explained why he turned and exited the restaurant so rapidly.

Realizing what might have happened, I started to shake, and I looked in the rearview mirror at Athena, remembering that I almost hadn't brought her along, aware of the magnitude of what she had unwittingly done.

"Athena," I said, and she moved so her front paws were lying on my center console, her head near my shoulder. "You saved my life, girl," I whispered, lifting my arm up and draping it around her shoulders as I drove home. Athena, who was just happy to be next to me, not to mention closer to the bag redolent with food smells, was unfazed, and she smiled at me with her tail sweeping back and forth on the seat behind her.

After I'd talked to my mom and a couple of my friends about what had happened, I decided to report the incident to the police, even though technically nothing had really happened. I gave detailed descriptions of both men and the pickup truck. The police officer agreed that it had been a good idea to call, if only just in case they tried something again with someone who didn't have a big German shepherd in her car.

I never looked at Athena quite the same way after that. I sent a thank-you email to Megan, giving her details of what had happened and telling her how grateful I was that she had sold Athena to me. Megan was so thrilled that she asked if she could use the story on her website. I readily agreed.

I know in the deepest part of me that Athena saved me that night. I was glad she hadn't actually had to defend me, but just knowing she scared the crap out of two bad guys was wonderful enough.

21. Agility

Athena and I seemed to lose our enthusiasm for Schutzhund at the same time. It became more difficult to wake her up from her naps in my back seat, and her passes at Pedro's sleeve became half-hearted, as if the whole thing were a bother. Liz and I had become fast friends by that time, and we spent a good part of each class giggling and talking on the sidelines, so much so that Pedro interrupted us one night and chastised us for not paying attention to the others working, missing valuable tips. During his lecture, Liz worked her mouth into a puffed-out balloon, trying to stifle her laughter, and I stared at the ground shame-faced. I think I may have even answered, "Yes sir. No sir," to several of his questions, feeling like I was thirteen years old again. Kiera was going through a phase as well where she seemed indifferent to the training, too, so Liz and I decided to take a break from Schutzhund.

To take up the slack, I enrolled Athena in agility at the Animals' House Great Falls Club in Sterling, Virginia. Athena, due to her regular puppy obedience and strict Schutzhund obedience classes, was adept now at being reliably off-lead, and I thought she might enjoy the challenge of learning something new.

I met Kathy, the head trainer, and I instantly felt comfortable in her presence. A former dolphin trainer, she was upbeat and easygoing with a wickedly sharp sense of humor. Schutzhund was such a precise sport, the rules clad in steel, the execution of lessons grim and humorless. It was to agility what professional baseball was to a light-hearted T-Ball game for kindergartners. No one got yelled at in agility, and if someone made a mistake, Kathy and all the other students still clapped and shouted encouraging things like, "Good try! You'll get it next time!" The dogs had varying degrees of skill; some didn't exactly listen too well when they were off-leash, and more than one escaped out of the ring, leading their owners on a merry chase around the complex. Athena wouldn't have dreamed of doing that by now, so I felt we were ahead of the game.

Athena's agility classmates included a small, timid mixed-breed named Queenie; a female Pembroke corgi; a chocolate Standard Poodle named Coco; a cantankerous, fuzzy Parson Russell terrier misnamed Wags; and a Belgian Malinois mix. Wags and Athena wasted no time barking at each other, but the friendly Mal and Coco the poodle greeted Athena warmly. I loved to watch Coco. She wore pink bows at her ears and sashayed like a supermodel, all the time smiling like she had delicious gossip at a cocktail party about every guest. Athena overestimated how welcoming the rest of the pupils would be to her (I kept her far away from Wags), and when she leaned down to gently sniff the corgi while we were waiting in line to do the course, the smaller dog objected with a nasty nip at Athena's nose. Athena gave an outraged roar and pinned her underneath her forelegs. The Corgi was one of those beguiling round-eyed powder-puffs hiding a bratty snippy personality, but because of the size-difference, my dog on top of her looked in contrast like a monster Satan-wolf. The rest of the handlers looked on, horrified, as the Corgi screamed, and continued screaming after I had pulled Athena off her. There wasn't anything more serious than drooled-on fur as a result of the altercation. From that point on however, Athena got the reputation as the bully dog of the group. It didn't help her cause when after our lesson, while the next class was waiting outside the ring, four or five dogs waiting stared and then started barking at her, as Athena stood stiffly, ruffling her fur out, lifting her tail brazenly, barking back at all of them.

"She's just asking for a fight," Kathy commented.

"Well, all the dogs are staring at her, barking at her," I argued.

Kathy looked at me skeptically. "Athena is aggressive," she said.

I could feel my temper flare. "Because she's a German shepherd, she's being targeted unfairly," I said. "The corgi snapped at Athena's nose, not the other way around, and the other dogs started it by barking at her. She's just a dominant girl. Those other dogs were barking at her for no reason," I pouted.

"Okay," Kathy said reasonably, but she said it in such a way that I knew she disagreed with me. I knew she was humoring me, which usually has the impact of making me reevaluate my stance entirely. Kathy wasn't just an expert animal trainer; she was an expert at defusing human behavior.

"All right," I said. "I promise to work on Athena's temper and be more firm with her when things like this happen in the future."

Kathy nodded.

Other than Athena's Mafia don insistence on respect from her canine schoolmates, she excelled in agility. Well, that should be clarified. She excelled at the *obstacles* in agility. As far as having any particular order to a course, Athena much preferred to go over or through things freestyle. She learned any obstacle within a maximum of two attempts, and then looked at me like, "Are you *kidding* me? That's all you want me to do?"

As other dogs in the class hesitated, legs quivering, to go up the dog walk or climb onto the dreaded teeter-totter, Athena confidently did both, slamming the teeter down with a decisive crash as she galumphed over it. The fact that the obstacle moved up and down while the dogs were on it sent most of them into a knock-kneed panic, but Athena was not bothered in the least. During one lesson, the entire teeter-totter fell to the ground with her on it, but the next time I sent her to it after it was repaired, she acted as if nothing strange had ever happened.

Kathy demonstrated each obstacle, and then we waited in a single file line for our chance to practice. Athena so enjoyed learning the obstacles that when we successfully negotiated one, she would often pick another on the course to do on our way back to the end of the line. In doing so, she was breaking the one rule in agility that Kathy was strict about: dogs were not allowed to do obstacles by themselves without supervision, in case they got injured. Athena didn't seem to care about that rule, however, and I'd be walking along with her next to me one moment and then the next hear a great scratching of claws above me as she scrambled up the A-frame, her face blank, open-mouthed, and happily dopey. "Athena," I'd mutter, grabbing her just as she was eyeing the tunnel, another of her favorites. I had to make a habit of re-leashing her as soon as she was done so we wouldn't get in trouble.

She would also find other ways to amuse herself, as she did once when a particularly nervous dog went through the chute—a tunnel with a tube made of parachute fabric collapsed at one end. The obstacle design was such that the dogs had to fumble around blindly with slippery loud cloth entombing them until they found the opposite opening. For a few students in our class, the chute was a source of panic, but Athena bulldozed through it like she did everything as I stood at the flat exit screaming "Athena! Dee-dee-dee deeee!" clapping my hands like a moron. One day an anxious pupil who hated the chute to begin with got trapped inside it, and we all watched as the small lump moved in frantic zigzags under the rainbow fabric. Athena smiled with delight, her ears pricked forward, following the movement like she was at a tennis match. Then her prey drive kicked in, and she stretched out to the end of her leash and, looking as if she found the whole thing very entertaining, reared up and pounced, her front paws landing behind the retreating figure.

"Athena! That's not nice!" I admonished and pulled her away, even as some of my classmates burst into inappropriate but uncontrollable snickers. The smaller dog when it finally emerged was disheveled and quite shaken up. For the remainder of the lesson, Athena kept looking up at me with an expression that seemed to say, "Wasn't that funny?" as if jumping the dog had been a private joke we had come up with together.

The only two agility obstacles that gave Athena any trouble were the weave poles and the tire, mainly because she had the finesse of a lumberjack. Her other weakness was her lack of concentration. She detested the tire, which was suspended on a large metal frame that the dog had to jump through. It required her to tuck her paws and jump carefully, whereas the regular bar jumps she could sloppily leap over and still keep going. She tried to evade the tire, not because she didn't understand the concept but because she, I believe, found it vexing to have to think that hard. Her dislike increased after a particularly clumsy jump during which she caught one of her gargantuan circus paws and pulled the entire swinging affair to the ground behind her. I could usually bribe her to jump through it as long as something exciting like the A-frame or the tunnel could be her next obstacle.

Her giant paws were also a problem with the weave poles. Again, she knew what she was supposed to do, but she preferred the direct approach and found slowing down to mince through the poles an unnecessary bother. Most often she wound around a single pole and then tried to run over to a better obstacle to go over. Plus she was so graceless, her body so fluffy, that when she did weave through properly, she caused the poles to wave back and forth precariously and the platform into which they were inserted to almost tip over, as she slovenly bumped her way through it, her eye on the prized teeter or high platform coming up next.

We took three levels of agility, and each successful completion meant another certificate for my refrigerator. The certificates really didn't bespeak a great level of competence; every dog got one, regardless of skill level. The payoff for us was that we were invited to demonstrate agility at the Chantilly *Super Pet Expo!*—the same event where I'd first thought of getting a German shepherd a few years before. Liz and Kiera, who had just started agility themselves, were also invited by Kathy to demonstrate as advertisement for the Great Falls Club, and we four girls had a marvelous time.

It was at the Expo that I discovered what I had suspected about Athena all along: she loved big crowds of people. When entering a place teeming with humans, Athena seemed to hear voices calling, "Athena! Athena! Over here!" Click, click, flash! "Athena!" Surrounded by multitudes at the Expo, she had the time of her life, prancing, tilting her head at passersby, stopping periodically to throw a perfect stack. She had charisma pouring out of every hair follicle. Hordes of admirers stopped us to tell her she was gorgeous, her coat fabulous, her face so pretty. Athena seemed to preen and pose accordingly. She never barked or lunged or did anything ugly-spirited. She was on duty as the Paris Hilton of German shepherds on the red carpet. It amazed me to see people so drawn to her. There were multitudes of beautiful dogs at the event, both pure bred and mixed, but Athena drew them in.

The sales person at the Miracle Groom booth called out to us as we passed by, "Can I use your dog for our demonstration?" Miracle Groom is a spray cleaner that detangles and cleans dirt out of the coat. Athena sat next to the woman, smiling at the crowd that had gathered, throwing in her patented head tilt at several spectators, as though she had become the Miracle Groom spokesdog in her own mind. The Miracle Groom made the red, gold, and black in her fur glisten and her fluff stand up.

"That dog's so pretty!" I heard someone whisper with awe behind me.

Sensing she had to really pull out all the stops, Athena lay down at one point with her paws spread just so, her eyes never leaving the crowd, as the woman talked into her little headset microphone, brushing Athena's plume of a tail.

"Awww," said the crowd as one.

Athena "left makeup" ready to face her adoring public once more. On our way to the agility ring, we met a father with his little girl, who used metal forearm crutches to walk. She was heading a bit unsteadily for Athena.

"Can she pet your dog?" her father asked.

"Sure! She's very friendly. She loves people," I said. I encouraged people to pet her, especially children. Given her size, many children were afraid of her and approached her tentatively, some even darting in and then screeching and jumping away. Athena regarded all of them with a phlegmatic charm; I could see the affection in her eyes. I loved to watch the dawning pride on a child's face when he or she mustered up the courage to pat her.

This little girl was both excited and shy, and she was having a slight difficulty balancing when she reached up to pet Athena. Many times when people want to pet Athena, especially when they're a bit nervous, I will ask Athena to go into a platz, since on the ground she seems less imposing. Most often she would slide onto her belly gracelessly, uncaring if she plopped down on people's feet or if her back shoved against their shins. But as the little girl reached for her, Athena put herself into a platz, settling into it in a slow, gentle way I had not seen her do before. It was as if she realized that if she went down too fast she might throw the little girl off-balance.

The little girl brightened and, with the help of her father, disengaged herself from her crutches and sat next to Athena, leaning on her. She stroked Athena's back as Athena lay keeping her head immobile, even though swarms of people and their dogs walked right by her. Her father and I just watched the two of them, silent. The little girl culminated their session with a full hug around Athena's neck, and afterward, my dog, the clumsiest oaf, the wild-eyed former face biter, stretched up her nose and gave the girl the smallest, most tender lick on the cheek I had ever seen her give. I hadn't thought Athena even capable of such restraint. The girl beamed, and I told her, "She really likes you!" Her father then helped the little girl up and refastened her braces, and they started to leave. The father turned and gave me a warm smile that went deep into his eyes and thanked me. Amidst the chaos and endless feet and the noise and the smells, the simple connection between his child and my dog had been a momentary oasis of quiet beauty, and I felt grateful to have witnessed it.

The Athena I recognized reemerged during our Agility demonstration. We had the good fortune to be assigned the A-frame, the most dramatic of all dog obstacles. When her name was announced, we went to the center of the course and she looked out at all the seated people and stared. I had to tug on her leash to break her pandering, and with a flurry of claws she climbed the ramp and came back down wearing her vacant smile of secret amusement. In practice, after the successful completion of her task, she sat snottily in front of me, accepting her hot dog with the apathy of a dilettante, but this time she sat ramrod straight, lifting one front paw and then the other, her eyes blazing. On the way out of the ring, she lifted her feet like a Tennessee Walking Horse as applause rang out. Liz and I grinned and rolled our eyes at each other on the sidelines.

Since Liz and I were only able to demonstrate one obstacle at a time, a few of Kathy's advanced students ran the entire course, including her star, Cisco. It was a neck and neck tie as to who was a bigger attention whore—Athena or Cisco. Cisco was a jocund Golden Retriever with a light blond body and the sweet hooded eyes stereotypical of the breed. Cisco was owned by one of the assistant trainers at the Animals' House and was a veteran agility expert; he ran the entire course with enviable speed and panache. Cisco had only one weakness, which was the crowd, and the more noise they made, the sillier he got. One of the Cisco legends from a past *Pet Expo!* was when he slowed down mid-demonstration to steal a kid's ice cream cone from the sidelines. He grabbed the cone from the child's hands without ever stopping, and as the child began to cry, Cisco finished the rest of his run while gulping down the ice cream cone whole, like a pelican would a fish. Cisco behaved himself on this trip, but he still wore a sunny smile on his face the whole demonstration, convincing me that a happy dog is one thing—a happy Golden Retriever is in a league by itself. Watching Cisco do his run would have cheered up Sylvia Plath.

Kiera, for a newcomer, picked up agility quickly, and she did her two jumps perfectly. Athena and Kiera were such a hit in agility, in fact, that a man who ran another dog show stopped Liz and me as we were leaving the ring and asked if we wanted to be in his variety show with our shepherds. We agreed. We all convened behind a curtain before show time and were told the rules and the order of events. Athena was more interested in the crowd assembling on the other side of the curtain, hearing snatches of conversation and chairs scratching the floor. She kept lifting the bottom of the curtain with her muzzle, sticking her face out enough to see what was going on out there, until I firmly told her to quit it and made her face the other direction. Then she "accidentally" pushed her tail out under the curtain into the show ring instead.

Liz and my inability to keep a straight face had not abated since Schutzhund, and we kept looking at each other and trying not to laugh at the man running the show; he seemed to fancy himself a modern-day PT Barnum and took his job of instructing us very seriously. The first event would be a "parade of all the contestants," followed by a game played with musical mats, a performance by a cowgirl who country danced with her dog, and finally, a high-jump competition. Musical mats was a game similar to musical chairs. The larger dogs would be paired up with the smaller dogs, and the pairs would walk around a mat on the floor; when the music stopped, the dog that lay down on the mat first won. Kiera was paired up with a pit bull and Athena a Boston terrier, but to "please the crowd," PT Barnum told us that the small dogs would win. "The crowd loves to see the little guy beat the big guy," he reasoned.

Athena was so happy to bask in the anticipation of showing off that she didn't once bark at or pin any of her fellow competitors in the holding area, despite the close quarters. Liz and I made a quiet mutinous pact that we were going to screw the rules and try our hardest to get Athena or Kiera to win musical mats, figuring that our girls should have a chance for glory.

We waited behind the curtain for the man to finish his opening; he fired T-shirts and balls into the assembled crowd, which was quite large. Then he darted backstage and with the seriousness of a runway assistant at New York Fashion Week, he pointed at each of us in turn and said, "And okay, go! Now!" making sure there was enough room between all of us for the parade of contestants. To the strains of the Baja Men hit "Who Let the Dogs Out?" we paraded our dogs around the ring. Athena kept stopping and gazing at all the spectators; once or twice she held up the dogs behind her because she kept freezing and standing in stack, coquettishly glancing sideways without moving her head to ensure people were watching her. I had to subtly kick her in the rear end to get her to keep going.

"Who's your favorite, ladies and gentleman! Pick your favorite now!" the emcee boomed. I saw many small fingers pointing at Athena, which could only mean the self-promotion was working.

Then it was time for the musical mats game. Athena seemed to understand the concept after the first time I pointed at the mat. All around us dogs were eliminated, until Athena and the Boston terrier were the only two dogs left. When the music stopped, Athena executed a perfect platz on the mat at the same time the other owner pitched her Boston onto the mat, where it stood a second before she coaxed it into a down. By default, since he was the smaller dog, the Boston won. Liz was indignant for us, and we both agreed it was dumb, but the Boston was such a bright and cute little thing, it was hard to hold a grudge.

After the country dancing human/dog duo, the next contest was the high jump. I knew that Athena, with her heavy body and her careless feet, would be one of the first dogs eliminated, but Kiera, a more slender German shepherd with amazing leaping ability, was perfect for the exercise, and Liz and I both were excited to see her compete. The pit bull was the first to be eliminated, and Athena only lasted two more increments of the bar, crashing through the last one. The effort to jump it and musical mats had caught up with her, however, and she lay on the mat on top of the bar, panting. The host had his back turned, ready to announce the next contestant, and Athena looked up at him in that joking way she looked at me when I threw the ball inside and she came out carrying a stuffed animal. When he heard the amused commotion it caused, he turned to face Athena lying there, did a Catskills-worthy double take and scolded, "What are you doing? You lost. Get off the stage!" putting his hands on his hips.

As the crowd roared with laughter, Athena decided it was a good time to cool off her belly, so she rolled onto her back and wiggled, her four paws waving around crazily, looking for all intents and purposes like she was clownishly defying the host. The crowd laughed harder as I uncoiled myself from the back of the line and yanked her up off the mat. As I led her away, she wore a completely unrepentant expression, reminiscent of her high-spirited demeanor after running away to Starbucks. We couldn't have scripted a more hammy moment had I rehearsed it a hundred times, and once again, I marveled at my dog's seemingly innate ability to make a complete goon out of herself.

The little Boston terrier, one of the dogs left, sprang over the bar as if his feet contained pogo sticks, but at a height of almost four feet, he knocked it down. Kiera was next, and I watched Liz on the opposite side, holding her hand up before commanding Kiera to jump over. Athena reared and play-barked, as if she were cheering for her friend. I think she just wanted to be in the center of the action again. Kiera jumped the bar with ease, and I was so happy when Liz triumphantly clenched her fist, celebrating. We waited to hear the host announce Kiera the winner, but in typical carnie fashion, the host had something up his sleeve.

A lady with a hairdo like the Little Dutch Boy's from the paint can emerged from backstage, wearing a bronze glittery vest. She was followed by a slow-trotting saluki who had a neck decoration made of the same glittery material. The host moved the bar to over five feet, before announcing, "Ladies and gentlemen, please welcome Puzzle! The current world-record high jumper!" Liz's face fell as we watched Puzzle, who was likely trained to do nothing else, jump over the bar. The crowd clapped appreciatively both at Puzzle and at the question, "Did you have a good time everyone?" and Liz and I, both a little deflated, left with no prizes. I felt especially bad for Liz; although Kiera is a stunning dog from the champion Bad-Boll line, Athena with her long coat and her ravenous love of attention often draws the initial, "What a beautiful dog!" whenever we're together. It would have been nice for Kiera to be the center of attention.

When the *Pet Expo!* rolled into town again the following year, Athena and Kiera were ready once more to demonstrate for the Great Falls Club. Both dogs had become proficient enough that they could run the whole course. I was prepared this time, stacking the audience with numerous family members and friends. My uncle was on hand to videotape the show to make a DVD. I arrived prior to the crowds to practice the course, and other than flapping the teeter down with such enthusiasm that it sounded like a gunshot in the building, Athena's performance was flawless. Since we had time before the actual event, we walked around to look at the other booths. In the congested thoroughfare, Athena boarded her imaginary caravan through the Sahara, and even I, used by now to such public displays, had to admit a certain awe over the immensity of her pile. Ignoring those who had to maneuver around her, she poo kicked with a flourish.

The agility demonstration kicked off at one p.m. Highlights from the DVD include:

Scene 1: Athena, who is supposed to demonstrate the tunnel, stands as if petrified, staring out at the crowd. The announcer says, "Look at Athena, everyone! She's saying, 'Hellooo, everybody!'" Athena tilts her head. The crowd laughs. I interrupt her lovefest to remind her why she's in the ring.

Scene 2: A few moments later, Kiera—all business—demonstrates a bar jump, A-frame, and another bar jump. Liz rewards her with a tug toy and they do a jig out of the ring, as Kiera is basically walking along on two legs next to Liz, not letting go of the toy.

Scene 5: A black Chow mix named Kiki demonstrates the whole course. Kiki doesn't like other dogs and stares at Athena as she and her owner walk past us on their way back to the holding area. Athena lurches on her leash and barks crazily at Kiki at this family-friendly event. The camera catches me grabbing Athena's mouth and closing it, mid-bark.

Scene 7: Liz and Kiera execute a flawless full course. During the run, an irritating high-pitched keening can be heard in the background. It is Athena, watching her friend run and jump.

Scene 8: And finally, Athena is waiting in a dutiful sit at the beginning of the course while I walk to stand beside the A-frame. I begin by saying, "Over!" which means that Athena is supposed to perform the initial bar jump and then run straight to the A-frame, a combination she has done at least twenty times in her lessons. Instead, when I say, "Over!" Athena veers to the right and soars through the tunnel. The crowd laughs. When she comes back to me to start over again at the jump, she is wearing a cheeky, joyful expression. It is apparent that she thinks herself uproariously funny, as if I have thrown the ball and she has brought back an ironing board.

When she gets to the weave poles, she hunches down into a weird crawl, missing the first two before banging into the whole set, causing it to sway from side to side precariously. The crowd laughs. Coming out of the weave poles, she suddenly goes down on her shoulder, skidding for a few inches, before recovering and leaping onto the teeter and finishing with the tunnel. (Closer review with the slow motion function reveals that coming out of the weave poles, she trips over her own paw, not paying attention, excited to bang onto the teeter-totter, presumably because it is the loudest most attention-getting obstacle on the course.)

The announcer at this point is inaudible, mainly because the laughter of my uncle and other family members sitting in the vicinity drown her out. When Athena executes a perfect sit at my feet for her reward, the camera pans to my face, and I am wearing the exasperated yet amused look my dog commonly engenders as I shake my head.

"She's such a clown!" my mom clapped and beamed at us afterwards. The rest of my friends, clutching their sides, still laughing, walked up to us.

"I thought you said your dog does the whole course," one of them reminded me.

"She was perfect the first round, our practice round, when no one was here yet! I swear!" I wailed. "She can do the weave poles! Really!" By then they were all dispersing to look at other booths, clearly skeptical.

22. Other Activities

After we had graduated from every level of agility class offered at the Great Falls Center, there wasn't anywhere higher to go, unless I wanted to start competing with Athena. Realizing that she didn't have the patient discipline required to really master the weave poles or hanging tire, and I didn't have the needed coordination to learn the more complicated patterns, we didn't go in that direction. She got hot, bored and moody between runs, and it was a sport dominated by Border collies, whose intense hyperactive mania irrationally angered her. Liz and Kiera continued agility, eventually finding an elite training school with a private coach that readied them for competitions throughout Virginia. Slender light Kiera, with her laser focus and boundless energy, won many blue ribbons in the AKC competitions they ran together. Watching how amazing and fast they were reinforced my decision not to pursue agility further with Athena. The only dog I ever saw bulkier and fluffier than Athena competing on the circuit was sweet giant Harry, a long-coated Mastiff. Poor Harry was so large he once got stuck in the tunnel and trotted along with it swaddling him like a sandwich bun, dragging it through the sawdust.

I tried to find other creative activities to keep Athena busy. One Athena liked to play was called the "Hot Dog Game" I invented for inside when it was too hot and disgusting outside as it often is in Washington, DC in summer. It kept her thinking, and she got to use her tracking skills. Making her lie down in the kitchen, I hid tiny pieces of hot dog around the house for her to find. Inevitably, I picked many of the same spots she went directly to, much as my family had done when I was little and used to hunt for Easter eggs at my grandmother's house. I always knew there was going to be one hidden in the piano bench. She therefore knew I stuck hot dog into her swinging baby gate. We also played "detection dog", a variation of the hot dog game. I took her to a place with a lot of cars, dumpsters, and drains and said in an urgent voice, "Check it! Check it!" Athena took her mission, even though she had no idea what the mission was, very seriously. She sniffed audibly around the cars and stood up on her hind paws on walls, among other techniques, with a workmanlike focus. We played detection dog at the Vienna, Virginia,

Metro station once while we waited for a friend. Athena was thoroughly enjoying herself, sniffing and checking magazine racks, trashcans, and cars, when I noticed that one or two people at the bus stop had become visibly alarmed. I stopped playing immediately. Even though I wasn't wearing a uniform or Athena a vest, I realized we looked like a bomb-sniffing team. After that, we limited detection dog to areas where there weren't any people.

Our last foray into a formal class came when my friend and neighbor Lauren enrolled her younger dog Cody in a sheep-herding course in Berryville, Virginia, at a working farm. Cody was a shepherd mix we were convinced was Athena's bastard son. We joked that Athena had snuck down to New Orleans where Cody had been found and had a wild night involving beads and an illicit mongrel affair. Athena, if she were human, would doubtless be in a *Girls Gone Wild* video.

I wanted Athena to try sheep herding, so she and I went to Berryville one day with Lauren and Cody. When we first walked by the flock standing on the other side of the fence, Athena bristled and barked at them, as if they were large dogs. Watching Cody, however, she quickly learned that the large dog-things ran away, and she was quite overcome and was shrieking and gabbling so much that I had to take her back to the car and leave her there, because she was distracting Cody from his lesson.

When it was her turn, at first Athena thought the goal of the exercise was to grab the crook in the instructor's hand and pull on it; a few sharp whacks on her nose from the teacher dissuaded her from doing it again. Finally, emitting choked, yippy noises, Athena started "herding" the sheep. The point for her wasn't to shepherd them so much as it was to chase and bite, and the instructor yelled "HAH! Get off there!" waving the crook at her wildly whenever Athena grabbed a mouthful of wooly haunch. She suggested that Athena might listen better to me, so she handed me my own shepherd's crook and told me to stand in the middle of the chase. I quickly got dizzy, spinning around with my staff trying to "push her away", which meant using the crook to poke at her shoulder to turn the opposite direction and chase the sheep the other way. She was very enthusiastic about running the whole herd around and around in a circle, which caused me mild nausea. It reminded me of the incompetent twirling I would end up performing during Schutzhund when she had her harness tied to the pole. At the command "push her away and change direction," I impotently inched forward like I was trying to enter a fast-moving traffic circle in a foreign country, careful not to be knocked down by smoothly cantering sheep or a galloping Athena, who now sounded like she was a rubber-soled sneaker scuffing a linoleum floor. I was embarrassed to note that just as she had with Schutzhund, she made noises from home that I preferred to keep between us and a few close friends. Instead of her "Yep!" play-bark, she did her "chasing noise," which was a loud rhythmic "*Heh*! . . . *Heh*! . . . *Heh*!" of excitement that resounded whenever she chased one of her dog friends around the common area. Some of my neighbors looked out their windows when she did that; the volume and cadence were such that it sounded like I was beating her sides using the same brutal rhythm the man in the hold of a pirate ship drums to keep the oarsmen in synch.

"Can you get her to stop that noise?" the instructor shouted at me from the sidelines.

"*Heh*! . . . *Heh*! . . . *Heh*!" Athena screamed, rushing by me again.

"Athena! Quiet!" I yelled to her.

"HEH! . . . HEH! . . . HEH!" she replied.

I kept missing at the push and change, and eventually the instructor stepped in and expertly blocked Athena so that she and the sheep ran in the other direction. After our lesson, I weaved out of the pen, as though a little drunk, to sit down at a picnic table, while Athena panted heavily next to me, practically gasping for air, but looking crazily happy.

The instructor whistled and called her Border collies out of her house to move the herd to a different field. Athena scowled at the Border collies and recovered breath enough to bark disapprovingly at them. Seriously professional, the Border collies never even twitched an ear behind them. The instructor came back and eyed Athena with the mild confusion I recognized from most of any of the teachers we had already had, telling me "Well, she tried very hard, didn't she?" I was acquainted with the tone by now to recognize that it meant "don't call us; we'll call you" but I agreed that she was zestful about life in general, fondly patting her head. "One thing that concerns me is she bit the sheep so much. With a lot of work, she could be trained out of that, though. She's certainly a sweet dog, and she seems to like the running part." I sighed, and said I'd think about herding lessons. In the end neither Lauren nor I decided to keep going; Athena had committed the fundamental herding breed sin of biting her charges, and while Cody liked herding, he liked pausing in his lesson to eat sheep poop even better. Later at Lauren's house we cracked beers, laughing and saying cheers to our disastrous sheep herders, who lay next to each other with the same dim, happy gazes, panting and content.

23. Trollop

Although my dog was spayed, every male she came in contact with fell head over heels for her and tried to win her affections. Besides Kaiser, her original pit bull suitor, many other males worked hard to win her paw. She was by turns indifferent, cruelly flirtatious, or both, depending on her mood.

We were at the dog park one afternoon with Jim and Mindi. Athena was, of course, loping along with her baseball in her mouth. Although she was lost in her own little world, as usual, she apparently still managed to weave a magic spell over Wrigley, a young Rhodesian ridgeback. She passed him on her urgent way to nowhere, and he began to follow her. Wrigley play bowed to her, barked at her, and tried to get her to notice him any way he could. Athena paid him not a lick of attention. When she stood still, Wrigley bounced on all fours like, "Look at me!" Meanwhile, Athena focused her gaze just beyond him. Finally, out of frustration, Wrigley grabbed a nearby ball from the ground and practically threw it at her, looking down at the ball and back to her. He smartly seemed to realize that a ball was the only thing she cared about. He bowed to her and barked again. Although the ball rolled and stopped just shy of her feet, Athena didn't even bother to glance at it. Acting as though Wrigley were invisible, she turned and trotted away. Poor Wrigley looked dejectedly after her.

"Poor Wrigley! Your dog's a snob," Jim said in a hurt voice.

"I know," I said. "I just don't know what her problem is."

"Poor Wrigley!" Jim said again, and then I got a lecture about how beautiful women shoot guys down and how hard it is to be a guy, as if I had trained her Miss Havisham-style to spurn gentleman callers.

Even older dogs seemed to hear Athena's siren song floating on the wind. Raleigh, a seven-year-old yellow Labrador owned by my friend Mike seemed to regard Athena as canine Viagra. Although it was true that Raleigh was not altered, it was also true that as large dogs go, he was more in his twilight years. One look at Athena, however, and the old get-up-and-go returned. He got especially frisky if they played in water together, as they did in Burke Lake when they first met. Raleigh was deceptively neutral toward Athena when they first walked along together; he barely looked at her. He was too busy marking every vertical object to trifle with such things as flirtation. The water seemed to act as an aphrodisiac, however, and after a refreshing dip he tried to put his paw over her back numerous times. Athena whirled around and gave a clipped "Rrr!" which even I knew was a completely nonthreatening noise.

Prancing to just a few feet beyond him, Athena then bent down and picked her stick up, mincing by him as he tried to catch her mid-mince with his forelegs.

"Rrr!" she'd say, as in, "Now, you stop that right now, Raleigh! I mean it!" followed by a giggle. It was only if he pushed the issue to full chest-to-back contact that she would spin and yell an angry, "Arr rarrr!" Comically undaunted by her reaction, he would happily try again a few minutes later. If he put a testing foreleg on her back and she growled, he put it quickly back down and looked away, the gesture said, "Wasn't me."

Mike apologized for his randy dog, but I always thought Athena was acting like a bit of a floozy. Of course, she didn't seem to mind the attention. Mike assured me that Raleigh, once he got familiar with a dog, would stop his advances, but for a few weeks, whenever they met, he put the moves on her. When his attempts were spurned—sometimes she got more forceful if she was irritable—he was pleased to just lie next to her, guarding his younger woman. It made me wonder if animals thought other animals of the opposite gender "pretty" and weren't just mindlessly reacting to hormones. Athena was never in season, so there was no logical reason for her to attract males, but apparently, they fell for her anyway.

Like the archetypal Mean Girl, Athena would toy with male dogs' affections if it suited her. Conner, an adolescent soft hound mix owned by my acquaintance Simon, naturally worshipped Athena from the first time they met in my living room. Conner not only recognized her as the dominant female; just being near her sent him into a besotted frenzy of muzzle licking, crawling, and flopping onto his back. Athena would deliberately turn her head away when he went to lick under her chin. Desperate to demonstrate his slavish devotion, Conner would cry and wiggle and try even harder. Athena would walk away. If, however, Conner got interested in something else, like a toy, Athena would push her way up to him to make sure he stopped to try to lick her muzzle again. This went on several times, until she realized she could play Conner like a fiddle without even having to get near him. Once when he was being too rambunctious for her taste, she strode up to within a few feet of him and gave a clipped yip. Conner's reaction was to howl his contrition, hurl himself onto his back, and pee.

I actually watched the evil wheels turn and clink into place inside Athena's head. When Conner started up again, Athena did a trot-by and gave the same loud high-pitched bark as she flew by him. She then stopped and turned to watch him with an open grin as he again cartwheeled onto his back, baying. She did her sadistic little trick one more time and then stopped when I scolded her. I didn't think she ever would have tired of the game on her own. Even after I scolded her, she looked at me, grinning. Again, like her conspiratorial look when she pounced on the stuck dog in agility, she acted like we had just had our own private joke together. Conner didn't seem to have any hard feelings, and Simon didn't either; in fact, he seemed to regard Conner's lovesick enthusiasm as extremely funny.

24. Search-and-Rescue Dog

Mike and Raleigh became a bigger part of Athena's and my lives the year we all met. Raleigh did eventually stop trying to flirt with Athena, just as Mike had predicted. If anything, Raleigh later regarded her with an ill-concealed distaste that occurs in many instances when there's been an initial foolhardy and passionate romantic attraction. Raleigh was similar to Mike in temperament. Both liked things quiet and orderly, and they could get snappish when irritated. Athena and I are similar in that we're both clumsy and boisterous, although we can also both get snappish when irritated.

Deceptively regal at first, Athena started revealing her true nature to Mike, unfolding her inner clown, overheated imagination, and joyful earnestness, and I caught Mike looking at her quizzically from time to time whenever she stumbled rushing for her baseball or stared at me with too much addle-brained enthusiasm.

Mike's first brush with Athena's goofiness came when we were at my friend Diana's mother's house for a pool party thrown for my birthday. Athena had always loved it there. The property consisted of a manorial house, three decks, over an acre of landscaped yard, and a fenced-in pool. From the very first time I let her explore the expansive yard, she acted as if the place were her home away from home. It amused Diana's family, the familiar way she floated around the grounds like a royal sentry. In fact, on our first visit, I let her off her leash and watched her confidently trot, disappearing, around the corner of the house into the back area.

"Where's she going?" Diana giggled. "It's like she owns the place."

By far her favorite place while visiting was the pool area. While she didn't like to swim in the pool (I once tried to show her it wasn't scary by pulling her in, and I was summarily stripped of my bathing suit top and mercilessly clawed by four thrashing paws.), she liked to be close to the action. She seemed to think it fun to be sprayed with Super Soaker water guns and especially enjoyed violently nosing large inflatable balls back into the pool when someone threw them at her, a bastardized game of catch. The highlight of all the pool parties Athena attended was one during which she got to bite and pull out of the water a large floating watermelon. She grunted and flounced up the stairs to the deck, proudly lop-sided, cheek fur dripping.

On the day of my pool party, Mike was sitting on the deck when Athena bounded up, taking two steps at a time, so focused on reaching him that she ran nose-first into one of the heavy iron legs of a table. She gave a piercing squeal, and Mike told me, "I felt so bad for her. She just ran right into the table leg. I was about to reach down and pet her to see if she was okay, when she suddenly did *this* and then turned around and ran back down." At "this" he executed a perfect imitation of Athena's mindless grin as she whirled around and, just as if nothing had happened, ran back down the deck steps to the pool. It was his first taste of the real Athena, and he sounded perplexed. "Then she almost fell going down the stairs, she was going so fast," he said. I explained that something more fun must have distracted her, and I left it at that. I didn't elaborate that had splashes and laughter not coaxed her back to the pool, she might have screamed like a sirocco until I or preferably everyone at the party had shown up to comfort her.

A month or so later, Mike and I took our dogs for a walk around his neighborhood one afternoon, where I knew Athena would shine. She is quite a show-off when on walks. Sure enough, she pranced showily and eyeballed the terrain like an expert guard dog on duty. Suddenly, she caught sight of a rabbit in someone's yard, and she darted forward, yanking, as it leisurely hopped across the driveway. I held her and told her to stop, and although she reared and danced sideways back and forth with excitement, she looked elegant and deadly doing it. Raleigh stood on the sidewalk staring at Athena with bored superiority. He, too, had seen the rabbit, but he was unconcerned with such nonsense as jumping after it, making a fool of himself.

"She really wanted that rabbit," I told Mike as we resumed our walk.

A few blocks further, Athena and I were a few feet ahead of Mike and Raleigh on the sidewalk when Athena again lurched forward, hopping from side to side, ready to chase and attack. Thinking that there sure were a lot of rabbits in Mike's neighborhood, I followed her animated eyes to a trio of lawn gnomes and a brown plastic raccoon gathered under a tree in someone's front yard. I hoped it was a coincidence and that a squirrel had just jumped into the tree, but nothing moved, including and especially not the gnomes.

By now Mike had caught up to us; he cocked his head and with a knowing, amused glint in his expression asked, "Is she excited over the lawn gnomes?"

"No, no!" I stammered indignantly. "She saw a squirrel, I think!"

"I didn't see any squirrels," Mike answered in his typical deadpan way. The corner of his mouth turned up; he might even have been smirking.

"Well I'm pretty sure one is up in that tree now," I said, squinting up into the branches.

Athena had frozen and was still staring at the lawn ornaments, tilting her head.

Mike gave me a long look but dropped the subject, or perhaps I changed it, and we continued on our way back to his house.

The incident wasn't forgotten. "Your dog chases lawn gnomes," he later teased. Unable to hide the truth any longer, I blurted out, "Yes, it would seem so, but it was the plastic raccoon that looked very similar to a rabbit that fooled her."

"It didn't fool Raleigh," he explained. We both looked at Athena, who lay smiling blankly and watching television.

I sighed. "She has a very vivid imagination." It was the best excuse I could think of at the time, and anyway, her cover was already permanently blown.

Then Raleigh got lost, and it was time for Athena to redeem herself in Mike's eyes by finding him. Mike had gone up to his childhood home in rural Pennsylvania to attend the funeral of his maternal grandmother. It was just before Labor Day weekend, and the plan was that upon his return to Virginia, we were going to take the dogs on a holiday to Virginia Beach.

I received word from him the night before his return that Raleigh had run off and had been missing for six hours. While Mike was at the funeral, Raleigh had darted through an open door at the place where he was staying. That alone wouldn't have been perilous, but a loud noise down the street startled Raleigh, and he had darted into dense woods and become lost. In actuality, for at least a few hours he likely wasn't lost as much as enjoying his freedom in the country; he was spotted by neighbors chasing ducks into a nearby pond and ambling along the wooded paths. Soon, however, it became apparent that the fun was over, because Raleigh, a devoted Daddy's boy, had never been away from Mike's side for very long.

I asked Mike if he wanted me to come up to help search. He said yes. I asked if he wanted me to bring Athena. Grief and shock must have weakened him, because he seemed to think it was a good idea. We both had heroic delusions that Athena would transfer her excellent skills at the hot dog game to locating Raleigh.

I was too rattled to drive, as well as being likely to end up in Kentucky, due to my poor navigation skills, so stalwart, tough-as-nails Lauren loaded Athena, her two dogs, and me into her SUV and hauled us the five hours up to Pennsylvania. She declined Mike's family's offer to stay the night and instead drove all the way back to Virginia the same night, stopping only twice for quick naps along the side of the road. It was too dark to resume the search at that late hour, so Mike, Athena, and I checked into a dog-friendly hotel and waited until morning.

The next morning I was prepared with Athena's thirty-foot tracking lead and a command to "Such Raleigh!" She led me along paths, seemingly efficient and single-minded in her mission. She led me into back yards, across fields, through creeks. I could barely keep up with her.

Labor Day weekend was unseasonably hot, and the temperature climbed into the eighties by ten a.m. We left the air conditioning running in Mike's truck, and if I felt Athena was getting overheated, I let her recuperate in the back seat. The only problem with this arrangement was that Athena learned very quickly that working in the sun wasn't as enjoyable as lying in the truck, so after a good showing of leading me around, sniffing the ground, she kept pulling me back there. I didn't want her collapsing in the rural locale; the nearest vet was not close and likely not open, so I had to respect her when she got too hot.

It got to be easier and easier to leave her in the truck when we were all searching, and when the day ended and we hadn't found Raleigh, I realized with a sinking heart that I wasn't even sure if Athena knew what she was supposed to be looking for. I feared her tracking was similar to our detection dog game, where she wanted to look busy, like she was doing a real job to please me but really only went through the motions.

I thought I'd try having her off-lead, that maybe if I let her go she would perhaps find Raleigh and then coax him back to us. When I urged her to "Such Raleigh!" she did in fact find Mike and his older brother Rich in a clearing up the path. By the time I caught up to her, out of breath, she was jumping on both of them, monkey whining. She ran to me and then back to them, looking at me with a "See? I found them!" I praised her because she seemed overjoyed that she had found at least something. She obviously thought her workday was over then, because she dragged me back to the truck so she could again rest in the air conditioning.

After the fourth fruitless day, we decided to adjust our search strategy. Walking miles of trails calling for Raleigh had not worked, and in fact, we suspected we were merely scaring him in confused circles. Rich, who had known Raleigh his whole life, did see him one day. When Rich called for him, however, Raleigh ran away, probably disoriented. It was not uncommon, we learned, for dogs that got lost to run from even their own masters when they had been out for a while.

Instead we decided to set up camp on the property of two affable brothers who had spotted Raleigh several times emerging from their woods. In fact, one of the times they had seen him, they came to get me as I sat alone in Mike's giant pickup standing watch. I followed them in the truck, bouncing along the gravel road, feeling like a little kid playing dress up because I could barely see over the steering wheel. They pointed across a vast expanse of thigh-high wildflowers and grass, and, tucking Mike's keychain into the waistband of my sweatpants, I took off running through the field, yelling Raleigh's name. But he had already disappeared back into the forest.

When I turned and saw that the truck was a distant gray speck, I ran back to it through the field, imagining myself as nimble and light as a white-tailed deer. I was about halfway back to the truck when I patted the waistband and realized the keychain was missing. I stood, dizzy, in the field, which buzzed and shimmered with insects, knowing that the chance of my finding the keys was zero. I tried, anyway, retracing my steps through the grass, praying for a glint of metal. After a half hour of tromping back and forth, no keys materialized, so I made my way back to the truck. I walked along the road until I found Mike's mom, and we were able to find a locksmith, luckily, to grind new truck keys. The house key was gone. Even though it was before noon, I cracked a beer from the ever-present cooler and waited for Mike to join us so I could break this latest bit of bad news to him. He took it remarkably well, probably because it appealed to his rather cynical sense of humor.

On the day we camped out waiting for Raleigh to make an appearance, we had two coolers full of beer and soda, a blanket, and many sandwiches. Athena thought, apparently, that we had set up a picnic for her amusement, and she went to find a stick for me to throw for her. She always gets unreasonably attached to sticks. Even though she always whittles her stick to the size of a pen cap, she is diligent about finding that piece, even if there are twenty-five suitable replacement sticks within easy reach. So on our stakeout, I would look up from my book to find Athena backing away, quivering, staring at a wet shard of bark she had laid next to me on the blanket. No matter how far I threw the piece into the same dense field that had swallowed Mike's keys, she was able to always find that tiny sliver. Mike and I shared a look of bemusement that she could perform this impressive feat but had trouble locating an eighty-five-pound yellow Labrador.

Then, after a long round of fetching, Athena marched with no hesitation up to one of the coolers, flipped the lid open with her nose, and drank noisily from the melted ice water. Mike and I looked at each other again. Days of observing us opening the lids to the coolers for drinks had apparently paid off for Athena.

"Did she just get herself a drink?" Mike asked.

"Yes," I said, watching her frantically search for—and reclaim—her inch-long sodden twig.

"That's pretty awesome," he conceded, laughing.

"She's never seen a cooler before this weekend," I admitted. I had to hand it to her. Athena chose the oddest times to display her momentary flashes of ingenuity.

Athena spent much of our time in Pennsylvania showing off, as usual, whether in the parking lot at our hotel, walking past the other guests, or while with me out on the balcony of our room, where she amused herself by standing on her hind feet to look over the wall at the people using the pool below us. The people below saw her and laughed, startled by the mammoth German shepherd head popping up from nowhere. "Ohhhh, so pretty!" I heard someone say, and Athena got in a head tilt before losing her balance and falling to all fours again.

I think her jolly obliviousness helped Mike keep his spirits up. Hers was the only presence that didn't have a whiff of worry to it; even though we all kept things light and joking, the sorrow at potentially losing Raleigh and the impact it would have on Mike floated like a miasma around us all.

Except when she had been particularly diligent "searching" through creeks or in mud, Athena was allowed on the hotel bed with us. She flopped heavily and mindlessly against Mike at night and was apt to watch him do things like open his laptop or brush his teeth as if they were the most fascinating things she had ever seen.

"We bonded during this trip," Mike joked. I think Athena felt the same way.

Finally, the day before Mike and I absolutely had to leave Pennsylvania to go back to work, a neighbor spotted Raleigh in her yard. Mike was on foot, and as soon as he caught sight of the dog, he began walking away from him instead of toward him, and Raleigh followed. Mike knelt down, his back to Raleigh, and Raleigh folded and ran to him, howling.

Everyone was so relieved that Raleigh, the soft city dog, had survived over five days in the rural wilds. When Mike took him to a vet for an examination, Raleigh was in amazingly good shape. He had a few burrs in his coat, and his paw pads were torn and bleeding, but he looked as if he had eaten, and a pull up of his back skin revealed no dehydration. We surmised that he had survived by stealing food from the outdoor dogs many people in the country had. He also displayed admirable survival instincts by holding his urine. Once Mike had him back on a leash, he peed a comically long time, easily almost two minutes. We drove back to Virginia smiling and happy, glancing into the back seat periodically to see Raleigh curled in a ball sound asleep and Athena with her nose pressed against the window, watching passing cars.

Neither Mike nor I wanted to go back to Pennsylvania for a long while, and I'm not sure Raleigh particularly wanted to either. I don't think that Athena would have minded one bit. As with most experiences, she had the time of her life and seemed to believe we had gone on some sort of special vacation designed specifically for her entertainment.

25. Bad Dog, Bad Dog, Whatchu Gonna Do?

Athena was fine in public and territorial when she needed to be, or so I thought. I had to rethink this philosophy one afternoon. We were waiting in my vet's tiny examination room, but our usual vet, Dr. Tohill, wasn't who came through the back door. Instead it was another man whom Athena had never met before. Athena, who was lying at my feet on the floor as I sat in a chair, went berserk when he came in, uncoiling herself and barking explosively, showing teeth, backing up to be in front of me, her front legs up off the ground. The vet, who I'm sure was used to handling big dogs, nevertheless recoiled and jumped back from her. "Whoa," he breathed. "You have a very aggressive dog. She could become very dangerous."

Dangerous?

My lovable clumsy loon who tripped on her own feet and bumped into things? The goofball who greeted friends with flattened ears and a wagging tail, doing a high-pitched monkey whine, holding a stuffed toy, trotting a circular course around my living room? My baby, who allowed children to foist any kind of indignity upon her and who loved to be fussed over by strangers? Dangerous?

I had to admit to myself that, yes, without a firmer hand from me, Athena could very well become dangerous. She had never once tried to inflict an actual bite, but her spastic jumping at the end of her leash like a hooked game fish while she barked and showed teeth was not warranted against people who hadn't attempted to harm us in any way. If her violent reaction to people she deemed dangerous escalated, I realized that she could possibly go the way of—at best—using her body weight to knock someone over or—at worst—biting someone who had done nothing wrong. Afraid that she was going to turn into Maxel, I worked with her on lessening her over-the-top response to strangers by rewarding quiet with treats, and that coupled with aging and losing some of her impulse control issues, succeeded. When she hit around two years old, a significant change happened. She finally seemed to connect her brain to events going on around her. When I gave her a command now, she metaphorically clicked her heels together and executed near-perfect obedience to me, looking up, waiting for her next instruction. Off-lead, we amazed people at outdoor venues, who remarked, "Wow, I wish *my* dog would listen that well."

We finally had meshed into a team. When I walked, she trotted alongside me, looking up at me, her body curled around my legs. My body positioning or eye contact was almost enough to elicit a certain behavior from her. When I added the guttural German commands we'd learned in Schutzhund, it was pretty impressive. "Platz!" I'd yell, and Athena would instantly drop to her belly. "Zeet!" and she'd freeze into a perfect triangular sit. "Aus!" meant she had to spit out what she was holding. "Fuss!" meant she should come around the front of my body to sit at my side, looking up at me. "Hier!" meant canter up to me and sit in front at attention, and "Come!" meant "You come *now* Athena," and woe to her if she failed to do so.

She casually ignored my calls to her once during a visit to the dog park with Liz and Kiera, and it only took once for her to understand the consequences. She was in a full-out "heh..heh..heh" gallop after a running dog, and given her propensity to go over the top of her victim and pull it to the ground by its collar, I didn't want her chasing dogs anymore. What was cute as a puppy was no longer cute when she hit sixty-eight pounds.

"Athena, come!" I yelled. I saw her ear flick back. She continued to run. "*Come! Now!*" I screamed. She acted like I was not there. Then she made her fatal mistake. The dog she was chasing ran by me, so she ran by me as well. I still don't know how, but as she passed I was able to reach out with both hands and grab the scruff at the base of her neck. She kept going, but her skin did not, and she let out one of her banshee screeches that once upon a time would have sent me into conciliatory pats and coos. In the split second that she was off the ground, I managed to flip her onto her side in the sand.

"Yeaaah!" Liz shouted from across the park. Liz had rigid, absolute control over Kiera, and compared to her, I was a creampuff who let Athena routinely get away with murder. I dropped my forearm onto Athena's neck, pinning her, as her sides heaved, and her eyes rolled around, and her tongue lolled out of her mouth as she panted from all that running.

"You need to come when you're called," I said to Athena with menacing calmness. She didn't struggle, but she looked mortified, which got even worse when other dogs came to stand around to watch the most dominant bitch at the dog park get her comeuppance.

"Free," I said as I gave her release command and removed my arm. Athena stood up and shook the sand out of her coat and meekly trotted away to get a drink at the water bowls across the park. I watched her and waited until she was finished and then called, "Come!" Athena perked up her head and ran full tilt over to me, sitting at my feet, perfectly still. "Good girl," I patted her sides and let her go again.

From that moment forward at the dog park, even if she was in mid-chase—mid-anything—when I called, Athena stopped what she was doing and came back to me. She probably didn't want to risk being shown up like that again in front of everyone. And I needed to be in charge in order to train her out of her dominant attitude when it came to other dogs.

From the time she was four months old, Athena had already asserted dominance over one of her best girlfriends, Mindi. A few days after meeting each other as puppies, Athena and Mindi played nicely, until something ticked off one of them, and before we could say, "Boo," they became a thrashing mass of high-pitched puppy snarls. I had read that dogs needed to establish who was dominant and that to intervene in such conflicts would cause the cycle to repeat itself over and over. So I recommended we let them hash out whatever they were arguing over.

Athena had an expression on her face that I hadn't seen yet. She had her hackles up and her lips pulled back so that her gums were exposed and I could see all her teeth; she was snarling. I dubbed it "Alien Face," because it reminded me of when the alien in the movie pushes its teeth and gums forward from its mouth and snaps. It was outright ugly.

With both front legs, Athena pinned Mindi to the ground, snarling and staring straight ahead, until Mindi moved, and then she grabbed the back of Mindi's neck between her jaws. With her forepaws and teeth, she held Mindi down for a few seconds, pinning her. They broke apart then, and Mindi shook as though shaking water off her coat, and they both acted like the scuffle had never happened.

"Your puppy is mean!" Jim told me. I couldn't argue with him.

Athena often made Alien Face at other dogs. Sometimes Athena just making Alien Face made other dogs skulk away, licking their lips nervously in an appeasement gesture. When Athena was dead serious, she made Alien Face and flicked her tongue out quickly back and forth like an angry snake's (it made her snarling go up and down in pitch), her muzzle wrinkled, her eyes squinting, her ruff completely puffed out.

Later when I watched footage of wolves disciplining each other, I recognized Alien Face. "They're doing Alien Face!" I yelled to Liz during a wolf documentary.

"Yeah . . . uh . . . your dog *is* a wolf. I'm convinced," Liz said, eyeing Athena with slight disapproval. Athena had made Alien Face and pinned Kiera upon first meeting her, and I don't think Liz ever truly forgave her. Apparently there were no hard feelings on either dog's part, because Kiera always humped Athena when they played together, and Athena didn't seem bothered by it.

As I liked to explain to people, Athena never started fights at the dog park, but she did finish them. The resulting melee never caused either dog to get punctured or cut, but a fluffed-out enraged German shepherd pinning another dog to the ground while displaying full Alien Face understandably unnerved and angered a lot of other dog owners. As the dominant bitch—with her high tail carriage and arrogant lope—she was pinpointed frequently by other dogs who had the idea that it was they who were, in fact, boss. Athena took it as a challenge when any strange dog snapped at her face, ignored her signals that she didn't want to be stared at, or tried to mount her.

Small dogs with Napoleon complexes were the worst of her enemies. No dog was too small or light to be put in its place, as evidenced by her disciplining the nipping Corgi in agility. The notion of David versus Goliath was just not in her DNA, and, an upstart challenging her was, in her eyes, wrong no matter what size that upstart was. I was at the dog park one day with Lauren and her dogs when we witnessed a Parson Russell terrier bitch latch onto Athena's forehead as she leaned down to pick up her baseball. Athena gave a relatively quiet yelp, which quickly changed to a deep rumbling warning growl. Lauren and I both reached in to help, but Athena had dislodged the terrier with an explosive shake and was attempting to pin it, the Parson Russell shrieking and snapping underneath her. She did pin it before we could drag her off, which seemed to signal other dogs nearby to join the riot, as dogs in dog parks are wont to do. They formed a dog pile from which the terrier eventually emerged, seemingly unhurt, although her sweater was covered in dust.

I was glad Lauren had been with me, because to people not paying full attention and who hadn't seen the terrier bite first, it looked like Athena went after the smaller dog unprovoked. The owners hustled their dusty terrier out of the park, not saying a word to me or any other owners.

"Nervous little dogs in sweaters" Lauren said, rolling her eyes. "They're usually the worst. I saw trouble. Her owners told me she's afraid of big dogs, and I wanted to say 'then why would you bring it in the big dog park?'"

"Yeah, that's the kind of dog that should have been in the small dog area; not in the main area." I muttered. "Do you think it's okay though? We got Athena off really fast. I didn't see any blood."

"Actually, Athena has blood on her lip. I think she got bitten, or maybe bit her own lip." Lauren said, holding Athena's lip up. It was bleeding. "If any dog bit that stupid little terrier, it might have been one of my two. They jumped in to back up Athena."

"Well, it bit Athena's forehead and was hanging. I don't know what Athena should have done." I said, helpless and angry. I hated that the whole thing happened. Lauren and I were frequently exasperated by nervous fear-aggressive small dogs and their inattentive owners. It made the dog park extremely dangerous.

In her favor, Athena never was trying to injure a dog when she pinned it. When it submitted, she didn't push the issue; she released the other dog and resumed whatever it was she had been doing. She never went after a dog that was minding its own business. If a dog snapped directly at her face or bit her as the Parson Russell had done, I reasoned that she was within her right to object. Fellow dog park customers who watched their dog get practically smothered by a snarling German shepherd did not agree.

At the time, I saw her as being in the right. In her dog judgment, she was only meting out fair punishment to dogs who didn't know proper etiquette when meeting their better. I believed that since she didn't inflict any damage on the other dogs and since she was merely operating per a dominant instinct, she was justified. In addition, when I touched her collar to pull her out of a conflict, she did the equivalent of throwing up her hands and saying, "I'm good! I'm good! I made my point!" I always put her in a platz after any altercation, and she lay there with a self-satisfied, relaxed air, as if she didn't have a care in the world.

And so it went at the dog park, until someone called the police. We were there with Liz and Kiera that day. An aggressive golden retriever (an oxymoron if ever there was one) was charging at other dogs, growling, and just being a bully. Athena was trotting through the throng of dogs near where the male was standing. She stopped in the group and stood for a second, looking over at the golden. It didn't seem to me to be a particularly hard or threatening stare, but the golden didn't like it and pushed up to her, chest out, body stiff, his face inches away from hers. The dogs erupted into a screaming argument, in which neither moved in for bites, but Athena took it to the next level by bucking up in the air and crashing over the top of the golden with her forelegs. She had just pinned him underneath her when the owner of the golden's wife reached in and pulled Athena off, hurling her a few feet away. At the first feel of human contact, Athena stopped, quietly let the woman pull her away, and rolled until she sat in a cloud of dirt. The golden was still in a frenzy of fighting the air, and it took a spell for him to realize Athena had been removed. Shaken, I called Athena over to me and put her in a platz. Liz shrugged next to me. It was over in approximately three seconds, and in her mind, Athena had made her point. The owners of the golden thought otherwise.

"You need to leave," the man said, coming up to me and jabbing his finger in my face.

"What for?" I asked.

"Your dog's aggressive!" he yelled.

"So is your dog," I replied.

"*That's why I'm taking him out!*" the man yelled.

"Now you are," I said. "I've watched your dog behave aggressively toward other dogs for the last twenty minutes. You didn't take him out then."

"If you don't leave, I'm calling the police," the man said, getting out his cell phone.

"Go ahead," I said, acting braver and more nonchalant than I really felt.

He and his wife left with their dog and sat in their car in the parking lot, staring at Liz and me. I saw the man using his cell phone.

"What should I do?" I asked Liz, my bravado starting to crumble.

"Screw him! Athena did nothing wrong!" Liz said, wrinkling her face in an expression of annoyance.

"Well, should I leave? I don't think I should leave, because then when the police get here it'll look like I fled the scene."

"No. Don't leave. Screw them," Liz said.

I sheepishly studied my fellow dog park patrons to see if they were going to get involved, while Athena lay panting and gentle as a lamb at my feet, but with a certain smugness to her demeanor. I didn't want to be known at the park as the lady with the vicious German shepherd, and I felt Athena was simply misunderstood.

Liz and I decided to take Athena and Kiera into the separate fenced-in area specifically for small dogs adjacent to the big-dog park. As it was most days, it sat empty. When we took the dogs out to enter the small-dog park, the man and his wife drove away.

Forty-five minutes later, a squad car pulled up and all of a sudden, Liz's defiance vanished.

"Oh my God. Oh my God. Oh my God, the police are here!" she said, jumping around waving her arms like Ed Grimley. She wanted to go somewhere and hide, leaving me there, and I sharply reminded her whose idea it had been to stay at the park in the first place. While she dissolved into a panicked puddle, I went to the fence to talk to the officer, prepared to give my statement about how Athena had pinned the golden but hadn't hurt him. Athena followed me to the fence and stood, wagging, with her baseball sticking out of her mouth, looking extremely dumb.

"Everyone having a good time today?" the officer asked, taking a notepad out of his pocket, looking bored.

"Yes. She pinned a dog that growled in her face, but as you can see, everything is calm now, sir," I said.

"Good-looking dog," the officer said, pausing in his note-taking, giving Athena the once-over. The good-looking master of spin tilted her head, looking quite coquettish and friendly.

"Athena, zeet," I said, to show the officer that I could control her, as well as to remind her not to flirt with everything in pants. Athena plunked down, still staring at the cop, adoring twinkles shining in her eyes.

"Well, you all have a good afternoon," the cop said, nodding and closing his notepad.

"You too, sir. I'm sorry you had to come out all this way for . . . this." I swept my hand over grass.

Just then a snarling erupted in the large-dog area as two dogs momentarily clashed.

The police officer glanced at them and then lazily strolled back to his squad car.

"What did he say?" Liz sidled up to me, whispering.

"Nothing," I said.

"Oh." Liz sounded disappointed. Overall our brush with the law turned out to be quite dull.

26. Dog-Park Pariah

Even a mild taste of law enforcement helped me decide that Athena's behavior at the dog park had to change. I contacted Victoria Schade, Athena's original trainer, for advice. She thought Athena had "a bit of a complex," and she suggested that I focus on her the entire time we were there. She advised me to move around a lot. She said that when dogs know where their owners are at all times, they can get complacent, but if the owner moves around, the dog has to maintain focus: "Where did my pesky mom go?" Victoria also told me that I needed to watch for signs of the situation escalating and stop Athena before she pinned again. If worst came to worst, she said, maybe a dog park wasn't a good place for Athena. I decided I would try Victoria's instructions first, because to deny Athena a place where she could chase her baseball and trot around a large fenced-in area seemed excessive. I vowed to turn her into a model citizen who learned to turn the other cheek, even if she felt a pin was justified.

So for the next six months, Athena was on a strict regimen at the dog park. I no longer allowed her to join in groups of dogs chasing a lone dog. I kept her occupied with her baseball and never let her far away from me for long stretches of time. I moved around the dog park frequently. I didn't stand and talk to people without checking every so often to see what she was doing. I forbade her from greeting dogs coming in at the gate, as I saw so many dogs do. "Welcoming Committee," several people would laugh, as groups of dogs stood, excited, waiting for the newcomer. I had seen way too many fights erupt during that very ritual, and I didn't want Athena to be involved.

I recognized dominant behavior in her even before it escalated to Alien Face. If I saw her and a dog sniffing each other and the other dog started to tense up, I said, "Athena, that was a nice hello, and now that's enough. Come."

I didn't allow her to become possessive over balls other than her own. She and a tall male Weimaraner ran to a deflated basketball someone had thrown and almost simultaneously reached for it with their snouts. I saw Athena's ruff start to go up. She lowered her head. On her face, I saw the embryo of the Alien Face lip curl. "Eh! No, *ma'am*!" I yelled. "Come!" When she reached me, I said, "*Such* baseball!" *Such* meant search, something she did with single-minded urgency when it was her baseball, which she had dropped to grab hold of the basketball.

It was always endearing to watch her retrieve her baseball at the dog park, where many balls were always strewn around on the ground. She would come upon a ball with an air of relief and briefly set her mouth around it, and I could imagine the cogs in her brain moving: "No . . . that's not it," as she spit the ball out and kept meandering along, until she spotted her baseball and picked it up with an air of joyful recognition. Finding her ball seemed to set the balance of the universe right again, so she could then resume her mindless trotting, satisfied.

Athena even found a loophole in the embargo on tennis balls. Keeping her baseball in her mouth, she alternately rolled a tennis ball along in front of her with her snout or pounced on it with her feet. As she did with the bench game, she attracted many snickers and "Would you look at that?" from spectators. "She likes soccer," I said weakly, as she ran along, a faraway figure who looked like she was vacuuming the dog park. She was able to push the tennis ball great distances, and like the bench game, she was happiest when she found suitable victims. She pushed the tennis ball to people's feet, glancing up at them, back at the tennis ball, up to them again, so they got the message that they were supposed to kick it for her. "But you already have one," was the inevitable reply, since she kept her baseball in her mouth. They kicked the tennis ball for her, except she never got the hang of waiting. Half the time I watched as the tennis ball ricocheted violently off her face, because she jumped in, too excited to wait for the ball to go by. "Oh! Sorry," the kicker would say, but no matter how many times people kicked the ball in my dog's face, it never seemed to faze her. The same dog who would step on a stick and run shrieking over to me holding her paw up so I could examine the nonexistent cut was perfectly content to use her face like a bumper in a pinball machine during soccer.

My strict rules for her at the dog park paid off. One afternoon, I entered the park with her, and a spotted, medium-sized male Australian shepherd mix began barking at her, showing teeth. It charged at her from across the park, stiff-legged, not playful in the least. The old Athena when faced with such a grievous infraction would have pinned him instantly, but she blithely ignored him and ran after her baseball which I had thrown upon entry. The fact that she ignored him seemed to further enrage the dog, and hackles up, snarling, he charged after her, barking at her retreating fluffy rump. She scooped up her baseball fluidly and then happily began her fast lope back to me. The dog darted in at her, flashing an ugly set of teeth. Athena glanced at him as she went by, but made no attempt to get into it with him. The dog then blocked her path and barked angrily a few feet away from her face. Athena looked at him quizzically, as if noticing him for the first time, and as he continued to bark at her aggressively, she seemed very confused. With the base-ball sticking out of her open mouth, the effect was quite comical. She again tried to return to me, but the dog would not relent. I watched her cut her eyes to me and turn away from the dog, presenting her back to him. She knew she wasn't supposed to fight. The dog ratcheted up his screaming and flew around the side and faced her, his face inches from hers. Athena looked at him a little more sharply, and the dog retreated slightly, still barking, teeth exposed, hackles raised.

Reminding me of the pacifist hero in a movie who the villain doesn't know is a black belt in karate, Athena squared her shoulders and deliber-ately laid her baseball next to her on the sand. She looked sad and resigned, but also resolute, and I saw her put her chest forward and plant her front legs. Her head lowered as she stared at her adversary, and her ruff started to rise. I watched her muzzle wrinkle and the lip flutter very slightly up and down, exposing one canine tooth. I knew she was growling.

I stepped in. I didn't want Athena to have to fight this dog, although he was aching to, and I figured the owner wouldn't want them to, either. I planted myself in front of Athena, leaned towards the snarling male, and with the force of a drill sergeant hoarsely yelled, "*Enough!*" The dog looked up at me, startled, and then averted his eyes and backed away. He turned around and walked off, throwing one last glower at me over his shoulder as he did.

A guy who appeared to be in his mid- to late twenties, built like a hulking bouncer, came forward. I figured it was to apologize and thank me for breaking up the fight before it happened.

"You don't gotta yell at my dog like that," he said, walking up to me. He towered over me and probably outweighed me by a hundred pounds. I was flabbergasted by his response.

"Obviously I do, because your dog is in my dog's face."

"*He's not doing anything!*" the guy said sharply, advancing on me, looking down at me. "You better watch your own dog," he concluded, gesturing toward me with two fingers pressed together, now well within the sphere of my personal space. I felt a powerful yet calm anger surge inside of me, and like my dog, I squared my shoulders and all five foot five 125 pounds of me took a step toward him.

"I am watching my dog, you *bleep bleep!*" I spat, leaning towards him stiffly. To this day I don't know what came over me, but I felt waves of energy coming out of my body. I hadn't been that angry in a long time. I think if he had raised a hand to me, I would have miraculously been able to roundhouse kick him in the head. He looked stunned; he probably was used to smaller people and especially women timidly taking whatever he doled out, and like his own dog, the bully averted his eyes and backed up.

"He's not doing anything" he added sulkily, still backing away.

"That's fine," I continued. "But when your dog gets *pinned* by my dog—which is what's going to happen— don't say *bleep* to me about it." I gave him a look of dismissive contempt and walked away.

The rest of the people at the dog park, I noticed, were looking at the ground, shuffling nervously. The park had become dead quiet during our argument. Even the other dogs seemed to be waiting.

Sure enough, not three minutes after I had warned him, his dog again charged Athena, snarling. She did not give him a second chance this time to back down. She outweighed the dog and was taller, and it was over very quickly. She pinned the dog to the ground in a terrifying wolf-like display while the dog screamed and struggled underneath her. I grabbed the top of her collar, and she went quiet, allowing me to lift her sideways. The look she gave me almost broke my heart. Her sorrowful eyes had an eerily human quality, and she put her ears back, expecting me to chastise her. Her message, "I'm sorry, Mom, I know I'm not supposed to do that," couldn't have been clearer had she spoken perfect English.

"Zeet," I told her, still holding her collar, but after that I said nothing; I only patted her side. We both watched as the man went to retrieve his dog, which was still howling and snapping and snarling in an unhinged meltdown.

"Come on . . . you're not being very nice," the guy said, trying to cover up his embarrassment. I imagine he was pretty humiliated, both because his dog was still thrashing around out of control, growling and struggling on its leash and almost biting him, as well as because my dog had kicked his dog's ass. As he was dragging his lurching mess of a dog to the exit gate, I looked again at Athena. She wouldn't look at me; instead she stared shamefaced at the ground. Seeing her look so sad enraged me further, and to the bully's and his dog's retreating backs, I screamed, *"Learn how to control your bleeping dog!"* He didn't look back, and I never saw him at that dog park again. A part of me thinks that he enjoyed the idea that his dog was taking on a big German shepherd, and I momentarily felt sorry for it. I released Athena and began to tremble. I looked around, and no one would meet my eyes. Except one person.

A taciturn Russian gentleman frequented the dog park with an aloof, dignified female Chinese shar pei. He wasn't a chatty individual and seemed to like to hang out alone. He usually would give a brief wave to other patrons and then stroll around the perimeter of the park, smoking cigarettes. His dog was much the same. She liked to keep to herself near the fence and only once in a while would pay attention to other dogs. He and I always cordially nodded to each other whenever there, but we had never spoken before this day. The man walked toward me slowly, and I worried that he was going to suggest we leave, or that Athena was aggressive, or any number of things. Instead, he stopped next to me. He looked down as if gathering his thoughts and then right up at me and said in a guttural voice, "I vant you to know. Your dog? Is so patient."

"Thank you for saying that," I said. "I really appreciate it. Really."

Then he walked away. I looked at Athena. I was inordinately proud of her. She had done her best to avoid the conflict and had only fought when she felt she had no choice. And someone had noticed my dog's newfound patience. When we left the dog park, I took her for her favorite treat—vanilla custard on a cone. She wouldn't make any connection whatsoever between our visit to Milwaukee Frozen Custard and what had happened earlier that day, but I think she understood that I thought she was a very, very good dog. I was finally realizing that, while my dog was indeed a badass, she would hardly ever display her forceful skills again. Like the secret martial artist in the movie, she would only react in a truly defensive situation like this one or the incident with the Parson Russell terrier.

I was starting to like dog parks less and less, because after the unbalanced Aussie mix and the terrier who bit Athena's forehead, I realized what I disliked about dog parks wasn't necessarily the dogs. It was their owners. One week after our incidents at our regular dog park, I took Athena to another one in Vienna, thinking maybe the mix of dogs and people there would be more polite. I had already ruled out the Reston Dog Park, because when Athena was just a puppy, I had taken her to Reston and watched as a man let his 120-pound Bernese Mountain Dog try to hump her. "Please get him off of her," I said as nicely as possible. "Her hips are still developing, and I don't want her to get hurt." The man shrugged and said "You shouldn't bring a dog in heat in here." Athena, still obviously a puppy, was at least a month away from her first heat, and I told him that. The man turned and started talking to someone else, so I ended up pulling his dog off of her myself. The Reston Dog Park I learned later had a reputation of "every dog for him/herself", since it also had the reputation where singles went to mingle, chat, check their cellphones and drink their Starbucks. Owners, according to the gossip, tended to use the Reston park, which was very large, as a giant playpen where dogs ran out of control, and my experience with it unfortunately supported that viewpoint.

Vienna's dog park was smaller, and I liked that a lot of it was in the shade and that the substrate was bark chips instead of sharp gravel. The dogs seemed less rowdy, the crowd older and more serious. As a park, it was perfect, but as with other parks, there was again an owner who made Athena's and my experience there difficult.

A sleek, very handsome young male Doberman pinscher was there with his owner, and at first the woman seemed agreeable and logical. That impression changed the moment the Dobie raced to Athena's baseball first and scooped it up. Athena looked at me with mild panic, knowing that she wasn't allowed to play with other balls, and she quickly trotted after the Doberman, who enjoyed this new keep-away game. I laughed, because it was cute, and I let Athena chase the other dog a bit. When it became apparent he didn't want to give up her baseball, I smilingly asked the owner if she wouldn't mind letting Athena have her baseball back, since I always brought it to the park especially for Athena. "There are other balls here. She can get another ball," she replied. I explained that yes, there were, and normally I wouldn't care, but I brought that specific type of ball for Athena's teeth. I patiently told her about Athena's visit with the dentist and "tennis ball attrition", but I might as well have been talking to a trash can. "That's ridiculous," she huffed. "One time isn't going to make a difference."

"Well, maybe not, but really, that's the one she likes, and I brought it here for her on purpose. We can find your dog another ball to play with. Here; I'll look for one for him, and they can both play with a ball," I said, wondering how I had time traveled back to kindergarten.

"Well," she chuckled nastily, "if she can get it back from him, she can have it back," watching as Athena was getting more frantic.

I was starting to get angry, but I realized that this had turned into some kind of contest of wills that she seemed to be relishing, and losing my temper would have fed into her strange need to deny my dog her stupid damn ball. So I changed tactics.

"Wow," I said, starting to laugh as if I appeared to pity her. "So are you not able to tell your dog to drop something? My dog has a command to drop whatever she has, but sometimes dogs just don't listen, huh. Well, okay, you're right. If you can't tell him to drop it, we'll just wait and I'll grab it later when he decides to drop it himself." I told Athena to come, and we started to walk away, as if unconcerned. My change in method worked immediately, because she scurried over and got her dog to drop Athena's baseball, rather than have someone think she couldn't control her dog. Athena reclaimed her baseball, and the lady pointedly ignored us the rest of the visit. Fighting the urge to pelt the woman's head with Athena's baseball, I took Athena and left. At least I was used to the crazy owners at my customary dog park, comfortable with the fact that the regulars respected my dog's attachment to her baseball and my reasoning behind it.

Upon our return to our usual hang out, despite Athena's admirable restraint with the Aussie mix that day, she had gotten a bad reputation after the Parson Russell terrier skirmish. Unbeknownst to me, the little dog had left the park that day with a puncture wound to her neck. Her owners had left with her immediately following the fight, and she hadn't had any obvious outward marks, and no one said anything to Lauren or me. I was grateful Lauren had been there to witness the dog clamping onto Athena's forehead first, because when I returned to the dog park a few weeks later, two board members sitting in the park with their dogs accused Athena of attacking the dog out of the blue and almost killing it. I explained that the dog had bitten Athena first and that I had a friend who saw it happen, but they weren't impressed. I told them I honestly hadn't known that the dog had been injured, and I told them that Athena had pinned it only a short time before Lauren and I broke it up and that a group of other dogs jumped in and kept the fighting going. Athena's canines were flattened, I told them, and I doubted her tooth could puncture very deep.

"Your dog is always causing trouble," one of the ladies snipped. "We're going to put a vote to the rest of the board members to ban her from coming here."

"My dog runs around with her baseball and minds her own business. I've worked really hard with her to keep her out of trouble," I argued.

"Well, I heard she was acting aggressively just two days ago," the same woman continued.

I was starting to get annoyed. "We haven't even been here in two weeks," I said, "so it wasn't her. Is it possible you're thinking of Maggie?" I didn't add "Athena's evil twin," but I could have, even though I really liked Maggie. Maggie was another long-coated German shepherd, who looked a lot like Athena, except she had darker markings and was taller and heavier. She also had, if possible, a shorter fuse than Athena and had been involved in more than a few dog-park scrapes. She was *very* protective of her owner and didn't like other dogs coming near him. Her owner was a suave older European man who wore expensive button-downs and well-cut dress slacks. "Oh, now, Maggie, Maggie, please!" he said whenever Maggie chased dogs away from him, growling. Most of the dogs were startled because they had no earthly idea what they had done wrong. Athena made an error in judgment the day she protested Maggie's demeanor by growling in her face. Maggie outweighed her and had a nastier temper, and she beat the figurative crap out of Athena. When we pulled the two apart, Athena ran behind me and stuck her head and shoulders through my legs peeking out at Maggie in what Jim coined her "docking station" position, like she was a laptop computer stuck securely in its base. "Docking station!" he would chuckle, every time she put her head through my legs, looking out. It was her way of saying either "I want to go home now" or sometimes, "Save me Mom!"

Maggie's owner apologized as Maggie strained, glowering, against his hold on her collar, and I swung my leg over Athena's back so she was out in the open, and told her, laughing, "You started it that time! Don't hide behind me!"

"Oh, poor Athena!" Maggie's dad said. "Maggie, you're a very bad girl. You be nice to poor Athena!"

I really wasn't upset over the scuffle. I was by now used to the fighting style of two rival German shepherds to know that rarely did they ever hurt each other; most of the conflicts were loud bluster and posturing with raised hackles. I examined Athena thoroughly, and other than being a little wet and sandy, she didn't have a single mark on her, and neither did Maggie. Even still, after that, Athena learned her lesson and gave Maggie a wide berth and wisely ignored Maggie's mumbling grumbles from that point on.

The board member who had yelled at us as we entered the dog park shrugged when I asked if she was thinking of Maggie and repeated, "We're going to vote to ban your dog."

Ironically, the whole time this conversation was occurring, Athena, who was chasing her baseball, was being harassed by one of the second board member's two cocker spaniels. I detested both the cocker spaniel, whose name was Murphy, and the board member, who never stood up from the bench the whole time she was at the dog park and would instead sit like a fat empress toad, launching critiques at other owners in between screaming "*MUR-PHY! MUR-PHY!*" Then she would laugh, bragging "I don't own my dogs; they own me!" whenever Murphy paid her no attention; Murphy never relented unless she bribed him with food. An obnoxious, hyper dog who barked constantly and was spoiled and pushy, Murphy ran after Athena every time we were both at the dog park, yapping repeatedly and nipping at her rear end. It was a good thing Athena never stopped suddenly—his nose could have ended up jammed into her anus.

I had asked the board member on prior visits to please get Murphy to stop chasing Athena, saying, "My dog's patience will wear out one day, and he's a lot smaller than she is. And if she gets sick of it and retaliates, she'll be the one in trouble."

Her response was, "He just doesn't like German shepherds. Never has."

I waited for her to elaborate or to say something like, "I'll try to get him to stop," but it never came.

The first board member and I had to raise our voices to be heard over Murphy's loud barking, and I pointed at him chasing Athena and said, "He always bothers her the second she comes here. Why aren't you doing anything about *that*?"

She screeched "*MUR-PHY! MUR-PHY!* Come!" He ignored her completely, as usual, still yapping at Athena's behind.

"*Great* recall, by the way," I said sarcastically. "Your dog listens *so well*!" and gave her a thumbs up. She looked embarrassed and huffy. I didn't care. I had reached my limit.

"Athena, come!" I yelled, and Athena turned and cantered to me, Murphy still at her heels. "Zeet," I commanded, and she sat, ignoring Murphy. "Aus, one more," I said and threw her baseball one last time.

Although a third board member e-mailed me a few days later and told me it was ridiculous that Athena should even be considered a candidate for banning from the park, and although several of my incredulous dog park acquaintances offered to write letters on Athena's behalf, it was just not fun to go there anymore. The whole point of the dog park was to have fun, and I felt like Athena's reputation and mine as an owner would never be free of suspicion, even if Athena was found innocent of an unprovoked attack.

Furthermore, I was upset that owners seemed to have little to no control over their dogs, particularly their small dogs, and allowed them to behave badly. Aggressive little dogs were allowed by some owners to chase and snap at bigger dogs, and while many people found that cute, I did not. I considered it dangerous, and I felt I was asking too much of Athena. I decided not to put her in such a pressured environment ever again, and we stopped visiting dog parks. My dog would never be okay with another dog hanging off her forehead, no matter how much training she had.

27. There's a Doggy on TV, Sports Fans!

I had the only dog in my (admittedly small) circle of dog-owning friends that regularly watched television. Athena didn't just occasionally show interest in a random image; she actively watched from the couch while lying next to me. I glanced at her sideways and saw her eyes moving, sometimes her whole head; she was transfixed by the screen. Any animal—live, animated, person in a suit—excited her to the degree that she pushed herself from the couch, stood in front of the screen barking furiously, sometimes standing and balancing on her hind legs, her front paws braced on my television cabinet. She looked like a jumbo hand puppet from behind, blocking the screen. She bobbed and dipped her head, following the image until she didn't want to stand up anymore, and then she dropped and circled to peek warily at the back of the television cabinet.

Often, she would briskly trot out into the back yard to find the interloper who may have slipped past her. These instances where she went outside were primarily when a dog on television had done the unthinkable—it had growled at, or even worse, bitten a person.

Athena had a fully developed sense of right and wrong when it came to dog-person relations. In her mind, no dog should ever growl at or bite a human. Mindi, Jim's dog, got very possessive over Athena's long-scraped-clean beef bones and would when visiting often take one under her paws while she was lying down and snarl at anyone who got too near her. Mindi made the woeful mistake of growling at me when I accidentally brushed her with my foot as she lay on the floor in front of the couch with one of these bones. Athena, who was in the kitchen at the time, burst into the living room like an avenging spirit, took what seemed to only be two bounds, and had Mindi pinned amidst a cacophony of snarls before I even realized what was happening. I cautioned Jim that he needed to handle his dog and not allow her to become possessive like that. One, it was potentially dangerous to a child if Mindi ever escalated to biting, and two, Athena would take it upon herself to discipline Mindi every time she did that, and sometimes Mindi was alarmingly close to Jim or me or both of us when Athena launched herself. Heedless, she would dive in, Alien Face in full effect, and they would scrap within inches of tender bitable limbs.

Athena's lessons were not very successful. Mindi continued to growl whenever she had a bone underneath her paws, and Jim never corrected her. After a while, unless Mindi turned and snarled at me (a rarity), Athena took to merely giving her a warning glare.

Athena and I enjoyed watching Animal Planet together. Doggies on TV were Athena's favorite thing, and any other animal on TV was a good source of amusement. "Down in front!" I shouted, as she sat right in front of the screen. It was hard to see around her dandelion-puff head and thick pointy ears, especially when she tilted her head first one way and then the other. I always started the viewing by forcing her to sit with me on the couch, but she couldn't seem to keep herself from moving to the floor for a better view.

The only program she didn't care for was the animal shelter rescue show where they temperament-tested a rescued canine using a fake rubber hand. More than one dog reacted badly to the fake hand poking it, and whenever a dog turned and bit the hand, Athena barked furiously at the culprit while standing inches away from the screen before racing out into the yard to find and punish the evildoer. For a while, there was a commercial for gum that featured a terrier who attached itself to a mailman's pant leg, aggressively shaking the material. Because the mailman chewed the particular gum, he stayed cool in the situation; even though the sound effects made it sound like the terrier was skinning the man's thigh. When Athena saw the commercial initially, she got more furious than I have ever seen her at a virtual dog, and she sprang halfway across the room toward the TV screen, not only barking and growling but baring her teeth, her whole ruff and the fur along her spine standing up as her front end bounced up and down with the force of her wrath. She whirled around and goggled at me, her astonished expression asking, "Did you *see that*? Can you *believe* that?" and I had to reassure her that "Yes, Athena, you're right. It is very *naughty* of that doggy on TV to do that. You're right."

She was so incensed that she raised her snout to the ceiling and let out a long howling bark of anger, and then, still fluffed out in her entirety, she stomped outside into the yard. Within seconds she was back in the living room, throwing a glance at the television, staring into the hallway, bobbing her head, trying to locate the terrier. Unsuccessful in her search, she briskly circumnavigated the living room, pausing only to push my front curtain aside with her nose to check for the terrier out front. She peered once more behind the television console, and then she picked up one of her stuffed animals and vigorously shook it. Often, she took out her vengeance on bad dogs on TV by shaking her stuffed animals. It seemed to calm her down. The fur on her neck didn't lie down completely after the gum commercial until she had vicariously punished her giraffe and gotten back up onto the couch. Even so, she remained quite rattled at this blatant disregard for decorum.

The ad was so egregious to Athena, so inflammatory, that I had to quickly change the channel whenever it came on. Even with my hasty snatch of the remote and flick of the button, Athena still raised her head from the couch, snapping to attention, coiled to spring.

"It's nothing, Athena, huh, huh," I'd say, laughing nervously.

She would stare at me with what can only be described as suspicion and then would grudgingly put her head back down.

Like me, Athena enjoys watching sports. She does her excited play-yip when we watch football, baseball, hockey, or basketball. During Major League Baseball, just the pitcher winding up to throw the ball causes her to spring forward, babbling. We go out at halftime during football season and play with her mini-football. For goofs, I put a Chris Cooley jersey on her, and when we play—I'm sure to the annoyance of anyone watching—I instruct her in fake plays as if we were in an imaginary huddle. She has an impressive talent for receiving the snap and catching long bombs. She unfortunately also has an impressive talent for chewing on the football and filling it so full of spit that the inside walls stick together, and I have to wait for it to gasp and wheeze open when she drops it or I won't be able to throw anything resembling a spiral. She knows when number forty-seven comes out that it's time for football, and since she understands the difference between "baseball" "football" and "basketball," when I tell her to go find her "football," she is able to retrieve it from her basket. She wears her Ovechkin shirt during Capitals season, although we don't have a puck to play with. We settle for her deflated basketball, which serves a dual purpose.

One time, during the NCAA basketball tournament, I was cheering a particularly close game, and she was carrying on with me. She must have overheard "basketball" from the announcers, since I never told her to get her basketball; in fact, I never said basketball, period, but somehow she made the connection, because I felt something repeatedly hit my leg, which I ignored until the commercial. When I turned to look at her, she was standing staring at me and wagging her tail, holding her deflated basketball, with which she had been smacking my calf, trying to get my attention so I'd kick it or try and steal it from her. I was amazed, and we played tug for the rest of the game. When my team won, I jumped up and down, yelling, and so did Athena, screaming, "*Wee whoo ur aurrr!*"

If we go to someone's house, and we decide to watch any program on TV, but especially sports, I have to put Athena in a different room.

28. Vanity, Thy Name is Athena

Whenever famous performers are interviewed later in life, not many of them say they were particularly retiring growing up. Most, if not all, brag that they couldn't get enough attention, and relatives confirm that from their earliest age, they were vibrant natural performers. Pint-sized celebrities in *Before They Were Famous* television specials pirouette and shout, looking into the camera the whole time.

That Athena loved a live audience was apparent the first time I visited Megan's and watched Athena's diva-armed entrance into the kitchen. She honed her performing skills with her one-dog show, *I'm Pooping!* that toured wherever she could find an audience. There was also the matter of her stacking at crowded events. I even think that some of the ball games she invented at the dog park were her way to draw attention to herself.

But nothing, nothing, captured Athena's rapt attention like a camera. Somehow she knew instinctively when someone was taking her photograph. From the tiniest digital camera to the bulkiest Polaroid, she managed to turn and look directly into the lens. We had her first "photo shoot" when she was six months old, at Petco. One day they sponsored an animal photographer, much like the one who attempted to take portrait shots of the misbehaving young long-haired shepherd at the *Super Pet Expo!*

The photographer set people's pets against an elegant tan backdrop. At six months, Athena was still a little iffy on following my stay command for longer than thirty seconds, particularly if she was visiting somewhere as stimulating as Petco. Like the budding pro she was, however, she tamped her impatience down long enough to get her picture taken. In fact, she seemed hypnotized by the lens when it was focused on her. As soon as the photographer had captured her image, however, she quickly bounced away into the belly of the store.

"Athena!" I called and had to leave the photographer to retrieve her. I kept barely missing her, as I looked down an aisle and saw her passing at the other end. She looked no guiltier evading me than if she had been out for a perfectly legitimate stroll; in fact, I don't think she had any idea she wasn't supposed to traverse Petco by herself, despite my stern insistence to the contrary. Lauren helped me fetch her by releasing Carman, her Ridgeback mix; Carman was the only individual who Athena listened to one hundred percent of the time, and Carman found her and led her back to me. I fastened Athena's lead—she had finally graduated out of her cat collar and leash—and glowered at her. Since she was six months old and full comprehension wouldn't dawn for another eighteen months or so, she looked up at me with no hesitation, beaming.

"Look at her picture," the photographer showed me. "It's beautiful!"

"Wow. That *is* really nice," I agreed.

The shot showed Athena looking directly into the camera. She hadn't really needed the squeaky toy the photographer used get her attention. The contrast between her picture and Carman's was noteworthy.

Carman was three when she and Athena met. Carman had started out life in a trash bag in West Virginia with several siblings and a feral mother who didn't realize that the rescuers who found the family were trying to help them. Tragically, she died of a gunshot wound when she tried to defend her puppies. Carman retained some of the wildness of her humble beginnings, and she had a gravity about her—a sadness and a wisdom and a natural sensitivity to Lauren and other people around her that was slightly disconcerting in a dog. When you looked into Carman's eyes, you saw something soulful. Athena's eyes, conversely, reflected a vacuous happiness that revealed she had never had a truly harrowing experience in her life. Athena's portraits were quite a hit among her relatives. Since I didn't have children with school pictures to pass out, I gave her grandmother one of the large pictures as well as one of the wallet-sized she could put in her purse. My mother wasted no time in showing everyone her "granddaughter," or as Jim said, her "granddogter." She proudly reported back to me that everyone thought Athena was lovely. Lauren and I traded photos, and she put Athena's on her refrigerator, next to pictures of her actual nieces and nephews.

Athena's next modeling assignment was around Christmas time, when PetSmart hired a Santa Claus to pose with people's pets. With his arm around her, and her forelegs in his lap, Santa and Athena both looked directly at the camera lens; I could hear him mumbling to her during the picture-taking that her "ears were very pretty," and being a sucker for a compliment, she looks bedazzled in the photograph. Carman had her picture taken the same day. Being naturally wary of strangers, she wears an expression that says, "My mother told me to sit with you, but I don't really want to."

Athena always had a natural affinity for the camera. No matter what she was doing, if someone pointed the magic lens at her, she stopped and posed. Even if she were tranquilized, barely able to lift her head, she'd be like Caroline the prom queen in *Sixteen Candles*:

"Smile pumpkin!"

"What? Ohhh, pictures!" Athena would slur, recovering just long enough for the shutter to snap closed.

In public places, Asians of all nationalities want to take her picture. When Liz and I took Athena and Kiera to the Cherry Blossom Festival in Washington, DC, the two shepherds received a lot of attention. Kiera wore her backpack and a bandana around her neck that read "Kiera." Athena just had on her bandana that read "Athena." She seemed hot and uncomfortable in her bandana though, so I removed it. We four stood in line at the snack court. The line to get food and water was long, and Athena started panting quite heavily in the direct sunlight. Liz had started talking to people next to and in front of her in line, and I decided to sit with Athena on a bench nearby in the shade, just so she could cool down a little bit. Athena immediately attracted fans who wanted to pet her.

"What is she?" asked several of the people, which is a question that if I had my way would earn me money every time I heard it. I would fill my swimming pool with doubloons and sidestroke through them. I could play tennis on my adjoining courts based on the second question, "What is she a mix of?" The guesses usually had shepherd in them, paired with everything from golden retriever, collie, and husky. Many people have asked if she's a wolf hybrid, and she has been mistaken for a Belgian Tervuren. Answering the questions gives me an opportunity to talk about long-coated shepherds and how they can't be shown, how it's just a recessive gene, and how, yes, she sheds a lot.

That day in front of the Cherry Blossom food stand, I noticed that Athena, usually a glowing vortex while people petted her and talked about her, was not paying attention. I was mildly surprised and irritated to see her staring, fixated, at something behind me. Her head was turned over her own shoulder like some Hollywood pinup girl, and I turned around to see what she was so busy staring at when there were perfectly nice people to head-tilt for right in front of her. I jumped, taken aback as I found myself inches away from a very large and wide camera lens, pointing almost against the back of my head, but angled toward Athena, who hadn't moved from her pose. An Asian man was busy rotating the lens, getting the focus just right, but he peeked around the viewfinder and gave me a friendly smile before darting back to resume his minute adjustments. I don't know how my dog could possibly have known that someone behind her was taking a picture of her, but she was locked onto the glassy sphere of his lens like a missile. Liz saw all this from the line where she was still waiting, and when we rejoined her and Kiera, she asked, "What was that man doing?"

"Taking Athena's picture," I said.

"Why?" she asked.

"I'm not sure," I admitted.

But that was just the tip of the iceberg. Athena got her picture taken three more times on that trip alone, each time by Asians who were presumably tourists as well. I would hear a gasp, followed by excited exchanges and then the rapid clicks of shutters.

"You're not walking an elephant," Liz said, out of the side of her mouth.

"I know," I said, out of the side of my mouth. "I think they think she might be a wolf."

Whatever it was, Athena's caché as some wild unheard-of beast extended to the most pedestrian of locales, Burke Lake Park in Burke, Virginia. The park features miles of trails around a large lake, a train ride through the woods, a carousel, mini-golf, and Frisbee golf. It's a pleasurable if not particularly exotic place; the most exciting thing we do is when I disobey the signs and let Athena cool off with a dip in the lake. I'm not the only scofflaw, as evidenced by the damp retrievers, spaniels and terriers we pass on the trail.

Athena swimming for the first time was something that I wish I could relive somehow. Until she was two and a half years old, Athena's policy about water was that as long as her feet felt solid ground, she was fine. I was mindful to throw her stick in only so far, because if she had to leave the bottom with her feet, she would complain loudly in her tooth-jarring fashion that the stick was out of her reach and she couldn't possibly fetch it. The crying would start in the water, as she whooshed forward, watching the prize recede, but then she would turn back, emerge, and pace back and forth on the bank, wailing for the stick like it was her long-lost friend drifting away, and I'd have to find her another stick to shut her up. Given that we were flouting the rules by allowing her in the water in the first place, coupled with the echoing properties therein, I wanted to make sure her stick was always in reach for her humpy bounces into the lake. Also, it was harder than it looked to find just the right stick. I had picked up what I thought were sticks to find they were makeshift fishing poles with fishing line and hooks still dangling from them, and I had to put Athena in an emergency platz on the bank so she wouldn't rush forward and truss up her face or impale her lips.

No amount of rah-rah coaching and no number of stern commands would coax her into the water to retrieve her stick if it drifted out of range. One day, however, I was with a male friend on whom Athena had a particularly strong crush, and not knowing the ramifications of throwing her stick too far, he tossed it out beyond what I knew she would brave. Athena surprised me however, by galumphing into the water, intent on getting the stick. I watched her hesitate when she realized that not all four of her feet were on the ground. She bobbed, surged forward, grabbed the stick in her mouth, hurriedly swiveled in the water and turned back. Her paws lost contact with the bottom for maybe two seconds, but she swam back to the bank in a flapping, exaggerated doggy paddle, each front leg breaching the surface of the water entirely before slapping back down. She held the stick carefully, stiffly, her snout raised far above the water. She resembled an old lady in a swimming cap who didn't want her permanent to get wet. We still cheered her as if she had swum the English Channel. Her long hair dripping off her like Spanish moss, she trotted back and forth on the bank carrying her stick, sashaying as flamboyantly as a Lipizzaner.

After that maiden triumph, Athena continued to swim in the lake. It took another nine or so tries before she could actually swim in a fluid dog paddle, which most dogs seen to know instinctively. Before she learned it, Athena splashed and kicked as loudly as she did everything else.

When she learned to swim more quietly, she added a different soundtrack to her stick-fetching routine. After reaching a challenging stick, she grabbed it in her mouth and, on the way back to the bank, began to make the whining, fussy noises she used to make when trying to hide her bone as a puppy. It was a cross between low-level muttering and her chase "*Heh! . . . Heh! . . . Heh!*" She frowned as if deeply concentrating on something. She reached the bank and began her usual flouncing back and forth, imminently cocky about her accomplishment. It was as though in the process of swimming out to the stick and bringing it back to shore, she was conquering her own personal demons.

It was prior to a stick-throwing episode at Burke Lake Park that she and I had the oddest photo opportunity yet. An avuncular-looking Asian man was standing with his camera by the water, taking pictures of ducks. When we walked by, he sucked in his breath and then walked up to us, grinning, gesticulating. Using pantomime, because he didn't speak English, he motioned that he would like to take a picture of Athena by pointing at her and then his camera. "Sure!" I said, smiling, and put her in a perfect Emily Post sit, the lake shining behind her. Athena was already riveted to the camera, ready for her close up. The man moved to stand next to me, and I wondered if he meant to curl his arm in front á la *Thelma and Louise* and take our photo from there, which confused me, because then only the points of her ears would make the shot. Still smiling, he grabbed Athena's leash from my hand and jutted the camera out, twitching it up and down slightly in the universal way of saying "Here, you take it." He showed me the button I would need to push. I stepped in front of the two of them and pointed the camera. Athena didn't seem overly concerned that a strange man had her leash; she seemed to understand that it was a necessary sacrifice in order to get her picture taken. "Okay, look this way!" I said, and the man stood grinning, proudly holding my dog's leash. Afterward, he giggled and bobbed his head slightly, and he continued to chuckle to himself as he walked away, waving. I considered joking, "I charge $5 a photo," but with the language barrier, the humor probably would have been lost. I'm still not sure why he wanted a picture of himself standing with my dog, but Athena did not mind.

Kashka, on the other hand, was like a reclusive double agent when it came to photographs. He had an uncanny ability to know when you were even thinking of picking up a camera. There were, over the years, many perfect Kashka moments I would have loved to immortalize on film, but as soon as I grabbed the camera, he gave me a look of haughty disgust and broke his pose, usually leaving the room entirely. The other trick he performed was to walk directly toward me while I aimed the

camera so THAT HE WAS REALLY CLOSE TO THE LENS; I have many pictures of him that are just a hazy blob of gray. This reticence surprised me, since he made a dramatic entrance into any room, showing up fashionably late so that all my guests could marvel at his beauty. Athena shamelessly made up for his shyness. She never had an unguarded moment in a photograph.

29. Dewey Defeats Truman

In November of 1948, no one expected such an unlikely outcome as Thomas Dewey losing to Harry Truman, and there were things I surely never expected, either. It was a lovely spring day, one of the first warm days of the season. I was out doing some work in my postage-stamp yard with a friend, and Athena was "helping." Helping for her meant she dropped her tennis ball (she hadn't graduated to her baseball yet) into my bubbling pond and watched it bob around.

Using her paw, she tried to pull it toward her to grab it in her mouth again, but usually all she managed to do was push it further away. She went to the other side of the pond and tried to paw it again, but the effect was the same as before. I had to pause in my weeding to retrieve it for her. "No, Athena! Leave it!" I said when I caught sight of her preparing to drop the ball into the water again. She paused and squelched it around in her mouth like a large piece of bubble gum and waited for me to turn my back. "Plop!" I heard, followed by desperate splashing, as she tried to row the ball back to her.

During all this, I was aware of Kashka meowing at me. I looked at my bedroom window, which overlooked my garden, and saw him lying against the screen, looking outside. "Hi, Kashi," I called to him, and I went over to pet the screen, like I was visiting him in jail. He meowed louder. "Do you want me to come in and visit you?" I asked, only dimly realizing that I asked my animals a lot of questions. Kashka gurgled. I halted my chores and went inside to see him. Athena didn't follow me, because she still had helping to do, and, also, she had a crush on my friend and wanted to stay outside with him.

"Hi, Kash," I said, as I petted Kashka's fur, warm from the patch of sunlight in which he was lying. He looked, I thought, rather longingly outside. "You can come outside," I told him, and even though Athena was already outside, I saw her perk up at the favorite word and walk over to the window where Kashka was lying. I was expecting Kashi to hiss and spring from his window seat, but he stayed put. Perhaps the screen offered some sense of security. "Well, come outside if you want," I told him without much hope that he would listen to me.

When I started to leave my bedroom, I was surprised to hear the jingle of his tag and bell as he jumped down and followed me out into the living room, then into the kitchen. I opened the screen door and stepped outside, and he stopped, sitting on the threshold. I left the screen slightly ajar and turned away. I turned back just in time to see him step gingerly down into the yard. Athena was interested to see Kashka in a position other than running away from her or hiding underneath a bed, and she came over to investigate.

I thought for sure that Kashka's nerve would fail and that he'd rush back indoors, but instead I saw him freeze, wince, close his eyes, and hunker down. His demeanor seemed to say, "Just take me!" Athena sniffed him for a few seconds, but then she simply stared at him. Kashka opened his eyes and stood up. Eyeing a particularly green section of grass, he turned his head sideways and began chewing on it. Athena found this activity enthralling, and so she put her nose down and began chewing from the same patch of grass, mere centimeters away from Kashka, who lifted his head and stared at her. His look, however, was different from any he had previously given her. Since the beginning, his expression when he looked at her always contained unconcealed disgust and hatred, but as she nibbled the grass next to him, I watched his eye-lids lower halfway in the contented happy way he regarded friends. He sent his whiskers forward and leaned toward her.

What occurred next caused my jaw to actually drop. I never believed people when they said their jaws dropped over something, but mine really did. Kashka gently but convivially bumped Athena's long nose with his forehead and then stood up and rubbed his cheek, shoulder, and side along her face, ending with a slight curl of his tail around her muzzle like he was giving it a brief hug. Athena responded by licking Kashka's head, unfortunately a little too eagerly, because he shook rapidly, setting his tag and bell ajangle. Then he just plodded away in the heavy lion-like way I had missed over the past several months.

"Did you see that?" I whispered to my friend. He nodded, equally shocked. "Good *boy*, Kashka! Good *girl*, Athena!" I praised quietly. I was suddenly aware that behind my sunglasses, my eyes were filling with tears.

As he was wont to do, Kashka threw up the grass a little bit later, and convinced he had been ill, perhaps delirious, I chalked up his bravery

192

around and downright affection for Athena as a fluke. But that evening, Kashka came into the living room like there was nothing unusual about it, even though Athena was lying on her "Athena" pillow in plain view. "Eh, eh, eh, *eh?*" he asked.

"Hi, Kashi," I said, my voice indicating that he was honoring us with his presence.

Athena got up and stood over him, sniffing his entire body loudly. Kashka flinched slightly but let her. When she got a little too interested in his rear end, he turned in a flash, sat on his haunches, and grabbed either side of her snout with his large front paws. He was holding her muzzle with his claws slightly out, but it was more emphatic than violent, and he licked her nose and then gave her a soft bite. Athena averted her eyes and didn't move. When he released her and sat back down, Athena backed up. I thought it was an extraordinary interspecies interaction, one animal gently but firmly indicating a boundary, and the other respecting it.

Athena panted and wagged her tail, staring at her newfound friend, following his every move. Each flick of his tail, motion to jump, and paw lick was mesmerizing to her. What she didn't find fascinating was that Kashka decided the most comfortable, coveted spot to lie down was dead center of her "Athena" pillow. With his paws tucked in, he was a small gray loaf ensconced in the vast square Washington Redskins' burgundy and gold of her bed. Athena didn't approve of this turn of events, and she tried without success to nose him off. She didn't quite dare use full force and instead made little darts in, whining. My cat, who used to quake at the very idea of Athena, sat like a spoiled pasha, blinking up at her unconcernedly. When she came in once too closely, he hissed and swatted at her nose. But he didn't get further agitated, and indeed there was something very smug in the way he stayed put.

Athena turned and looked at me then with an almost human look of stunned chagrin. "She looks like she might actually cry," my friend said, and it was true: her eyes had a sheen. Kashka, my little Napoleon, meanwhile, was by now sound asleep. Athena kept looking at me and then back at Kashka, and the look clearly said, "Do something!" I explained that Athena would have to learn how to share, and to ease the confusion of being suddenly second in command to her big little brother who was approximately an eighth of her weight, I coaxed her onto the couch next to me.

After that, I made sure to feed both of them hot dog in the kitchen together, so I could demonstrate to Athena that I got a bite, then Kashka, then her. She tried to steal his hot dog at first, because she of course finished hers without chewing and he purr-gnawed his with excruciating slowness. She learned very quickly that Kashka was the dominant animal, because I never allowed her to steal his food. So Athena would watch this tiny blob that barely came up to her knees chew his meat, and she would wait patiently and politely for him to finish before she would lick the floor, in case he had missed any.

She learned the rules quickly and displayed honorable patience and good manners whenever they got treats. As I passed out delicious tidbits like Rotisserie turkey or leftover chicken, she didn't even attempt to get his and sat with earnest restraint, awaiting her turn.

Kashka's renaissance of bravery, however, also meant he got a little too pushy sometimes, and although I discouraged him from throwing his weight around, sometimes he sniffed around Athena's food bowl while she was eating or stretched his nose towards one of the stuffed animals she was holding. The first time Athena growled at him, I had to—just for the simple fact that one bite from her could kill him—severely discipline her. A growl at Kashka meant a decisive and strong pin from me. It got so that if Kashka so much as even walked into the kitchen while Athena was eating, she turned her head sideways, and backed away from her own food bowl just in case he might want her dinner. With my assurance that she could eat—I always pushed Kashka away—she relaxed. Soon she paid him not an ounce of attention when he would daintily drink water from her bowl, right next to her, while she snuffled and crunched the contents of her meal.

Once Kashka had returned from self-exile, he learned quickly how to use the dog door, and he crawled through it regularly. Whether he recognized his yard now, or just didn't go very far, I don't know, but he never ran away or got lost. And Athena was always perfectly happy to "Such Kashka!" if I didn't see him right away. She played search-and-rescue dog and could locate him in the most obscure places indoors. Outside, she would make a direct path to one of my bushes, and I could always tell she had located him, because her puffy tail would start to wag. She seemed very pleased to herd him back through the flap for me.

Kashka resumed doing things he hadn't done since he was younger, such as watch birds and go outside in the rain. One night, as I listened to a downpour whispering outside, I heard the dog flap open, realizing it was Kashka going out. He didn't want to stay in the rain for long, apparently, because I heard him claw his way back inside within a minute or two. He bounced, chirruping, into the living room, demanding to be dried. Kashka's fur was uniquely downy, and when it got rained on, it didn't really get wet but stood up in peaks like gray meringue. Still, I would always wipe him off with paper towels. I got up and he followed me, still gurgling and now purring loudly as well, into the kitchen, circling my ankles as I ripped off several paper towels.

"Look at you! Oh, my, you were in the rain, Kashi," I said, as I had said countless times before. I rubbed his soft fur rather vigorously, turning the paper towel over and draping it over his back like a saddle, as the ritual dictated. Kashka walked along with it on his back for a few paces before I picked it up again and dried his tail, something he still seemed to enjoy especially well.

Athena demonstrated just how much she viewed Kashka as her superior one morning when she tried to go outside to eat her chicken leg. Whenever she got chicken parts, she always liked to eat them alfresco, on my walkway, whereas eggs she preferred to eat in the kitchen, where she could hurl them down onto the floor to crack them open and then lap them up. On this particular morning, Kashka was lying in front of the dog door, as if he wasn't sure he wanted to go out or not. Athena was so nervous to step over him to go outside that she instead tried to maneuver around him, and, glancing at him sorrowfully, holding her drumstick, she voluntarily banged her own forehead on the top of the flap rather than crouch down properly, which might have inflamed him, being so close. I lifted Kashka out of her way, but it was amazing to see Athena so hesitant and willing to endure discomfort. I praised her and thanked her for her nice gesture, rubbing her head where she had hit it. She seemed relieved to be able to glide through her flap normally with Kashka out of the way.

I began to notice when I came home from work that Kashka would often greet me with his hair suspiciously wet and lying against the grain on his forehead and shoulders. Since Athena greeted me without a single scratch on her, I figured her cleanings were not unwelcome. Kashka was still shy around her Redwood legs, as Athena wasn't too discriminating as to where she put her feet when she was excited, and he liked to stay between the rocking chair and the wall when she trotted around the room. Not long after their miraculous truce, they began to sit on the couch with me at the same time, one on either side of me. I made sure to pet them both equally, and although it was slightly claustrophobic, it was also soothing to sit there all together.

Kashka's novelty wore off quickly for Athena, as did his terror of her. Often, I would get up in the morning to find the baby gate pushed open, Athena on her back looking at me upside down, and Kashka standing impatiently next to her, yowling for his Fancy Feast. He often got buffeted while she scrambled to get up and bring me a stuffed animal, her standard greeting, but hunger made her flailing limbs merely a bother to Kashka rather than an ordeal. He flinched and ducked, still meowing.

For Halloween that year, I went to a friend's costume party dressed as the Julie Newmar version of Catwoman from the *Batman* television series. It was quite late when I started the drive home, and I realized with dismay that Kashka was out of Fancy Feast. I had dry food, but he would no more eat that than turtle turds, so I knew I would be in trouble if I came home empty-handed. The only store still open at that hour was 7-Eleven, so I had to go into the store dressed as Catwoman in my black suit, ears, and mask. The proprietor was a short wizened man in a turban, and, clearly delighted by my getup, he brightened and followed me around the store as I perused the aisles looking for the pet food section. My face hot, I took several cans from the shelf, pausing to also grab a can of Alpo, the only dog food I could see, just to let him and anyone else know that I had a dog, a big dog, at home waiting for me. I was not unaware of how bizarre it looked, being in a Julie Newmar outfit, buying Fancy Feast. I looked like some fetish call girl, on my way to a strange date.

When I got to the counter, the man couldn't have been more tickled by my purchases. "You buy cat food . . . And you are a cat," he sang, and if memory serves me correctly, I think he even clapped.

"Yeah, it's for Halloween," I said, laughing, pointing at myself. He grinned, but no recognition registered on his face.

"Have a good night," I mumbled, hightailing it out of the store.

When I fed Kashka, I told him he had better be grateful. The next morning, I dumped the Alpo into Athena's bowl, snickering, because it was so far removed from what I normally gave her. When I placed her bowl back into her raised wire holder, I said words I never thought I'd ever utter in my life: "Kashka, please get your face out of Athena's bowl and let her eat her Alpo."

His tiny gray head jammed up tight next to her large dog mouth, both of them gobbled with unnerving hillbilly zeal. I tried to pull him away and hold his chest, but he could still be strong when he wanted something, and he wanted her Alpo more than he had ever wanted almost anything in his life. He squirmed out of my clasp, and to ensure that he got his fair share, he stood on his hind legs, forcing his front paws into her bowl and then struggled to get traction to climb completely into it. Athena was not bothered by this at all, and merely ate around his feet. Kashka and Athena from that point on shared leftover plates of food I set down, ravishing the contents like two feral strays; he was unfazed being millimeters away from her huge crushing teeth, and she was similarly unconcerned by his interference. On these occasions, both acted like I never fed them.

Kashka's behavior on Christmas Eve one year solidified just how far he had come. I was in the middle of my traditional viewing of *It's a Wonderful Life*, and Athena, who had been visiting with me at Gamma's that day, was lying against me on the couch, sleepily holding a stuffed animal in her mouth, and struggling to keep her eyes open. When she is about to go to sleep, often she will cuddle a soft toy in her mouth, which I think of as the equivalent of a child's pacifier or security blanket.

Christmas Eve at my mother's was a fun but draining time for her. My family had all convened at my mother's for dinner, and Athena promptly inserted herself as the obvious star guest of the gathering. My mother had bought Athena Christmas presents, and she asked if I wouldn't mind her opening them there, since the next morning we were re-reconvening at another relative's who didn't have a particularly dog-friendly house, and Athena was not invited. Curious, boldly sticking her snout into the bag of goodies, Athena watched as my mom pulled out various wrapped packages. I opened the paper for her, after dutifully reading the tag (the niceties always must be observed in my family), and Athena watched every tear and rustle like a hawk, with shiny eyes and open mouth.

Athena and Kashka both seemed to understand when they were getting presents. I'm sure other pet owners can vouch that as silly as it sounds, their pets are the same way. One of Athena's gifts was a squeaky toy, and she pulled it from me before the paper was even completely off, her tail crazily spiraling, and wasted no time in squeaking it at the approximate speed of a jackhammer. This caused everyone to laugh, which only encouraged her to stand in front of every single seated family member in turn, taking care to show each person for a suitable duration just how enjoyable she found her new toy. She politely left no one out, and even carefully negotiated her way around the coffee table, where she stared at the next person in the receiving line like she was a loud, squeaky Queen Elizabeth. She was quite concerned that all assembled benefit from a private audience.

"She really likes it," my mom crowed, which was difficult to hear over the rapid squealing of the toy. When she got to the end of the circle, I had to grab Athena's collar so she didn't start round two.

Glad handing always exhausted her, and she lay sleepily on the couch as I geared up for the cathartic, happy tears I would shed watching George Bailey celebrate with his friends and Clarence getting his wings. Suddenly, I heard a series of short pulsing growls coming from Athena, not scary growls but the sound she made when something was irritating her, like her version of grumbling.

"What is it, Ath—" I started to say, and then I looked at her and burst out laughing. Kashka had decided that he wanted to be on the other side of me to cuddle, and he figured the shortest distance between Athena and me was over Athena's body. So taking halting steps on the uneven terrain, he made his unsteady way over her, pausing to regain his footing here and there. At one point he had to balance partially on her neck and forehead, bracing his hind foot against her brow bone. Athena rolled her eyes at him grumpily but didn't move her mouth from around her stuffed animal. Kashka mewed brightly at me when he reached me, not intimidated at all.   Kashka was by now fourteen years old, and certainly he looked it. Although he had the spirit of a younger cat, his body had shrunk, and he was starting to waver slightly physically; he occasionally missed jumps that before he would have sailed with ease. His kidneys were diagnosed as in failure, so he had to drink a lot of water and urinate frequently, and he had unfortunate poo accidents outside his litter box sometimes. I supplemented his one box with three others strategically placed around his bedroom, but he still occasionally missed.

Athena had made me immune to picking up crap, however, and I just cleaned them off the floor and praised him mightily when I came across any he had properly left in one of his boxes. He also was more cantankerous than he used to be and more demanding, and I mimicked how he would sound if he could talk: "Give me mah food! Dagnabbit! I don't *care* if I just ate fifteen minutes ago. Just give it tah me!"

Given his advanced age, the first time Kashka met Kiera, I was apprehensive. Athena was a calm glassy sea next to the roiling storm that was Kiera, and I was certain that she would either stomp him to death or petrify him into heart failure with her antics. But Kashka's partisanship of Athena seemed to have fed a latent adoration in him of all things canine, and Kiera calibrated her energy down to previously unseen levels around Kashka. As a result, Kashka fell head over heels in love with Kiera. Athena still was a bit rough in showing love, and she kissed him rather sloppily, whereas Kiera gave him slow tender baths that caused him to close his eyes in bliss. Whenever Kiera visited now, no matter where he was in the house, he quickly inserted himself into the middle of the shepherd mix, unconcerned if he got knocked almost completely over by the beige tree trunks of Athena's legs. Emitting an irritated squawk, he shook his head violently, but recovered and twisted his way underneath Kiera, insistent on getting his wash, which she caressingly administered, head to tail base.

"Kashka, your girlfriend is here!" I always called when Kiera skittered through the front door. When we all went to the kitchen for snacks, Kiera learned within seconds who was the most important member of the household. Like Athena, she sat in perfect obedience waiting for him to eat his treat first. Watching him, my frail little old man, confidently chew his tidbit next to two hulking dogs towering over him was both endearing and comical.

When I ate, and whenever I had guests over to eat, I shut Kashka in his bedroom, because Kashka, when he wanted something, was borderline scary. He had, growing up, restrained table manners around people eating; the most blatant naughty thing he did was to walk near my plate once and "accidentally" wipe his tail completely through what I was eating. After that, however, a sharp, "No!" dissuaded him from getting near anyone's food, and he would stay at a respectable distance, glancing at you periodically, waiting to see if anything interesting was coming his way.

Age had caused him to throw out any semblance of good manners. He routinely coiled his arm around my hand as it was poised to put food into my mouth, as he attempted to pull it to *his* mouth. Using the force of his strong shoulder, it was an effective technique, and even though I yelled at him to stop, elbowing him to the floor, he was undeterred and would jump on me repeatedly. I would have to finally pick him up as he went dead weight and carry him into his bedroom and shut the door. He had also gotten surprisingly indiscriminate as to what he begged for; the obvious contenders—chicken, turkey and fish—had been supplemented by pancakes, chips, pastries, and even the occasional green bean.

So one night when Liz and Kiera were visiting, I knew our chicken nuggets would cause Kashka to crawl all over us, demanding, "Give it tah me! I don't care if it's yours! I want it! Feed me! I don't care!" So I put him in his room with a freshly opened can of Fancy Feast to placate him. Kiera and Athena both knew the ramifications of even staring at us while we ate and sat at a discreet distance. Neither of us permitted our dogs to sit and stare at us with long icicles of drool coming off their mouths. When we finished, I let Kashka out of his room. He came out with the handles of a plastic bag wrapped around his waist, empty cat food cans clanking and dragging behind him like he had been decorated as a "just married" car.

"Kashka! What did you do?" I asked, and he blinked at me and stood waiting for me to extricate him from his trash apron. Liz decided I had, in fact, the calmest cat alive. She said if her family's cat had managed to do the same thing, he would have zoomed around in a complete melt down before disappearing for a week. Kashka merely seemed mildly annoyed, and in fact, I think there was a part of him that enjoyed shocking us.

Although Kiera was his girlfriend, he reserved his most ardent love for a mystery admirer. Kashka by this time liked to come outside at lunch with Athena and me; he seemed to enjoy watching her chase her baseball and took the opportunity to also scratch sticks, eat grass, or weave between my legs. He was back to his old vigor, at least mentally. Although he was tottery and skinny with hardly any muscle mass left— a shadow of his former bodybuilder physique—he exhibited none of the timidity he used to before Athena came along. Indeed, he seemed much braver now, as if sensing that his giant younger sister would protect him, as doubtless she would.

Athena was blasé about him by this point, and the tables had turned to him elaborately rubbing himself on her nose, turning and going back the other direction until she licked him. I could see the impatience in her face, and she would give him a few kisses to placate him, but her whole demeanor was, "Yeah, yeah, okay, here. Now move; I'm chewing something." So when Kashka came in from the yard for his first morning can of food one day and I saw his fur sodden, I was confused; Athena didn't lavish him with that much affection normally. It was Lauren who solved the mystery of his dishabille for me.

Cody and Carman were visiting one afternoon, and Cody made a beeline for Kashka's room, looking for him. Kashka emerged, sleepy, and I watched Cody slather him, almost tipping Kashi over in his enthusiasm. Rather than being alarmed, Kashka braced his paws and looked as ecstatic as I have ever seen him, save for infrequent hedonistic bouts rolling in catnip. After Cody was finished, Kashka was soaked, his coat turned up in crazy disarray.

"Wow, Cody and Kashka seem to really like each other!" I said to Lauren. We both watched then as Kashka thudded up to Carman, who gave him two brief tidy licks before turning away.

"Oh, you should see them together in the common area," Lauren said.

"What? They've been outside with him?" I asked, confused.

"Yeah," she said. "I take the two of them out in the early morning, so they can run, and he comes out from under your fence and goes right over to them. It's funny, because even if they are in mid-chase, both will stop and come over to him very slowly. It's like they know he's old and a little unsteady. Cody slobbers over him and then Kashka rubs himself underneath Carman's belly to wipe himself off." Lauren laughed.

"I didn't know he'd been doing this," I said, astonished. "How often?"

"Oh pretty much every morning he comes out to visit them. They love him," she assured me.

I looked over at Kashka as he slowly ambled into the kitchen. I was deeply touched that he went out of his way to visit his dog friends, even more so when I found out that they both halted their fun running and playing to approach him so gently.

Kashka's newfound love of canines spilled over to Mindi as well. Although she had a driving urge to chase cats while outside, Mindi responded to Kashka quietly and wagged her tail whenever he made an appearance. She especially liked to watch him eat his soft food in his bedroom. "Mindi," Jim would call from the next room in a warning tone, not wanting her to bother Kashka.

"She's in here," I'd call back. "She's fine; she's just hanging out."

Mindi, who turned into a demon-possessed witch around her borrowed bones, never growled at Kashka when he was in the living room. She snarled at anyone else who came near, but never him.

I don't know how his dog friends understood his frailty, but they did. And I had to give my tough little cat props. Even though he looked excessively leggy and his feet seemed even larger now that his body was so skinny and those same legs trembled slightly now when he stood still, and even though he had trouble grooming himself and often didn't (I had to brush mats out of his once luxuriant fur and wipe his bottom on several occasions), and even though he occasionally had accidents on the floor, he ate heartily at every hobbit meal, enthusiastically begged for treats in between meals, had mini-adventures in the yard, jumped on the countertops, and even left me a dismembered fledgling he had somehow caught.

And so, Kashka became one of the gang, so much so that he followed me to Lauren's one night to say hello to his friends. It was a blustery cold night in late winter. At Lauren's, whose back door faced mine, just across the common area, Cody, Carman and Athena were wreaking havoc in her living room, or as she referred to it, her "romper room," chasing each other. Lauren had just adopted a large female Persian named Fireball that no one could take in, and the cat was in a crate in a spare room; Lauren thought she would feel more secure if she wasn't left to roam around too much at first. I went home to grab my cell phone, and when I got there, Kashka was chatting and babbling, and I petted him and humored him with, "Yeah? Okay! Yeah! Oh, yes, that is interesting, Kashi!" We had many of these nonsensical conversations, but they seemed to please him; I know they pleased me.

When I made my way out the back to return to Lauren's, Kashka followed me out, still gurgling, using Athena's dog flap. "Kash, I have to go, okay?" I said. He wasn't done, apparently, because he followed me out of my yard into the common area. Still talking, he followed me as a cold wind swept through the open field. "Kashi, you're walking very far with me," I said. We were almost to Lauren's sidewalk. The wind ruffled his sparse fur, and I was worried he would get cold or blown over, so I picked him up and carried him partially in my coat.

"I think I know what you want," I told him.

I brought him into Lauren's, and Cody practically knocked me over, jumping in midair, trying to lick Kashka. It was mayhem in the house; Athena, Carman, and Cody were excited by my return as well as the fact that I had Kashka with me. When I put Kashka down, he walked around the house like he had been there hundreds of times, stalking around, exploring everything. I told Lauren that he couldn't stay long, because his weak kidneys meant he couldn't go long without urinating.

"Well, would he use Fireball's litter box, for the time being?" she asked. I said we could find out. I had already shown him where the water bowl was. I coaxed Kashka upstairs with me, and he walked into Fireball's room. Fireball screeched and yowled at him from within her crate, hissing. Kashka, even though Fireball was probably double his weight, got a little of his old swagger back and blinked calmly, staring at her. He climbed into her litter box, and, still staring at her, took a long, satisfying pee. He then walked by her as cool as a cucumber and went back downstairs, intent on seeing if Lauren had any food for him in the kitchen. He knew no matter where he was the significance of a refrigerator, and he stood under her refrigerator door, meowing. The small cat and the three big dogs all got something yummy, and then Kashka inserted himself in the middle of lapping tongues and drool spatters as he and all three dogs drank from the same water bowl.

I knew by looking at him when he was ready to go back home, so I picked him up and carried him back. This time, he didn't follow me when I turned around to return to Lauren's. It made me happier than anything in a long time to see my beloved Kashka confidently take matters into his own paws again. It was the confirmation I needed, to know that the large silly German shepherd I had brought home had made his life enjoyable again in his August years.

30. Shepherd Girl

Sometimes I still look at Athena, now with a white soul-patch on her muzzle, stretched on the floor unconscious, and I am stunned to realize that there's a *big dog* in my house. Even saying aloud, "I own a German shepherd," causes me to frown, slightly puzzled, as if the reality hasn't sunk in even all these years later. I'm always bubbling with warm pride when someone asks, "What kind of dog do you have?" and I say, with a crisp nod of my head, "A German shepherd," but in private, I'm secretly baffled. When I look at her or even picture her in my mind, I see vestiges of the puppy she used to be, trying to hide her bone or hold back vomit or destroy my living room, but most often I only see a long swath of pink tongue.

I read an article once that discussed what a dog meant when it wagged its tail more to the right versus to the left. It was interesting, but what caught my attention was that it stated that a dog that showed a lot of tongue and had a relaxed open mouth was content and happy, that it really was, in fact, the dog version of a smile. I'm sure most, if not all, dog owners who read that article thought, "Duh."

Indeed, if the article was accurate, Athena is the happiest, most contented dog imaginable. I don't take the bulk of the credit for this; Athena is by nature a carefree individual. I'm still amazed at what an easygoing, pleasant companion she is. Our favorite way to sit is with her in a platz, leaning against me, my arm draped around her shoulders. I love that she loves to eat crackers with me on the couch, and I love the way she hulas across the floor when she brings a toy to me. When I go out walking, anywhere, I feel secure. We watch out for one another. I get as giddily excited about asking her, "Would you like to come sleep with Mama?" as she does when I ask her.

I never allowed her in bed with me at night as a puppy, which in hindsight was probably a good choice, as it likely would have set her dominance-meter exploding. Now, however, I'll allow her to lie next to me on the bed while I read or go back to sleep in the morning. When I ask her, she gets so beside herself that she hunches her shoulders and opens her mouth to opossum-like proportions, her eyes gleaming crazily. When she takes the maiden leap onto my bed (she knows on which side she is allowed), she spends a few seconds on her back, emitting a low grunting noise that she only makes when deeply happy. It's a noise between Karl Childers's "Mmm hmm" from *Sling Blade* and a bassoon. Besides when doing the bed roll, the only other time she will make the noise is when Jim massages the base of her ear.

In the beginning, it took her a while to get settled. Having me lying next to her proved too novel, and she would either freeze in her upside-down position, staring at me whitely, her lips falling away from her teeth, or she would wait until I made a millisecond glance in her direction, and I would end up with a sopping face. Attempts to evade her licks sent her into playful bliss, and she would forget her size, flopping down on me or pawing me, both culminating with another subsonic grunt. After the first few times, she routinely made sure to grab whatever stuffed animal was her favorite at the moment, and she brought it to bed with us. Holding it in her mouth, she unheedingly lay down (occasionally next to rather than on top of me), grunted, and fell asleep with her head on the pillow. I feel strange now, trying to sleep without her next to me.

She and Kashka made my dreams come true by sleeping side by side on the couch, something I discovered when I was restless one night and turned on the light in the living room. Both winked at me blearily, back to back.

The abiding love I feel for her doesn't mask her bad habits she never outgrew, which I fully acknowledge. She does a radar-gun maneuver in the car, barking at rock-concert decibel levels at cars that we pass. The habit is slightly less annoying now that I traded in my Civic for a CR-V, so she has her own area in the back, blocked by a safety grate. Large trucks transport her barks to multi-syllabic bawling, and my windows are smeared with nose prints, since she presses her nose against them with almost every bark. I've gotten used to the noise, but she has caused many passengers of mine to jump in their seats. It gets particularly bad on two-lane roads. I can usually stop a bark before it comes out, but she still lets out a pinched yelp, which is something of an improvement, if not much for my unfortunate passengers.

Playing outside with her is sometimes undeniably boring, as she has not ever abandoned her love of creating her own games, paying me little mind. For all the trembling eagerness she shows when she knows I am taking her out to chase her baseball, it only lasts a throw or two.

Then she carries the ball around, laying it down next to her as she pulls out large sticks that always seem to be in piles. She alternates between holding the stick and the ball, lunging at both as if she has an imaginary playmate who is trying to steal them from her. I stand there with basically nothing to do but watch her. As per usual, she is content with this arrangement. When I see dogs who torment their owners with endless requests to throw their ball, bringing it back, dropping it, I feel mild envy; I have to interrupt Athena's ball/stick game to get her to bring me the ball so I can throw it.

As she grew from a puppy to an adult, Athena didn't seem to understand that she'd progressively gotten bigger. When she was a puppy, she liked to hide under my bent knees when I sat on the floor, as though hiding in her own private tepee. She found this spot most pleasant when she had something to chew. When she grew up, she still liked to burrow under my bent knees whenever I sat on the floor, but the end result was that I tipped over backward, because she dove underneath and had to squirm in. She never seemed to realize or mind that the only way we could still sit that way anymore was with my feet several inches off the ground, her tepee essentially collapsed on top of her.

My mother, sister, and I were sitting on my sister's tidy love seat one night, watching a melodramatic Lifetime movie, making wisecracks. My sister patted her lap (she was in between mom and me) for Athena to sit with us. Athena complied by jumping up on top of everyone, and after we'd all said some variant of "Oof," my mother promptly started to complain. Athena's rump and hind legs were on my lap, her stomach on my sister, and her front paws on Mom. She seemed to recognize that only one of us wanted her up there, really, and she gave a tiny tea-sandwich lick first to my mom's cheek, then to my sister's, and then somehow to me, by bending her head backwards like a seal. We watched the rest of the movie all crammed together on the sofa with giant Athena spread across our laps.

"Here we are, just us girls," my mom said, patting Athena's legs, finally accepting the circumstances. Athena didn't laugh or make fun of Meredith Baxter Birney's character's histrionics, but I think she had a good time just the same.

As mentioned, Athena hates swimming in a swimming pool. A murky, rocky, uneven-bottomed, slimy, stinking lake is just fine. Also fine: fountains and other inappropriate public monuments. Athena happily jumped into the hallowed Reflecting Pool on the Mall in Washington, DC, when Liz and I took her and Kiera to play Frisbee on the grassy expanses.

"Athena, get out of there!" I shouted at her, and she, as usual found a way to obey and disobey at the same time by detouring with the Frisbee in her mouth at the last second, plunging into the water, and quickly turning around, exiting the water. She jumped in the World War II Memorial fountain as well, using the jets of water like a Waterpik, squinting and biting quickly and repeatedly with her front teeth exposed.

"You can't go in there," I said as Kiera joined her and the two dogs began leaping and frolicking.

"No, girls," Liz and I moaned, trying with as little fanfare as possible to get them out of the fountain quietly.

"Athena!" I commanded, and I had to tighten my lips, because she looked at me with completely uninhibited, ridiculous joy, the fur on her forehead and mane sticking up like disarrayed hedgehog quills. We finally got them out, and I whispered, "I'm sorry. I'm so sorry," to a guard who came over to tell us to keep our dogs out of what is essentially a sacred, serious place of meditation and reflection honoring the brave men and women who fought for and died for our country. Athena and Kiera both looked up at the female guard with identical, guileless, beaming wet smiles, and she couldn't help but soften and laugh.

The guard wasn't the only spectator tickled by the dogs' exuberance. An elderly couple—a frail yet proud-looking soldier in a wheelchair, who was covered with a blanket in the eighty-two-degree heat, along with who I presume was his wife—were seated nearby, and I heard them chuckle as Liz and I walked Athena and Kiera out of range of temptation. I heard the man say in a tremulous voice, "They sure liked that fountain. I guess they were hot." His companion said fondly, "Oh, yesss. Yes." They gave us and the dogs friendly looks, and I wanted to hug them.

I never have figured out why Athena refuses to go into a swimming pool. Recently my condominium had an end-of-the-season "dog swim" at our community pool, and I took Athena, thinking that this time, maybe finally, would be the time she'd try. She did not. She had her shoulders shrugged up in glee as she loped around the pool, and many people tried to coax her in all the way. Instead, she went down two steps and then froze, blocking other dogs as she squashed herself against the wall of the pool and watched Labs and pointers splash and play. A fellow German shepherd passed within inches of her, back and forth, easily entering the pool and then climbing the stairs out again, but she remained firmly rooted to her spot. The pinnacle of humiliation was when we watched a long-haired Chihuahua the size of a guinea pig paddle by right in front of her. I tried to take her to the baby pool, where the water level was no higher than my shins, but she stood with her front paws splayed at the lip of the pool deck, and I ended up in the pool myself, scooping a ball out of the water for her so she could repeatedly drop it back in. An English bulldog wearing a buoyant safety vest floated by, wheezing and snorting.

As maddening, selectively bright, egotistical, clumsy, and goofy as Athena is, she is undeniably my shepherd girl.

I think back sometimes on her early puppyhood behavior, and I realize that she and I were dismayingly similar as youngsters. I was hyperactive, bossy, and not great with eye contact or empathy. I was also a drama queen whose feelings got hurt easily and who cried a lot. I was happiest when I was obsessively rocking on my spring horse, and I used to only feel completely secure when I had my worn flannel baby blankie shoved up against my nose. Athena's frantic obsession with first her bone, then her ball, reminded me of my addiction to my horse. Her holding a stuffed toy in her mouth when anxious or sleepy I recognized in myself with my blanket, and later, with my bite guard. I have TMJ, so I have to bite on a ridiculous rainbow-shaped piece of rubber when I sleep. I have made the mistake of talking while it was in, much to the delight of several friends and ex-boyfriends who thought it funny to mimic my garbled speech.

"Let me see your bite guard," Mike used to tease me, poking the corner of my mouth with his finger. When I removed it to lecture him on the rudeness of people poking their finger at other people's mouths, he said, "You're just like your dog. She has to have a toy in her mouth, and you have to have that thing!" I had to stop and concede his point.

Athena and I share being super-confident and gregarious in large crowds, although I think that we both are a bundle of over-stimulated nerves in them also. I know our backs both go out when we have exerted ourselves too much, and between us we have bumped into more objects than I can count. We are, also, quick to anger if we feel someone has slighted us unfairly. On the plus side, we both are joyful about simple pleasures and find amusement in most anything. I'm a happy person overall, if a bit vacuous, and in profile we look alarmingly similar—her with her "Yay, fun!" expression and me with a vague smile. I realize it's a cliché to say "Dogs and their owners start resembling each other." I know. With my dog and me, it's become some kind of symbiotic personality trade-off that happened as soon as I unconsciously picked the weird puppy I did. From then on we fed off each other. The bottom line though, is that I'm completely, unapologetically in love with my dog. I love her as openly and as madly as that first night I held her smelly sleeping puppy body to me.

On July Fourth, a few years ago, my grandmother, who used to secretly toss scraps to poor lonely Maxel, and who had been my cheerleader, defender, and all-around best pal, died. Her death, while inevitable, had always seemed impossible to me. I thought if anyone could debate her way out of or strong-arm death, it was she. It was altogether fitting that she died on July Fourth—our shared favorite holiday. She always loved summer. She used to quote Henry James: "Summer afternoon—Summer afternoon . . . the two most beautiful words in the English language." Death was her independence from the stroke that had left her unconscious in the hospital for four days. I knew on that balmy July night that she was somewhere on a beach eating lobster with way too much melted butter, waving happily to a humpback whale. She was unequivocally a dame in every way. She stayed sharply alert into her late eighties and righteously angry at injustice in the world, cursed colorfully, and lounged in elegant designer clothes while bedecked in gold bangles all up her wrists. This daughter of WASP New York City high society kept her house spotless, her silver tea set polished, but could be cajoled into belching "Sarsa-par-illaaa" by us grandkids, raising a bejeweled hand to her mouth afterwards exclaiming "Oh that's awful; that's just awful!" laughing her great battle ax laugh that sounded like a gravely oboe.

None of my friends was available to do anything that night. I was alone. Honestly, I wasn't fit company anyway, but I was disappointed that I wouldn't get to see any fireworks to commemorate my grandmother. Driving back to my house at dusk from shopping, I noticed people gathering along Route 50, sitting along the hillside adjacent to the street, watching the tree line across the way. I saw sparklers and blankets and coolers—some of my favorite symbols of summer. I decided to rush home, put my purchases away, and drive back up to park and watch the show; the best vantage point was Athena's favorite shopping center where Petco was located.

On impulse, I invited Athena with me. I don't know what made me think to bring her; usually dogs and fireworks are not a great mix. Athena was always up for anything, though, and I had already committed by putting on her leash. We drove up to the shopping center and parked in the lot, which still allowed a good vantage point of the tree line. I lifted the hatch of my CR-V, spread out a blanket, sat next to Athena and waited. At the first puff of the released charge and the resulting bloom of color and noise, Athena barked, and bounced her front end up and down.

"Oh, sweetie, this was a bad idea," I said, prepared to shut the hatch, and drive her home. To see the fireworks wasn't worth terrifying her. But in the red glow of the descending sparks, I looked at her profile and saw that Athena wasn't scared at all. She was grinning, looking up at the sky, bobbing and tilting her head. Her bark, I realized, was the play yip of Schutzhund, and her round-eyed enthusiasm was the expression with which she watched the television screen during sporting events.

She looked at me as if to say, "Isn't this *great?*" I agreed and ruffled her chest and threw my arm around her shoulders. She even eventually lay down with her front paws dangling over the tailgate of my car, my arm across her back, our heads turning in unison, watching the flares light up the black furry sky. Once in a while she was overcome and had to sit up, raise her front paws and bark, but mostly she lay calmly beside me.

"Goodbye, Nonny," I whispered during the booming finale, laughingly remembering my grandmother's love of spectacle, as tears escaped my eyes and Athena jabbered next to me.

"What did you think?" I asked my dog, after it was over and the night was silent again. She responded by slathering my face. Fireworks had proven too much fun, however, because she also gave my nose and part of my cheekbone a happy bite, sounding her high-pitched monkey whine.

"Ouch! Athena!" I said, as she gazed at me adoringly. Some things, I gathered, didn't ever really change. I threw my arms around my crazy shepherd girl's neck and hugged her, thankful.

The End

Afterword

Goodbye to a Friend

Sunday, September 23, was pretty much like any other day. I came home Sunday morning after spending the night out, only slightly surprised that Athena alone greeted me at the front door. Normally Kashka was there, too, so close I had to remind him to move back. Often his and Athena's legs got tangled, or he got momentarily pushed over as she ran to get a toy.

But he wasn't there, and I figured he was outside, basking. He liked to do that on sunny days. I told Athena to find him for me, and she dutifully ran out into the yard, sniffing behind bushes. She looked anxious as she came inside that she hadn't been successful in the job I had assigned her. I went out to the yard and called for him. He squeezed underneath the fence then; he had just been out in the common area.

"Hi, Kashi. There you are," I said, but then I abruptly stopped, because he was meowing in a way that was not usual for him. He was mewing in a high-pitched way I had not heard since he was a kitten. He seemed stiff, and he lay on my walkway, still mewing. I petted him and asked what was wrong, but when I got up to feed him in his room, he followed me willingly, albeit slowly. He ate his soft food, purr-chewing, and I petted his bony back as he ate, doing my usual ritual prattle about how he loved soft food and "It's very good! Yes, it's very good soft food!"

Afterward, I went to the refrigerator and called out, "Who wants hot dog?" One giant and one little triangle sat in perfectly polite anticipation as I got the package out of the cheese drawer. As usual, Kashka held his piece down with his paw and nibbled at it. Athena inhaled hers like she was in a competitive eating contest yet never tried to take his piece.

I got ready to go to my hair appointment but was puzzled when Kashka followed me to the front door, walking rather fast. He was meowing urgently, but I thought it was just because he had forgotten already that I had fed him (he seemed to be forgetting things more frequently). When I got home from the salon, he was lying underneath Athena's dog bowl stand, in the sun. I left after that to watch the Redskins game with my friend Greg. When I came home, around 7:30 p.m., Kashka came in from the kitchen but walked very slowly and stiffly, facing the ground. I went into his bedroom and opened a can of food, emptying it out for him. He sniffed it and then fell chin-first into the plate. He then left the bedroom and jumped onto the couch, where he lay, his legs splayed at odd angles.

"Kashi? Kashi?" I cried, alarmed, lifting his chin to look into his eyes. They were miserable, sunken. I petted him and put my head down on his side. Faintly, like far away rain, I heard soft purring. He jumped down from the couch then and wobbled, lurching like a drunk toward his room. I picked him up and held him to my chest; it was like lifting a feather duster. I had started to cry, because I knew he wasn't just under the weather. I had looked into his eyes and seen that he was dying, and very soon.

I lay him back down on the couch. I wet my fingers with water from Athena's dog bowl and wiped his lips. Athena stood next to me, looking at me and at him, alarmed. I called Lauren.

"Kashka is dying," I choked out. She ran over with a nutritional supplement paste and rubbed some on her finger and offered it. He averted his head and lay it down. Lauren gently lifted his lip, which in my panic I had forgotten to do, and we both winced with silent knowledge when we saw his gums. They were a horrible slimy gray.

"We need to get him to the emergency vet," I said. Lauren told me to get a towel, and she wrapped him up so just his head and tail were sticking out. Being Kashka, he had wiggled just enough so that his right forepaw was hanging out, too. Lauren carried him to the car as I wept and called Craig, one of my ex-boyfriends with whom I had remained friends and who still loved Kashka to distraction. I told him to come to the Hope Center Emergency Clinic in Vienna. Right away.

Lauren passed Kashka to me, and I held him on his back, like a baby. He and I locked eyes and held them for the fifteen minutes it took to drive to the clinic. My tears fell onto his forehead, as I told him over and over, "Mama's here. Mama's here. It's okay, my love. I know, it's time, and it's okay if you have to go, if it hurts too much. Mama's here. My love. My angel." I croaked out my bastardized version of "You Are My Sunshine," his song:

You are my sunshine, my only sunshine
You make me hap-py, because you're gray!
You'll never know dear, how much I love you
Pleeease don't take my Ka-shi away.
Kashi's song!

"I've never heard you sing that before," Lauren said softly. It wasn't a song I sang in front of people, only for him.

"Nutley Street, Nutley Street," I reminded Lauren, because she was about to take Route 123 towards Vienna, which was an exit too early. Lauren, whom I viewed as super-human in a crisis, displayed tiny microscopic fissures in her composure, proving that her love and concern for both Kashka and me were affecting her. They touched me, the little moments of confusion she had that night.

The fifteen minutes we drove I was hardly aware of anything but the tiny, light, gray bundle in my arms. Kashka and I continued to look deeply into each other's eyes, and it was only fitting, because we started out our life together locking eyes, and we were ending our life together doing the same thing. He stared at me, his second eyelid showing, but his gaze was unwavering, and the look was one of somber trust. I had tried in our sixteen and a half years together to never let him down, and he trusted me if I told him things were okay. When it proved too much for him, he turned his head and buried his face in my arm. He pushed with his paw, squirming in his towel a little. I laughed slightly. That was Kashka—stubbornly fighting for optimal comfort until the end. I soothed him by holding him a little tighter, though, admonishing him gently not to struggle and to just lie still. He listened to me.

We arrived at the clinic, and they took him back into the back, assuring me that if he started to falter that they would get me immediately. Tests weren't necessary. The vet came out after thirty seconds, before I could even finish my preliminary paperwork, and shook her head. She led Lauren and me into a small examination room and shut the door.

"Everything is failing," she said. His kidneys, so weak over the years, had finally given out completely, and he was in end-stage renal failure. She couldn't even feel his bladder, so the toxins were in his system. He was severely dehydrated, and she said his heart was beating erratically.

She explained that they could try an IV to give him fluids, but that many times such action caused shock to the system, an overload, and in addition, he'd be in the hospital for several days in isolation.

I shook my head violently. "No. There's no way I would do that to him, put him through something so iffy and leave him here alone." I also marveled at how just the day before he had been normal. The vet nodded, saying that when the kidneys finally do go for good, it can be quite sudden.

Lauren looked at the vet and asked, "Could you excuse us a second?" The vet agreed and left. Lauren gripped my forearm. "Sweetie, what do you think he's telling you?" she asked. "This is your decision; you know him best."

"He's telling me it's time," I said, gasping for air and sobbing. "He's not. He's not Kashka. That's not Kashka. His eyes . . . "

Lauren agreed. Just then, I saw Craig through the tiny window of our examination room. He came in and hugged me. Craig worked his lips, which were trembling, and then I saw his face fold and he was crying. I began crying harder, hugging him, and I said I felt so bad for Athena; she didn't even get to say goodbye.

Lauren pointed to one of the many pictures of cats on the wall of the room, and said, "Well, look at this little black and white kitty here. Look. Her name is Athena." It was true. The label on the cat's picture was "Athena." A vet assistant came in with some paperwork, and I told her we weren't going to explore treatment options.

Craig, Lauren, and I waited. The vet brought Kashi in, still wrapped in his towel, and lay him down on the examination table. He was on his left side, and his right arm was still out of the towel, and the end of his fluffy tail was sticking out the other end. He already had gauze on his arm, in preparation; they had to find a vein and give him a light sedative, the vet explained. The vet, so kind, said to take as much time as I needed and to get her only when I was ready. She left the room. Lauren left and brought in more paperwork for me to sign, as well as a discreet request for my credit card to pay the four hundred dollars I would owe. For his cremation inscription, one form had three lines to write something.

"How do I sum up this cat's life in three lines?" I asked, wailing, losing my grip momentarily. Eventually, I chose:

"You're the best friend
That I ever had.
My sunshine. I love you gray guy."

The first two lines of the inscription were from the Queen song "Best Friend," which I used to sing in secret ode to him whenever it came on the radio.

Craig and I went outside so I could quickly collect myself. "We need to do it soon, I think. He looks miserable," Craig said, his eyes wide and shocked. I agreed. "You know how you feel when you're dehydrated; you want to die," he said, and we laughed through sobs.

When we went back into the room, I saw Lauren bent over Kashka, petting his head and his body through the towel. Later she told me she had assured Kashka that Carman and Cody and Fireball loved him a lot and would miss him, and they said to say goodbye, too. Lauren went to the waiting room; Craig and I stayed behind.

"I'm ready," I said to the vet. She gently told me what I could expect. What might happen. She also assured me that it was completely pain-less. For a place accustomed to doing this sort of thing doubtless many times daily, I was comforted by how compassionate they were. I bent over Kashka, kissing his head over and over, and I whispered, "Mommy is here, and so is Daddy."

Craig reached and rubbed Kashka's forehead. "Hey, Kashi," he said, sobbing freely now.

The vet slipped the needle with the sedative into Kashi's arm; it would render him unconscious. "Now we do the second one," she said.

"I love you Kashka, so much," I cried, and I reached out and gripped Craig's hand.

The vet put her stethoscope under the towel, and after one second said, "He's passed now."

I cried unabashedly then, as did Craig.

"I loved him," he said.

"I know you did. He loved you. You'll always be his daddy."

"Look." Craig pointed. "Look at his eyes." I looked. They were open, but the sunken pained look he had had earlier was gone.

"Now he looks like Kashi!" Craig said. He was right. Kashka looked like himself again, finally, in death.

Craig left me then on my request, and I petted Kashka's soft fur, pinched gently his cold little ears. I bawled, knowing that I'd never touch his fur again, feel his surprisingly hard forehead; his fur there always felt like it was covering a rock. I nuzzled his head. I stroked his tail and rubbed his foreleg. I held his large pickle-chip paw, flicking my fingertip over his claws, which he wasn't able to retract completely in his old age. His paw pads were cold. All of him was turning cold. Even in death, I expected him to pull his paw away sharply. He never liked anyone touching his paws. I finally picked some fur out of his tail; again, I winced, because I expected him to turn and croak in protest. But I put the fur in my wallet. I told him one last time that I loved him, that he was my best friend, and that I would see him again, and I said something I said to him a lot over the years: "I promise."

As we left the clinic, a tech ran out with Kashka's collar in a plastic bag, asking if I wanted to keep it.

"Yes!" I screamed, guilty that I hadn't thought to take it off him. I clutched the bag to me. We dropped Craig off at the Metro, after I thanked him for coming. Lauren drove me home in silence, broken only when she cruised by the firehouse to see if any cute fireman were waiting outside. She took a rather long roundabout way, and I think it was because she was trying to delay the inevitable of when I would walk for the first time into a house where Kashka no longer lived.

I went into the house and sat on the couch. I called the relevant people. I was nauseated from shock and from crying, and I vomited. I ran the water all night; it's the only noise that soothes me when I'm that sad. Athena lay next to me; she was anxious and darted her long muzzle forward to lick the tears off my face constantly. I held the plastic bag open for her to sniff the collar. She took a long deep sniff, and then licked the outside of the bag. I slept with the collar on the pillow, between us. Athena moved to the living room when she got restless, but she ran hurriedly back into the room, jumped on the bed and frantically licked me when she heard me keening at 5:30 a.m.

Monday I sat at home, dazed. Athena was a constant presence, and I petted her often. I took Jim up on his offer of help, and I asked him to clean out Kashi's room. The idea of opening the door and seeing the litter boxes and food plate and no Kashka was just too much for me to bear. Mike came over, and we took Raleigh and Athena for a walk while Jim cleaned.

Athena, when we returned, blocked the back area of my house, where Kashka's now empty bedroom lay, raising her tail and growling at Raleigh, refusing him entrance to those areas.

After the house was empty, save for Athena and me, she lay next to me on the couch. Her eyes were deeply, gravely sad. Although she had looked for Kashka Sunday night, sniffing outside his closed bedroom door and doing a sweep of the bushes outside, Monday night she seemed to understand that he was gone. She looked at me as if for answers, and I stroked her beautiful shepherd head and told her I understood. I told her it was okay to be sad but that we both would be happy again. I told her she still had Carman and Cody and Fireball and Mindi and Kiera and Raleigh and that they loved her. At these familiar names, she tilted her head. But her eyes didn't lighten.

I got Kashka's collar out of the bag and extended it to her. She sniffed it and very gently took it in her front teeth. She then pulled her lips back into a grimace that appeared disgusted, like she smelled something bad, but in hindsight I recognized it as the exact expression people have when they pull their lips back right before they cry. She softly laid the collar onto her own curled-up tail and looked at me in the eyes. The corners were tilted down, and the look of pure mourning was as unfiltered and raw as the grief in my own heart. She didn't have the benefit of our human layers. Her sadness was as clear as a cloudless blue sky. She sighed and laid her head between her paws, leaving the collar on her tail. After a while I picked it back up and held it while I watched TV. The collar and tag felt warm in my hand, and I felt vibrations of grace from it. Silently, I let tears fall; Athena must have been attuned to the scent of them by now, because she was instantly up, licking them off, whining, her ears back. I hugged her and brightened, for her sake.

That night I slept holding the tag in my hand. I sniffed it. I smelled the smell of Kashka's fur on the shredded band. Athena, who needed some time and space of her own, I think, stayed in the living room.

The next night Lauren invited us over, thinking that having Carman and Cody to play with might be just the thing to help cheer Athena. We were about to walk into Lauren's house when Athena took a sharp detour and sniffed Lauren's Blazer, walking as if in a daze into the parking lot, by now a known no-no, and sniffed the passenger-side door. Lauren's tailgate was open. Athena ignored my entreaty to come into the house and instead jumped into the back of the truck. She didn't sit in the back as if she wanted to go for a ride; she hopped the seat backs into the passenger seat, sniffing every inch of the seat back and floor. She then sat on the seat and appeared both dejected and angry.

"Athena, come on," Lauren said. I clapped. "Come on Athena. Out." Lauren and I had glanced at each other during her frantic perusal of the truck, except we didn't hold eyes long, because neither of us wanted to tear up. We both knew full well that Athena had smelled and was now sitting in the last place where Kashka had been. Athena, normally responsive and obedient, obstinately sat in the passenger seat and refused to look at either of us for a good ten seconds, neither did she move. When we finally did coax her out, she had a defeated air about her, so opposite from her normal mania when she knew she was seeing her friends. It was as if her last hope of finding Kashka had been dashed.

When she went through the door to Lauren's house, rather than the usual mayhem of greetings, Carman and Cody instead slowly and respectfully sniffed her. Carman, usually a bit standoffish since their big fight that night at my house, licked Athena's muzzle and invited her to play. Cody merely stood staring at Athena with puzzled yellow-gold eyes, as if waiting to see what to do. I had brought Kashka's collar with me in its plastic bag, and I held it out for Carman and Cody to sniff. I felt as if maybe I should let them say goodbye, somehow. Cody sniffed deep into the bag and quietly sat down, a reaction I'd never seen in him before. Carman, like Athena, licked the outside of the bag. Afterwards, although it took some time, all three dogs began playing. It was a relief.

I had some reservations attributing Athena's initial reaction to independent feelings of sadness. After all, I was devastated upon my return home from the clinic; perhaps she was merely responding to my cues. I was convinced, however, after seeing her stalwart and pained expression, stubbornly not budging from the passenger seat of Lauren's truck, that my dog had been genuinely mourning her little big brother's death. She was never the same again. I noticed the change in her one night when Lauren and I watched *Steel Magnolias* at her house. During the climactic scene, when Sally Field cries and rends her garments over her daughter Shelby's death, I looked down at Athena, who was riveted to the screen, watching as Sally Field had her breakdown. Athena's mouth was closed, and she looked upset, her ears intently forward. When Sally Field was done crying, Athena turned to stare up at me with an expression I can only describe as worried. I had to assure her that Sally Field was just an actress and that she was okay. Neither Lauren nor I had been emotional during the movie; neither of us particularly even liked *Steel Magnolias*, and we even found Sally Field's scene slightly annoying. Athena apparently believed it a tour de force of sorrow, however. Athena's empathy has spilled over now onto anyone crying on television; it seems to affect her most grievously, and I always have to tell her that the person in question is all right.

I think, in both our ways, we miss Kashka terribly.

I realized over the two days after his death that Kashka had bestowed his greatest gift to Athena and me, his ultimate expression of love and sacrifice. He was in abject pain, I believe, all day, and he could have chosen a far away bush or ditch in which to die. But he chose to lie on the couch, in Athena's spot, where it smelled the most of Athena, and let both of us know it was his time. I firmly believe he held on in the car, knowing that we had some strange, ancient covenant to honor, he and I, and for that I will be forever grateful. It was his final act of goodness, mercy, and class and encapsulates why he was loved, strongly, by all who knew him. A week after he died, I held a small memorial service for him in my living room with his pretty sealed box of ashes set up on a table along with several pictures I had managed to capture of various stages of his life. Friends and family members who had known Kashka for years came to honor his memory and laugh over their favorite stories about him. Athena, Carman and Cody were in attendance.

Goodbye my dearest, truest friend. My little shadow. My bed-monster chaser. My brave, proud, badass explorer. May the rotisserie turkey breast, Gerber meat sticks, and chicken nuggets never run out, and may there always be green grass, warm sunshine, and hopefully, a friendly dog to keep you company over the Rainbow Bridge. I love you and will always love you. Athena and I will see you again. I promise.

Made in the USA
San Bernardino, CA
02 May 2014